EXAMINING RELIGIONS

Moral Issues in Six Religions

Edited by W. Owen Cole

Arye Forta
Joe Jenkins
V.P. (Hemant) Kanitkar
Rosalyn Kendrick

Heinemann Educational
a division of Heinemann Educational Books Ltd
Halley Court, Jordan Hill, Oxford OX2 8EJ

OXFORD   LONDON   EDINBURGH
MADRID   ATHENS   BOLOGNA   PARIS
MELBOURNE   SYDNEY   AUCKLAND   SINGAPORE
TOKYO   IBADAN   NAIROBI   HARARE   GABORONE
PORTSMOUTH NH (USA)

First published 1991

93 94 95 96 11 10 9 8 7 6 5 4

British Library Cataloguing in Publication Data

Moral issues in six religions.
   1. Religions. Doctrines
   I. Arye Forta, Joe Jenkins, V. P. (Hemant) Kanitkar,
   Rosalyn Kendrick, Piara Singh Sambhi, Andrea
   Willson. Ed. W. Owen Cole.
   291.56

   ISBN 0–435–30299–X

Authors' acknowledgements

Andrea Willson would like to thank the following people
for their help: Tessa Winterbotham, Owen Cole, Sue
Walton, James Belither, Chris Stark, Alex, V. Baar, Dennis
Sibley, The Friends of the Western Buddhist Order, Rev.
Chushin Passmore and his assistant at Throssel Hole
Priory, Ven. Ajahn Khemadhammo, Andy Weber, and all
my kind teachers. I apologize to all the traditions of
Buddhism for any shortcomings and errors due to my
own lack of knowledge and understanding of the
Dharma, and dedicate any merit I may have made in
contributing to this book to the welfare and happiness of
all sentient beings.

Joe Jenkins would like to thank the following people for
their help: Angela Mitchell, Owen Cole, Sue Walton,
Tony Hammond, John St John, Professor Matthew
Lipman, The Brothers of Belmont Abbey, Aileen Milne.

V. P. (Hemant) Kanitkar wishes to thank Ramesh Dogra,
Stephanie Ramamurthy and Dr W. Menski of the School
of Oriental and African Studies, London University for
their help in selecting and locating Hindu scriptural
material; Dr Owen Cole for his advice and guidance; his
wife, Dr Helen A. Kanitkar for her constant
encouragement and erudite comments, and Mrs Barbara
Nelson-Smith for preparing the final typescript.

Rosalyn Kendrick wishes to thank the following people
for their help: Shaikh Zahran Ibrahim, Imam at Islamic
Cultural Centre, 146 Park Rd, London, NW8 7RG; Saheb
Mustaqeem Bleher of the Islamic Party of Britain; Zarina
Choudry, of the Islamic Society for the Propagation of
Religious Tolerance in Britain, 20–22 Creffield Rd,
London, W5, and a very dear friend; Sara Sheriff – Islamic
Circle Organisation; Khola Hassan, Ameerah of HISAM;
Aurangzeb Khan; Ghulum Sarwar Khan; Hajji Aziz Ur-
Rahman; Hajji Mukhtar; my dear husband Waris Ali
Maqsood and his teacher Sufi Afsul. May Allah bless
them all, and keep them on His path always.
Taqabbal Allah minha wa minkum – May Allah accept the
work we have done for His sake.

Rabbi Arye Forta wishes to acknowledge the help given
by his wife Chana, without whose critical eye he would
have missed out a lot of important information; Rabbi Zvi
Telsner of Finchley Central Synagogue who checked the
entire text for accuracy; Mrs Feige Rabin of Lubavitch
Lending Library who provided much of the resource
material; Dr Owen Cole for his numerous helpful
suggestions; Su Newland, Public Relations Director of
Jewish Care, for her help with the chapter on the
Disadvantaged.

Designed and produced by Gecko Limited, Bicester, Oxon
Printed and bound in Great Britain by The Bath Press, Avon

CONTENTS

Morals and issues

Moral issues are part of being human. As babies we cry to demand attention and our parents, usually mum, have to decide whether to give in to us immediately or to let us wait. To let us cry may seem cruel. To give in may be the beginning of many demands, starting with 'I want sweets' and a tantrum on the shop floor and ending up with 'You can't make me! I'm bigger than you now!' Does life between parents and children have to be a battle? That is a moral issue. So is the question of whether mum should always be the person who has to deal with the crying baby.

In this book there is not space to set up more situations of this kind. That is something which you and your teacher will have to do. This book looks at what members of the six religions which we have included have to say. Please remember that although we have tried to give you reliable information you may easily find another member of the tradition who may disagree. No one need be wrong. Of course, no one from any of these religions is going to say that murder is right, but some might say that if you have two three-course meals a day, while people are dying of starvation in Africa or Asia, you are a murderer!

Morals can be very complicated. The issues that are seen as important can also vary from time to time and place to place. If we were writing before about 1850 we might have had to put in a section on slavery, but today no religion or society approves of it. However, there are still some people working in conditions that are perhaps like slavery. For example, bonded labourers in India or some low- or un-paid domestic servants in London! The issue of treating human beings properly has not been solved entirely.

Different religions also have different priorities or concerns. An example of this is vegetarianism. Vegetarians are to be found in every culture, but it isn't something which most Christians would usually include in a list of issues raising moral questions. For many Hindus, however, it would come near the top of their agenda. Also, some issues are ones which challenge Jews and Christians living in Europe and North America but not people living in Indian villages. When to turn off a life support machine is an example of this. Or whether

to resuscitate a seventy year old whose heart gives out during an operation. The Hindu in a village over five hundred miles away from the technology found in most Western hospitals might say, if she were asked her view, 'You should be so lucky!' On the other hand, people in Britain are unlikely to be invited to donate a kidney for money. Anyway, it is illegal; should it be? People living in Bombay, of whatever religion, could be made a tempting offer to sell one of their kidneys, by representatives of a European hospital. Even though it is illegal in India too, the chance to make enough money to educate their children, arrange their marriages, buy land and set themselves up in business, is something which they might find difficult to refuse.

How to use this book

Because the moral agenda varies between religions, we have dealt with each religion separately. The Index should help anyone who wants to use the book thematically.

Values and morals aren't like the list we might make when we go shopping. They arise from beliefs. It is therefore essential for you to read the introductory chapters about the religions you are studying and to try to learn more about those religions. The more you know about a religion, the more you are likely to understand its attitudes on moral issues.

Also we are able to understand the ideas, attitudes and behaviour of other people better if we are willing to put our own beliefs on one side while we listen to what they have to say. Your success in using this book will depend to a large extent on your ability to do this. It is like taking off your own shoes and putting on those of the person you are reading about.

Finally, please remember that this book has been written by believers, but that within every tradition there are many views and attitudes. For example, the discussion of arranged marriages is confined to Hinduism and Sikhism but it is also the usual practice in Islam too. In India many Christians, Jews and Buddhists have arranged marriages. To have covered every attitude to moral issues, even within these six religions, we would have needed to write an encyclopedia.

Owen Cole

1 INTRODUCTION – THE WORLD VIEW OF A BUDDHIST

Buddhism gets its name from the word **Buddha**, which means *enlightened one*. This title was given to **Siddhartha Gautama**, who became 'enlightened' and then taught others how to attain the state of **enlightenment**. The founder of Buddhism was born into an enviable lifestyle, yet he still suffered the same problem as every other human being – lack of satisfaction. His life story is a good example of the human condition, for although he seemed to have everything, he was still unhappy.

Shakyamuni Buddha, the founder of Buddhism in this world age

The life of the Buddha

In a northern state of India, 2500 years ago, a prince was born to a life of wealth and privilege. He grew up to be handsome and talented, and lived a pampered lifestyle, given everything he could possibly want, and protected from the unpleasant aspects of life. But by the time he was 29, he realized that, in spite of his rich lifestyle, he was not content. The continual pleasures did not fulfil him and he felt sure that there should be more to life. Although his surroundings seemed as close to paradise as anyone could wish, it was not enough. Bored and frustrated, the royal Prince Siddhartha Gautama started to travel outside his kingdom to search for something which would give his life meaning and purpose. What he saw on his travels would be commonplace to most of us but, because he had lived such a protected life, it was appalling to him. Siddhartha Gautama saw 'three sights' which were to change his life – old age, sickness and death. The effect was to prevent him from ever again feeling contentment, because he saw how fragile life really was.

'How can there be laughter, how can there be pleasure, when the whole world is burning? When you are in deep darkness will you not ask for a lamp?
Consider this body! A painted puppet with jointed limbs, sometimes suffering and covered with ulcers, full of imaginings, never permanent, for ever changing.
This body is decaying! A nest of diseases, a heap of corruption, bound to destruction, to dissolution. All life ends in death.'
(*Dhammapada, The Sayings of Buddha,* tr. Mascaro)

With this gloomy outlook alone, Siddhartha Gautama's dissatisfaction could only increase; now everything he saw seemed to be tainted. Then, on one of his journeys, he met a wandering **ascetic**. Although the man was homeless and alone, carrying only his essential possessions and wearing a simple robe, he appeared to be tranquil and calm. It was clear to Siddhartha Gautama that the man's happiness was not dependent on his external circumstances, but came from inside himself. This 'fourth sight' inspired Siddhartha Gautama to give up his royal lifestyle, leaving his home and his family, to search for the 'truth' about life.

For six years he practised and perfected various methods of meditation, under the guidance of great masters and following old traditions. Still Siddhartha Gautama did not find the perfect serenity that he was looking for. Eventually, he followed his own intuition and insight which led to his final 'enlightenment'.

The Wheel of the Dharma symbolizes the Buddhist Eightfold Path

The Buddha (Siddhartha Gautama) remained on Earth for 45 years, teaching his followers, before he died and entered **ParaNirvana**. He left behind a major religion which provides humankind with a profound system for understanding life.

'Cease to do evil. Learn to do good. Control the mind. This is the teaching of the Dhammapada.'
(*Dhammapada*, tr. Marahathi)

At the basis of all the 84 000 teachings the Buddha gave are his first teachings, called **The Four Noble Truths** and **The Eightfold Path**. All Buddhists, whatever their cultural backgrounds, believe that understanding these truths and abandoning all negative views to develop only good qualities will bring peace and happiness in this life. Eventually, when perfected, this will lead to the eternal peace and happiness of enlightenment or Buddhahood.

'He who, by his good deeds, transforms his evil acts is like the moon freed from the clouds.'
(*Dhammapada*, tr. Marahathi)

THE FOUR NOBLE TRUTHS

- Life is suffering. *This is to be comprehended.*
- The cause of suffering is desire. *This is to be abandoned.*
- The cessation of suffering is the cessation of desire. *This is to be realized.*
- The Path to the cessation of desire. *This is to be practised.*

The Buddha compared himself to a doctor whose work consists of four stages:

- the diagnosis of an illness
- identifying the cause of the illness
- finding the cure for the illness
- prescribing the medicine.

Using the doctor analogy, taking the medicine helps the patient feel better, and completing the course cures her. Buddhists say that taking the medicine of mind-training brings more and more peace and happiness until eventually the cure of enlightenment is attained.

THE EIGHTFOLD PATH

- **Right views** Knowing the difference between good and bad and the effects of your actions.
- **Right intentions** Doing things for the right reasons without expecting reward or recognition.
- **Right speech** Non-abusive language. Speaking without causing harm or offence to others.
- **Right action** Acting in a socially considerate way to others. Having equanimity for all beings.
- **Right livelihood** Not earning a living through the suffering of others, e.g. not selling alcohol or weapons or meat.
- **Right effort** Striving to perfect your spiritual path rather than improving your material wealth.
- **Right mindfulness** Having awareness of your thoughts and actions so that you live in harmony with the world.
- **Right concentration** Practising meditation to gain liberation, or **Nirvana**.

KEY IDEA

At the heart of the Buddha's teachings in the Eightfold Path is the idea of not causing harm or suffering to any other being.

FOR YOUR FOLDERS

▶ Write an essay about how important you think the Buddha's life-story is to Buddhists.
▶ Write and draw a cartoon-strip story of the Buddha's life, identifying the milestones which led to his enlightenment.

FOR DISCUSSION

▶ Why would Buddhists say that happiness does not depend on material success?

According to Buddhism, everyone has been circling in **samsara** for countless lifetimes. Buddhists believe they have been reborn as animals, humans and many other types of being again and again. All the beings they come into contact with in this lifetime are a result of the **karma** they have created with them in the past.

Buddhists believe that if they have a good relationship with someone it is a result of good karma. Every feeling of joy and pain they experience through relationships with others is dependent on past karma. So, if they want to have only pleasant relationships, Buddhists believe they must first of all understand karma.

The Knot of Eternity is a symbol of good luck and represents the continuous round of existence

> **Samsara** A Sanskrit word meaning the continuous cycle of life and death, which is pervaded by dissatisfaction. The Buddha called this mental and physical dissatisfaction and pain **suffering**.
> **Karma** A Sanskrit word meaning actions and their effects. Actions are wholesome, unwholesome or neutral. Wholesome actions create **good karma**, or happy and positive results, and unwholesome actions create **bad karma**.

Love

Buddhism says that what people call love is actually a feeling which stems from attachment and desire. It is a **need** for others, rather than the wish for their well-being. If someone truly loved a person they would never tire of working for their happiness. As it is, what people really never tire of is working for *their own* happiness.

Ironically, Buddhism says that it is precisely this need, or grasping, for happiness which creates obstacles in people's relationships with others. By generating compassionate and selfless love people can avoid harming others. In doing so they also create the good karma needed to receive love, and put an end to their own suffering.

KEY IDEAS

Life is suffering.

(The First Noble Truth)

The cause of suffering is desire.

(The Second Noble Truth)

To stop suffering, we must stop desire.

(The Third Noble Truth)

Friendship

The Buddha's code of social ethics for a layperson or **householder** was first taught to a young man called Sigala, a householder's son. The **Sigalavada Sutta**, as it came to be known, covers the six sets of ideal social relationships:

- parents
- teachers
- wife [partner] and children
- friends and companions
- servants
- religious teachers.

This is what the Buddha said about good friends.

21 *'There are four friends who should be reckoned as good-hearted: the helper; the friend who is the same in happiness and adversity; the friend of good counsel; the friend who sympathizes.'*

22 *'On four grounds the friend who is a helper is to be reckoned as good-hearted. He guards you when you are off your guard; he guards your property when you are off your guard; he is a refuge to you when you are afraid; when you have tasks to perform he provides a double supply of what you may need.'*

23 *'On four grounds the friend who is the same in happiness and adversity is to be reckoned as good-hearted. He tells you his secrets; he keeps secret your secrets; in your troubles he does not forsake you; he lays down even his life for your sake.'*

24 'On four grounds the friend who declares what you need to do is to be reckoned as good-hearted. He restrains you from doing wrong; he encourages you to do what is right; he informs you of what you had not heard before; he reveals to you the way to heaven.'

25 'On four grounds the friend who sympathizes is to be reckoned as good-hearted. He does not rejoice over your misfortunes; he rejoices over your prosperity; he restrains anyone who is speaking ill of you; he commends anyone who is praising you.'

26 When the Master had said this he recited another verse:

'The friend who is a helpmate, and the friend
Of bright days and of dark, and he who shows
What 'tis you need, and he who throbs for you
With sympathy: these four the wise should know
As friends, and should devote himself to them
As mother to her own, her bosom's child.'
(*The Buddha's Philosophy of Man, Early Indian Buddhist Dialogues*, arranged and edited by Trevor Ling, *The Layman's Social Ethics*, [Sigalavada Sutta])

Conflicts with others arise because people identify with a group or a view. They have rigid views about who their friends and enemies are, and these views affect their social behaviour.

This feeling of being close to some and distant from others is actually a source of suffering because it is inevitable that at some time everyone will be separated from those they are close to. Then people whom they dislike will disturb their minds.

The Buddhist practice of **equanimity** views all living creatures as equal in their desire for happiness and their potential for attaining enlightenment. They are also equal in their potential for committing wrong through ignorance.

KEY IDEA

Equanimity helps towards a caring, loving and unprejudiced attitude to all.

FOR DISCUSSION

▶ Discuss how the Buddhist view differs from the conventional view of love.

TALKING POINTS

● 'The cause of suffering is desire.'
● 'The Buddhist practice of equanimity helps to eliminate prejudices.'

FOR YOUR FOLDERS

▶ Look at what the Buddha said about good friends. Discuss how this compares with your own views about good friends.

THINGS TO DO

▶ Buddhists use meditation as a method for developing their good qualities. The following is a meditation on equanimity.

Close your eyes. Imagine you are seated in the centre of a large space. To your right and left, visualize your mother and father; next to them, your brothers and sisters; surrounding them, your close friends and relatives. See everyone you know, love and value, seated around you. In front, facing you, visualize those people you do not like. Concentrate on them until you see them quite clearly. Think about their problems, and why you don't like them. Encourage a feeling of tenderness towards them. Now imagine that all the beings of the world come and group themselves around you. The entire space, which is vast and devoid of objects, is filled with the countless beings of the world. Imagine you are all smiling, feeling at peace with one another. Generate a strong feeling that you have loved all these beings at some point in past countless lives. Finally, generate a feeling of equanimity. Mentally, you could think, 'We are all the same. We are all seeking happiness, and only through our ignorance going about it the wrong way. I forgive myself and every being for not previously seeing ourselves as equal.'

3 THE FAMILY

Karma

Buddhists believe that the body they inhabit is just a temporary home. When this 'house' gets old or is destroyed, the **subtle self** (the mind or consciousness, not to be confused with the brain) leaves the body at the time of death to inhabit a time and space called the **bardo**. This is an in-between-bodies state of being.

The karmic links they have created in the past direct people to their next **rebirth** or new body. This may be in one of any number of realms – god, hell, animal or human. Someone's future parents' karma combine with their own to provide the conditions which lead to their birth. At the time of the parents' union the subtle self enters the egg in the mother's womb and so begins a new existence in a new body. There is no death of the subtle self, only of the *forms it inhabits*. When someone's karma runs out in one body the subtle self just moves on to inhabit another.

'Of all the realms of samsara, there is none in which I was never born. I have been born in every single place throughout the entire extension of space.

Each and every physical form in existence, even the most ugly and miserable of all, seen or not seen by me, I have taken innumerable times.'

(from *The Wishfulfilling Golden Sun* by Lama Zopa Rinpoche, a Tibetan Buddhist Spiritual Master)

Buddhists believe that who someone is in this lifetime is a result of their karma, so is their home, their parents, and all the members of their family. In one way or another links have been created with them in the past and now, in this lifetime, more links are being created with them in the future.

KEY IDEA

Understanding the law of cause and effect (karma) helps us to understand being part of a family.

Mother love, or the kindness of mothers

Mother love is the closest parallel to pure love or **compassion** that an ordinary person can understand. By meditating on the kindness of

mothers, Buddhists believe that they start to have some understanding of what genuine, selfless love is all about.

Buddhists say that the kindness of the mother extends from conception until death.

'My mother's kindness is responsible for all the opportunities I have of making use of my physical body and of leading the sort of life that I do. If she hadn't taken care of me when I was in the womb, I wouldn't have been born alive. If she hadn't fed me well afterwards, I wouldn't have enjoyed the various functions of my physical body, such as using my eyes to see the most beautiful objects, my ears to hear the most beautiful sounds, my nose to smell the sweetest perfumes, my tongue to enjoy the most delicious tastes, or my body to enjoy sexual love, and have many children.

Also, becoming rich by working with my body, speech or mind, and being skilful and creative with my hands; all this depends on my mother's kindness. My mother always took good care of me, feeding me properly, protecting me from dangers, directing my life, and making me study so that I could have a comfortable life and good reputation. From the time of my conception she has been worried and concerned about me.'

(Lama Zopa Rinpoche *The Wishfulfilling Golden Sun*)

Buddhists believe that becoming **enlightened**, or **Buddha**, involves developing wisdom and compassion to perfection. So, by meditating on the kindness of mothers, they believe they will develop their compassion, and become closer to their goal.

Chenrezig is the embodiment of all the buddhas' compassion

KEY IDEA

A mother's love most closely resembles the pure love of a Buddha.

Loving compassion

Buddhists believe that all **sentient beings** have been their mother in another life.

Sentient beings Buddhists use this term to describe all the beings who live, breathe and have feelings, wishes and desires.

'If we divided this earth into pieces the size of juniper berries, the number of these would not be as great as the number of times that each sentient being has been our mother.'
(Nagarjuna, a Tibetan Buddhist Spiritual Master or Saint, who lived around 800 CE)

Contemplating that all beings have been their mothers through countless lifetimes helps Buddhists generate a feeling of loving kindness and gratitude to all beings and not just their parents of the present. This means that gradually they develop the view that all the beings of the world are as dear to them as their present family.

*'The mind that cherishes all other beings
and would secure their happiness
Is the gateway leading to infinite good qualities.
Seeing this I seek your blessings
to cherish these beings more than my life,
Even if they rise up as my enemies.'*
(a prayer from *Offering to the Spiritual Guide*, Panchen Lozang Chökyi Gyältsan, a Tibetan Buddhist Spiritual Master 1570–1662 CE)

KEY IDEA

Throughout time, all the beings of the world have been our family.

THINGS TO DO

▶ One of the Buddhist meditations is to contemplate the kindness of mothers. You might try the following exercise.

Close your eyes to avoid distractions and try to picture your mother, or someone whom you feel is the ideal mother, or someone whom you feel has been most like a mother to you. Think about the times when she looked after you when you were a child. Remember the games she played with you; the things she taught you; the things she gave you; the places she took you to; the way she looked after you when you were ill. Let all the memories of your mother return to you now. Then consider the following statements: A mother loves her child without expecting anything in return. Whether sick or tired, depressed or run-down, a mother will do everything within her power to give to her child. Even if her child abuses or neglects her, or the child turns out to be unpleasant and unkind, a mother will continue to love and care for that child. Try to generate a feeling of warmth and gratitude to your mother.

FOR DISCUSSION

▶ Buddhists seem to value a mother's love more than the love of a father. Why do you think this is? Do you think that a mother's love is in some way different to a father's? Explain your answer.

GROUP WORK

▶ Try acting out a recurring family argument you have with your parents. It could be about coming home late, or going out with someone your parents disapprove of. What advice might a Buddhist give the family to help put an end to the arguments?

Marriage as spiritual training

Buddhists believe that every situation we experience should help us to become better people, and ultimately to become enlightened. The spiritual path is not easy. Many Buddhists find that, although they really *want* to become enlightened, they still feel the need to live ordinary lives.

'To say that sexuality must eventually be transcended is not to deny it can be a vehicle for expressing much love; nor is it to deny there is a place for marriage and the procreation of children. It is precisely because Soto Zen recognizes that marriage can be a true medium of training that it has a ceremony to witness the sincerity of purpose and purity of such a relationship:

We are now being given the light of the Lord so that we will extinguish the light of selfishness. We will make the Lord's light sanctify our marriage, and we will be converted deeply to the Three Treasures. From now on we will purify our bodies and minds so that we will make no mistake in human morals and so as to help each other to be successful each in our own way. Our every action shall increase our respect for life and the merits of our relationship shall glorify all living things.'

(from *The Place of Sexuality in Training*, Rev. Daishin Morgan, Zen Monk of the Order of Buddhist Contemplatives)

The (*'We are . . .'*) marriage contract is read together by the bride and groom during the wedding ceremony (from *The Shasta Abbey Book of Ceremonies*).

The Two Golden Fishes represent spiritual release from samsara

Good conduct

The eight steps of The Noble Eightfold Path (see page 7) are divided into three types of practice:

● good conduct
● mental development
● wisdom.

The Buddha taught that by following the guidelines of **good conduct** everyone can find happiness and avoid harming other beings.

Good conduct includes right speech, right action and right livelihood and recognizes the fact that all beings wish for happiness and dislike suffering. **Right action** means having respect for life, property and personal relationships and therefore avoiding killing, stealing and sexual misconduct.

To maintain a good marriage, lay Buddhists practise virtues like loyalty, honesty and faithfulness, which help to destroy selfishness. Being married keeps Buddhists constantly aware of the meaning and rewards of good conduct.

In this society it is probably **sexual misconduct** which causes most problems in relationships. Anyone who becomes a Buddhist undertakes to observe the **five precepts** or rules. The third precept is to refrain from sexual misconduct. This reflects the Buddhists' respect for people and personal relationships.

Buddhists regard sexual misconduct as having any sexual relationship which will cause unhappiness to others, e.g. with someone else's partner. Buddhism regards marriage and the family as important units of society.

In the **Sermon on Blessing**, the Buddha defined the highest blessings which lead to happiness, now and in the future. Those concerning marriage and the family are contained in the following verses.

'To support one's father and mother, To care for one's wife and children, And to have a peaceful occupation. This is the highest blessing. Generosity, good conduct, Helping relatives, And blameless action. This is the highest blessing.'

(*Dhammapada*, tr. Maharathi)

KEY IDEA

Practising good conduct is a step on the Noble Eightfold Path to Enlightenment.

Responsibilities

The Buddha talked many times about the life of lay followers. One of these talks is called the **Sigalavada Sutta** and deals with the responsibilities of members within a family and society in general. Fulfilling these responsibilities results in everyone experiencing harmony, security and happiness.

The ideal husband would fulfil his responsibilities to his wife by:
● treating her with respect
● behaving in a courteous manner towards her
● being faithful
● sharing authority in family matters
● showing his appreciation by giving her presents.

The ideal wife would show her love for her husband by:
● managing the household well
● being hospitable to his family as well as her own
● being faithful
● taking care of the family's belongings
● skilfully and industriously completing her jobs.

In this way a marriage would be safe and secure.

Yogis or Yoginis devote all their time to attaining enlightenment

fetters. These latter drag men down, and though slack are hard to break. Men who have destroyed such bonds, who have abandoned the pleasures of the senses, who are free from longing, having become indifferent to them, go forth and retire from the world.

(From the section on Craving, *The Dhammapada, The Buddha's Path of Virtue*, an anthology of the sayings of the Buddha, tr. Maharathi)

KEY IDEA

A harmonious marriage will result in a happy family.

Divorce

When a marriage does fail and there seems to be no way of avoiding separation, then it is inevitable that everyone involved will suffer pain.

Buddhists would say that the only way of dealing with divorce is to go about it as sensitively as is possible. Hurting others can never bring satisfaction and happiness, according to Buddhist teachings.

Transcending desire

Buddhists believe that each life they live is a step on the path to enlightenment. Eventually, in order to attain enlightenment and escape the cycle of life and death, they must renounce the world of sensual enjoyments, which include attachments to people and comfort.

'The wise do not call that a strong fetter which is made of iron, wood or fibre. But jewels and precious stones, sons and wives form stronger

---

FOR DISCUSSION

▶ Buddhists consider that to be free from desire is to be free from suffering, and a necessary step on the spiritual path. In what ways, do you think, wanting or desiring to have things leads to suffering?

FOR YOUR FOLDERS

▶ The Sigalavada Sutta contains The Buddha's advice to his lay followers 2500 years ago. If he were alive today, how do you think he might adjust this advice to help 20th century couples? Rewrite the lists.
▶ In today's society divorce is a common fact of life, and easily obtained. What moral dilemmas might a Buddhist caught in an unhappy marriage face today? Can Buddhist morals survive alongside our society's view of personal freedom and the rights of the individual?

5 SEXUALITY

The Middle Way

The Buddha described the Buddhist spiritual path as the **Middle Way**, because it avoids the extremes of living. It neither **indulges** nor **deprives** human **senses** or desires. In our society people tend to be driven by the sensual side of life. They try to satisfy their desires with physical and material pleasures.

Buddhists believe that trying to satisfy our senses can cause suffering, both to ourselves and other people. Sex is viewed as natural, but most rewarding within a caring and loving relationship.

KEY IDEA

Sexual desire, like all desire, needs to be controlled to avoid causing suffering to others.

'There is a middle way wherein sexuality is fully acknowledged and regarded compassionately without the need to indulge in actions which lead to suffering.'
(Rev. Daishin Morgan *The Place of Sexuality in Training*)

Permissiveness

Buddhists believe that sexual permissiveness usually results in suffering. This is because it is based mainly on pleasure or desire, rather than affection or love. The Buddhist view is that an active sex life within a long-term partnership is better than a series of short-term affairs.

'. . . When you are a slave of your senses you cannot know what love really is. If you only use other people as a means of satisfying your own desires, then you can never really know them for who they are. This leads to a deep sense of loss and loneliness which many people foolishly try to fill by seeking still further indulgence, without realizing they are making things worse.'
(Rev. Daishin Morgan, *The Place of Sexuality in Training*)

KEY IDEA

Sexual permissiveness usually results in sexual misconduct.

Homosexuality and lesbianism

Homosexuality is the subject of widespread prejudice in our society. These attitudes can make this type of sexual expression emotionally very difficult for the people involved.

Again, the comment from a Buddhist spiritual teacher would be that it is important not to cause others pain, so 'marriage' is advised rather than the pursuit of sexual gratification.

'Buddhism does not make a song and dance about morality for its own sake, but points out that certain actions cause suffering and are therefore to be avoided.'
(Rev. Daishin Morgan, *The Place of Sexuality in Training*)

Abortion

The Buddhist belief in reincarnation puts abortion into a very clear light. Buddhists say that in between the death of an old body and birth into a new body, the consciousness, or **subtle self**, continues its spiritual life, although without form. Rebirth in the new mother's womb takes place at the time of **conception** when the father's sperm fertilizes the mother's egg.

The Buddha taught that life has no beginning that ordinary beings can understand. This means that whenever abortion takes place, the baby life-form is destroyed.

Birth control

Birth control prevents fertilization. This makes it impossible for a sentient being to take on a form in the mother's womb. So birth control protects the two partners who do not want a child from the pain of an unwelcome pregnancy, and protects the child itself from being unwanted. The consciousness is not killed; its new body is merely prevented from forming in that womb. The consciousness will take on a form elsewhere, with the ripening of its karma.

KEY IDEA

Abortion involves killing and is therefore seen as a wrong action, whereas birth control actually avoids wrong action.

Celibacy

'The place that sexuality has in the scheme of things is that ultimately it must be relinquished, like every other desire. This means that celibacy is the natural outcome of religious training. However, each of us must train where we are now and deal with sexuality like any other desire as it arises, without guilt. That we experience sexual desire is not a problem; what matters is how we deal with it . . . To say that sexuality must eventually be transcended is to point out a direction the road takes; that we may not have reached that point on the road should not cause us to doubt ourselves, become enmeshed in guilt and fear, nor to suppress our sexuality.'

(Rev. Daishin Morgan, *The Place of Sexuality in Training*)

The majority of Buddhists who are celibate are ordained. Taking ordination means becoming a monk or nun and making many more vows than lay Buddhists, with the purpose of renouncing all worldly attachments.

Sexual desire brings with it many kinds of attachment to worldly pleasures – to another person and to sexual pleasure itself. Monks and nuns take the vow of celibacy to free themselves from those worldly ties.

Taking a vow does not get rid of the desire, like unwanted rubbish. It acts as a reminder of an important decision arrived at through deep contemplation. When Buddhists are faced with the choice to commit an immoral act, the vows they have made remind them of their decision to follow a spiritual path.

KEY IDEA

Celibacy is a natural progression in religious training.

Tantric Buddhism

Tantric Buddhism is a method of unifying male and female energies in order to attain a perfect balance of the two, and reach spiritual completeness. Sexual symbolism is used in meditation to help the practitioners realize their inner potential.

'What we do not realize is that within each one of us is an unlimited source of both male and female energy. So many of our problems arise because we are either ignorant of, or we suppress, what we have within us. Men try to hide their female side and women are afraid of expressing their male energy. As a result we always feel cut off from something we need. We do not feel whole and therefore turn expectantly towards other people for the qualities missing in ourselves in the hope of gaining some sense of completeness. . .

(From *Introduction to Tantra*, by the late Lama Thubten Yeshe, a Tibetan Buddhist Spiritual Master)

FOR YOUR FOLDERS

► Write a letter from a Buddhist to a non-Buddhist friend who is considering having an abortion.
► Sexual misconduct and killing are viewed by Buddhists as wrong actions. Use this unit to write an essay from a Buddhist viewpoint on some of the issues discussed.

FOR DISCUSSION

► What advice do you think a Buddhist spiritual teacher would give to a homosexual or lesbian disciple about their lifestyle?
► In what situation do you think a Buddhist might consider abortion?

GROUP WORK

► A young person has become a Buddhist and has decided to be ordained. Their parents are perplexed by their choice. Act out the scene where the Buddhist tries to explain the reasons for a celibate and religious lifestyle.
► Non-Buddhists might interpret sexual permissiveness as sexual freedom. Act out a discussion between a Buddhist and a non-Buddhist who believes in sexual freedom.

The perfect human rebirth

An important Tibetan Buddhist teaching is about birth as a human – this lifetime and how it is used. Tibetan Buddhists call it the **perfect human rebirth** because they believe its many attributes and freedoms can enable them to reach spiritual enlightenment. Because of their belief in reincarnation, Buddhists call it **rebirth**, and because being born as a healthy human being is so rare, it is called **perfect**, or sometimes **precious**. It is only recognized as perfect, though, if the follower has the insight and wisdom to use their *physical* well-being to advance their *spiritual* awareness.

KEY IDEA

A healthy human life is rare and precious, giving the freedom and opportunities to practise a spiritual path.

'Wasting this very precious human rebirth is many millions of times worse than losing universes full of precious jewels because:
1 It wastes the numberless lives spent trying to gain this precious rebirth, which has resulted from good karma, created by morality and charity. These virtues have been practised mainly in the human realm during several previous lives, each of which was the result of many others.
2 It wastes the present opportunity of gaining Enlightenment and achieving all other realizations.
3 It wastes the possibility of better future lives, in which I could have achieved realizations and attained Enlightenment, stopping all suffering.'
(Lama Zopa Rinpoche, *The Wishfulfilling Golden Sun*)

The Tibetans use an analogy to illustrate the rarity of perfect human rebirth. It is said that gaining the precious human rebirth is as likely as a blind turtle, swimming in a vast ocean and surfacing only once every 100 years, putting its head through a small golden ring which is floating somewhere on the surface of the water (see page 17).

Drugs and alcohol

The **fifth precept** that a Buddhist promises to observe is to refrain from taking **intoxicants**. Drugs and alcohol are intoxicants. They can affect a person's mind and influence them to think or act in ways which normally they would not. With such an altered state of mind, people can be thoughtless and careless, and therefore more likely to cause suffering to others.

Some people would argue that using drugs and alcohol releases them from their inhibitions and depressed states of mind. If someone is inhibited and tense, though, intoxicants will just give them a false sense of temporary well-being. They won't fulfil their needs or provide a solution to their problems. The danger then is to keep on taking intoxicants again and again, which will only dull the mind still more.

KEY IDEA

What we do to the body, affects the mind.

Buddhism teaches that 'Buddha' is within *everyone*, but the Buddha-nature is hidden by endless layers of wrong attitudes which seek happiness from external sources. Buddhists say that, when someone becomes enlightened, they will discover their essentially pure nature, so it is important to clear – rather than dull – the mind, to reveal this purity.

The Japanese Buddhist Hakuin wrote: 'This very earth is the Lotus Land of Purity, And this very body is the body of Buddha.'

MEDITATION

There are many methods of meditation which Buddhists use to enhance their awareness of themselves and life. One meditation, used for calming the mind and creating a sense of physical well-being, is a simple breathing exercise.

Close your eyes. When you are still and comfortable, focus your attention on your breath as it enters and leaves your nostrils. Concentrate on the tip of your nose. Feel the coolness as you breathe in and the warmth as you breathe out.

If any thoughts come into your head let them go, without following them, like soap bubbles melting in the air. Bring your attention back to your quiet and regular breathing.

By doing nothing at all except breathing, Buddhists believe they can become aware of an inner source of peace.

Moderation

In the life story of the Buddha, there are two extreme lifestyles. The young prince, shielded from the suffering of the world and spoiled with sensory pleasures, is unable to think clearly. He later reacts to this pampering, by starving and neglecting his body until he almost dies.

Siddhartha also abandons this way of life when he realizes that, unless his body is healthy, his mind cannot concentrate. Having eaten a bowlful of pure, wholesome food he feels that his body is restored to health, the strength returns to his mind, and he is once more able to meditate.

His finding of a **middle way**, between two extremes, provided the example for all Buddhists to live in moderation.

Eating

VEGETARIANISM

Most Buddhists become vegetarian because they cannot reconcile eating meat with the first precept of refraining from killing.

Although, in order to eat meat, they do not actually have to do the killing, many Buddhists feel that eating meat conflicts with the view of not causing suffering. Buddhists who do eat meat, mainly do so for cultural or health reasons. A Western Tibetan Buddhist monk writes:

'A meat diet was necessary in Tibet. However, Tibetan people living in countries well-supplied in vegetables and fruits still maintain a diet relying on meat, it seems mainly because of physiological and cultural factors. His Holiness the Dalai Lama has pointed out on many occasions that, since it is a precept issuing directly from Mahayana trainings, a follower of this tradition would do very well in opting for a complete vegetarian diet if it does not harm one's health.'
(Thubten Dadak, 'On becoming vegetarian', *Mandala*)

FASTING

On some holy days, Buddhists fast to divert all their attention from the body to the mind, and enable them to concentrate entirely on their spiritual practice.

Fasting is usually only a temporary and short-term measure. Generally, it is viewed as an ascetic practice which does not lead to a healthy state of being.

Zen Master, Dogen-zenji said, 'We must care for food as if it is our own eye-sight.'

The blind turtle of the Tibetan analogy

FOR DISCUSSION

▶ In the cartoon, the blind turtle of the Tibetan analogy sunbathes on its golden ring, while sharks gather around. Explain what the sharks might symbolize to a Buddhist.

▶ Lama Zopa writes about how bad it is to *waste* our precious human rebirth. What does he mean by 'wasting' it?

FOR YOUR FOLDERS

▶ Write two lists to compare
 a) all the many things one might do in life, that a Buddhist would view as a waste of time
 b) the things that a Buddhist would view as meaningful.
   You could also write your own lists, e.g.
 a) trivial pursuits
 b) valuable achievements.

▶ When someone becomes a Buddhist, they vow to take refuge in the Buddha. What do you think is meant then, by 'taking refuge' in intoxicants?

7 WEALTH AND POVERTY

Greed

*'Not to commit any evil action.
To accumulate a wealth of excellent virtue
And to tame one's mind –
This is the teaching of the enlightened ones.'*
(Shakyamuni Buddha)

This quotation of the Buddha gives some insight into the Buddhist view of what it is to be wealthy. In Buddhist teachings there are many references to wealth and poverty. These have absolutely *nothing* to do with having material possessions.

According to Buddhism, the world we live in is governed by desire. It is often referred to as the **desire realm**. People's desires drag them through a continual search for satisfaction. They turn life into a search for happiness through the acquisition of wealth and objects.

Ironically, Buddhists say, it is this continual craving and dissatisfaction which brings us so much unhappiness.

The Wheel of Life

The **Wheel of Life** is a symbolic drawing of the suffering nature of existence. It is also called the **circle of the 12 dependent links.** The picture shows the wheel held in the mouth of the Lord of Death, showing how all beings are controlled by impermanence and death.

On the Wheel of Life, craving is symbolized by a man drinking wine. Just as this man's thirst is never satisfied, so the person deluded by greed is never satisfied and craves more things.

The important thing to understand about the Buddhist attitude to wealth is that it does not *in itself* bring happiness. If anyone thinks seriously about the lives of the wealthy and famous they can soon see that having a lot of money does not guarantee happiness.

KEY IDEA

Happiness does not arise from the accumulation of wealth and possessions.

Poverty and renunciation

The extreme opposite of enjoying a life of wealth and luxury is to live in such need that there is

The Wheel of Life

neither time nor energy to think about anything other than survival.

Buddhism says that people should aim for the balance *between* not having enough and wanting more. If people's minds are weighted towards greed then, rather than being able to enjoy their comfortable lifestyle, they become governed by their desires and experience the suffering of worry, meanness and craving. Yet if they don't have enough to live on they also suffer.

The Buddha encouraged his disciples to be well contained and have few possessions, because contact with objects leads to more greed and further suffering. This contact with objects is symbolized on the Wheel of Life by a man with an arrow in his eye.

'Better it were to swallow a ball of iron, red-hot and flaming, than to lead a wicked and unrestrained life eating the food of the people!'
(*The Dhammapada*, tr. Maharathi)

KEY IDEA

Poverty is not the same as renunciation. Poverty is to live in need, whereas renunciation is no longer to have greed.

Generosity and miserliness

Buddhists believe that if they are generous then they create the karma to be wealthy in this, or a future lifetime. If they experience poverty and need then this, too, is due to the karma they have created in the past by being mean and miserly.

Whatever anyone's present circumstances, they are not guaranteed to last, because of the basis of samsaric existence, which is ignorance. Ignorance is symbolized by the blind woman on the Wheel of Life in the first picture clockwise on the outer circle. Nobody knows where they are going, where they will be reborn, what they have suffered in the past, and what karma they have created for the future. No one can be certain about what lies ahead.

Buddhists believe that the only way to destroy ignorance and all other delusions, and start to have some control over life, is to practise a spiritual path of **Dharma Wisdom**. This is symbolized on the Wheel of Life by the Buddha, outside the circle, pointing towards the moon, the 'cool', peaceful state of mind free from all delusions and suffering.

> **Dharma** This is a Sanskrit word, literally meaning *that which holds one back from suffering*. The Pali spelling, **Dhamma**, is used by Theravadin Buddhists and the Sanskrit translation by Mahayanists. All Buddhists use the word to describe spiritual teachings.
> **Mahayana**. This is a title given to the school of Buddhism which believes in personal liberation for the sake of leading all sentient beings to enlightenment, rather than personal liberation as an end result. It is also known as **The Great Vehicle**.

The bodhisattva

The **Six Perfections** are the practices of giving, good conduct, patience, energy, meditation and wisdom. Someone who masters the Six Perfections is called, in Mahayana Buddhist terms, a **bodhisattva**.

A bodhisattva is someone who is motivated to attain enlightenment for the sake of all sentient beings.

'It is said that in one of his previous lives when the Buddha was still a bodhisattva, he was the leader of a tribe of monkeys. On one occasion, a huge fire spread through the forest endangering the lives of all the animals living there. The only way of escape was across a wide chasm. The chasm was too wide for the animals to jump across. It was too deep and its side was too steep for them to climb down into it to reach the other side. Only the monkey leader was strong and large enough to reach the other side of the chasm.

The great monkey, to save the lives of his fellow beings, then placed his feet firmly on the near side of the chasm and, stretching himself across, grasped the opposite edge with his hands. In this way, he made a bridge of his own body so that all the other animals could cross to safety. By the time all of them had reached the other side, the great monkey was exhausted by his tremendous effort. He had no more strength to hold on to the edge of the chasm and fell to his death below.'

(*Buddhism in Practice*, Singapore Buddhist Federation)

KEY IDEA

The giving of oneself, without regret, is seen as true generosity.

Offerings

As part of their daily prayers and regular religious rituals, many Buddhists make offerings to the Buddha by placing desirable objects, such as food, on their shrines. They believe this encourages the practice of giving, and develops their generosity.

FOR DISCUSSION

► What problems might Buddhists living in the West encounter in their practices of avoiding greed and desire?
► How might the Buddhist practice of giving, as described in the Six Perfections, become 'imperfect'? Make up a short play about someone who, in Buddhist terms, gives with the wrong motivation.
► How might placing something in front of an image encourage a generous state of mind? Make up a scene between two friends, one of whom is a Buddhist, the first time the non-Buddhist visits her friend's house.

8 SUFFERING AND EVIL

The truth of suffering

The truth of suffering is the **basic truth** from which the Buddha started teaching. His realization that cyclic existence, **samsara**, holds no lasting satisfaction or happiness, and that all beings are born from suffering to live and die in suffering, forms the central theme of Buddhism.

The term 'dissatisfaction' is sometimes used instead of suffering because suffering suggests actual physical pain. Closer examination of the nature of existence shows that suffering most clearly describes the physical and mental states anyone passes through repeatedly, even within one lifetime.

There are said to be eight types of suffering in samsara:

- the suffering of being born
- the suffering of old age
- the suffering of sickness
- the suffering of death
- the suffering of separation from loved ones and objects
- the suffering of encounters with unpleasant experiences and objects
- the suffering of not getting what we want
- the suffering of our own delusion and karma.

KEY IDEA

The very nature of life is dissatisfaction, or suffering.

That suffering is unavoidable is illustrated in this Buddhist story, about Kisa Gotami.

Ignorance and evil

Buddhists believe that all suffering has its source and its cure in the mind itself. Someone who commits evil is someone who acts out of ignorance and delusion, and although these acts harm others, the greatest harm is the suffering caused to the person committing the evil.

These words are the opening verses of The Dhammapada:

'All that we are is the consequence of what we have thought. All that we are is moulded on our thoughts and made up of our thoughts. If one speaks or acts with an evil mind, then pain follows him, even as the wheel, the hoof of the ox.

All that we are is the consequence of what we have thought. All that we are is moulded on our thoughts and made up of our thoughts. If one speaks or acts with pure mind, then happiness follows him, even as the shadow that never leaves.'

(*Dhammapada*, tr. Marahathi)

Buddhism teaches that to overcome their delusions people must first recognize that harmful acts do not create happiness. Having recognized this, they can then start training their minds to overcome these obstacles to happiness.

'Because of unwise choices, some people (the "monsters" of this world) push themselves to the extremes of cruelty and hate and cause horrendous suffering. But this does not destroy the seed of Buddhahood within; it is simply buried beneath layer upon layer of ignorance, misery, and pain. "Buddha-monsters" suffer from the delusion that to protect themselves they need to harm or destroy others.'

(Rev. Chushin Passmore, *There is Always a Choice*)

THE STORY OF KISA GOTAMI

Kisa Gotami had a beloved son, who, when he was just one year old, suddenly fell ill and died. Overcome with grief and unable to accept her son's death, she took the dead child in her arms and ran from house to house looking for medicine to restore the baby's life. No one knew what to do to console her, until someone mentioned that perhaps the Buddha might be able to help.

Kisa carried her son to the Buddha and begged for his help. He told her to go to the house of a family who had not experienced a death, and collect four or five mustard seeds. Convinced that this would bring her son back to life, she began her search.

Again and again doors were shut in her face. There was not one household which had not experienced the loss of a loved one. At last she understood what the Buddha was helping her to come to terms with – that death comes to all. She took her son away, and some time later returned to the Buddha to become one of his followers.

When Buddhists talk about studying, listening to and practising **dharma** they mean using one or more of the many different spiritual methods of overcoming delusions. The first step in removing ignorance and other delusions is recognizing the First Noble Truth (see page 7).

(see page 7)

KEY IDEA

People commit evil out of ignorance.

Pleasure and happiness

Suffering also describes the unsatisfactory nature of the pleasures people experience in life:

1 The indefinite nature of samsaric pleasures – whatever happiness they bring, it never lasts.
2 The sense of dissatisfaction which constantly strives for more and better samsaric pleasures.
3 The pain and discomfort of physical illness and mental unhappiness which accompanies the striving for samsaric pleasures.

'Using our present rebirth only to enjoy samsaric pleasures is being like a dumb animal that eats the grass at the edge of a cliff, in constant danger of falling off.'
(Lama Zopa Rinpoche, *The Wishfulfilling Golden Sun*)

The Banner of Victory symbolizes the victory of the Dharma over the forces of ignorance

Buddhists believe that people seek happiness through samsaric pleasures because of their delusions and karma, but that true happiness lies in the release from samsara.

Often people think that Buddhism, with its view of suffering, is a negative or pessimistic religion. This needs to be thought about carefully. Religion, in general, is often associated with the rejection of pleasure, and people who choose a spiritual path think that spiritual discipline requires the denial of pleasure. This attitude is *not* Buddhist and, in fact, is just another delusion . . . 'I am a good and spiritual person because I do not indulge in the pleasures of the world.'

When people experience pleasure they should allow themselves the enjoyment. Feeling miserable because the Buddha said life is suffering is *not* what Buddhism is about.

'If we wallow in misery the only result is that we experience even more misery. On the other hand, if we know how to experience happiness without the polluted attitudes of either grasping attachment or guilt, we can cultivate deeper levels of this experience and eventually attain the inconceivable happiness of our full human potential.'
(Lama Yeshe, *Introduction to Tantra*)

Buddhists see happiness as an *inner* experience – finding what is already *within* them, rather than pursuing what always seems to be just *beyond* them.

FOR YOUR FOLDERS

▶ In your own words say what you think Buddhists mean by
(a) suffering, (b) evil, (c) happiness.

FOR DISCUSSION

▶ *'The village I reach at last
deeper than the deep mountains
what joy
the capital
where I have always lived!'*

This enigmatic little poem, from *There is Always a Choice*, was written by the Great Zen Master Dogen. What 'place' do you think he is referring to?

Right livelihood

By following the guidelines within **right livelihood**, Buddhists avoid causing harm to others within their daily work, and so even in a situation in which they have to participate for the sake of survival, they are still able to create the cause for their own and others' happiness.

KEY IDEA

Right livelihood is a guideline to working without causing harm to others.

'What we have done will not be lost to all eternity. Everything ripens at its time and becomes fruit at its hour.'

(Divyavadana)

RIGHT LIVELIHOOD

To avoid work connected with:

- weapons
- animals for slaughter
- slavery
- intoxicants
- poisons and harmful drugs.

1 Work connected with deadly weapons
This provides people with the means to hurt and destroy others, which is the direct opposite of Buddhist intention.
2 Work connected with the slaughter of animals
This, too, involves harming others and shows disrespect for life.
3 Work connected with slavery
Slavery also shows disrespect for life and forces others to do what they do not want to do, for the sake of personal reward.
4 Work connected with intoxicants
Participating in a job such as selling alcohol is actually contributing to people's minds being clouded and to their being deluded. This frequently results in the harming of others through their own negligence and lack of self control.
5 Work connected with poisons
Poisons are manufactured to kill or maim and do not lead to the welfare of others.

Respect for life

Each of the prohibitions above corresponds to the positive value of respect for life. The helping careers, such as nursing, social work and teaching, are considered particularly worthy occupations, because they provide more opportunities to develop compassionate qualities.

If the motivation of someone in a caring career, however, is primarily for personal ambition and gain, then their karma is affected.

Stress

More and more it seems that people are suffering in stressful jobs because so much is expected of them, and the pace of life is so fast. This busy lifestyle creates a busy mind, and does not help anyone to be thoughtful for others.

'Grant yourself a moment of peace and you will understand how foolishly you have scurried about. Learn to be silent and you will notice that you have talked much too much. Be kind and you will realize that your judgement of others was too severe.'
(Tschen Tschi Ju, *Springs of Chinese Wisdom*)

Buddhists believe that even difficult work situations can be eased, by trying to cultivate a positive attitude towards their work. By thinking of the benefits to others that their work is providing, or merely by working with other people harmoniously and creatively they can improve their own, as well as other people's, daily lives.

Leisure

It is the Buddhist belief that in spite of progress, the nature of the mind remains the same. Human frustrations have not decreased but have simply changed.

The life story of the Buddha demonstrates that leisure in itself does not make people happy.

Alms giving

The traditional way for ordained Buddhists to survive, which is still practised today, particularly within the Theravadin tradition, is not by working for money, but by relying on the kindness of others.

Ajahn Teacher or guide.

MEDITATION FOR RELAXATION

The following meditation is a way of relaxing and healing the body, as well as pacifying the mind. You may like to try it.

Close your eyes and sit comfortably. Concentrate on the sensation of your breath as it passes in and out of your nostrils.

Imagine that the air is like light – very pure and healing, like a miracle medicine. As you breathe in, visualize the light entering your body through your nostrils. Imagine it gradually filling your body, from your toes upwards to the top of your head.

As you breathe out, visualize the tension and pain leaving your body through your nostrils, in the form of smoke, which disappears into the depths of the earth.

Eventually, you can imagine that the light is pouring out of every opening and pore of your body, as if you are radiating light. Enjoy the feeling of being calm, peaceful and relaxed.

Venerable Ajahn Sumedho, a Western monk of the Theravadin tradition has said,

'An alms-mendicant is one who gives the occasion for others to give alms. This is different from being a beggar going around scrounging off the neighbours . . . an alms-mendicant gives the occasion for others to give the alms that are necessary for existence – such as food, robes, shelter and medicine. You don't need very much and you have to live quite humbly and impeccably so you are worthy of alms.'

In Buddhist countries, the giving and accepting of alms is viewed as mutually beneficial for those involved. To give alms offers the opportunity for lay people to support a monastery as an important part of their own spiritual practice.

'This monastery is dependent on alms, there are no fees for staying – it just depends on what people offer. If it was an institution based on fees, we wouldn't really be samanas any more, we'd be businesspeople, making a business out of teaching the Dharma which has been freely given to us.'

. . . and the sangha's gratitude towards the benefactors helps their practice too.

'. . . as samanas, we give the occasion for people to give what they can, and that has a good effect on us as well as on the society. When you open up the opportunity in a society where people can give to things they respect and love, people get a lot of happiness and joy. But if we have a tyrannical society where we're constantly trying to squeeze everything out we can get, we have a miserable and depressed society.'
(Ajahn Sumedho, *Cittaviveka, Teachings from the Silent Mind*)

Theravada 'The Way of the Elders', the school of Buddhism which uses the Pali canon, the earliest recorded teachings of the Buddha.
Mendicant or samana Homeless, penniless practitioners, who rely on the kindness of others for their survival.
Sangha The Buddhist spiritual community. This usually refers to ordained Buddhists. The Sangha are the third of the Three Jewels of Refuge.

FOR DISCUSSION

► What moral dilemma faces the Buddhist who wishes to integrate into our society where so many people socialize in pubs? What would be the most skilful way of solving this problem without insulting or upsetting others?
► Think of a stressful situation. What advice might a Buddhist give for coping with it?

FOR YOUR FOLDERS

► If you were a Buddhist employer, what methods would you use to get the best from your employees, and how would you create a happy work environment?
► '. . . trying to squeeze everything out we can get . . .' What is Ajahn Sumedho referring to here, when he is explaining the philosophy behind alms-collecting and giving?

The Second Noble Truth

'The main problems which humankind is facing today are basically created by ourselves – created by the divisions we make, based on the secondary factors of ideology, nationalism, economic systems, racial differences, and so on. These issues are hard to reconcile if we think of them as having primary importance. Therefore, I believe that the time has come when we should think on a deeper level – the level of actual, human being – and try to act, from that level of appreciation and respect, for all other human beings. We must build a closer relationship among ourselves, based on mutual trust, mutual understanding, mutual respect, and mutual help, irrespective of culture, philosophy, religion or faith. . .

There is no need for us to agree philosophically, no need to share a temple or a belief. If we are full of good will, our own mind, our own heart, is the temple. Kindness, alone, is enough. This is my religion.'

A hand mudra; mudras are used mainly during prayers and meditation

The extract above is from *Voices of Survival in the Nuclear Age*, a piece by His Holiness the Dalai Lama, the spiritual and temporal leader of the Tibetan people.

Buddhism says that all problems – personal and shared – stem from the **deluded** or deceived mind. The deluded mind strives for happiness through external sources. This striving, also called **desirous attachment**, was identified by the Buddha in his second Noble Truth, that desire is the main cause of suffering. The Buddha taught that only when this desire is extinguished will we actually find true and lasting happiness.

KEY IDEA

The cause of suffering is desire.

The deluded mind

The six main delusions are:

1 Ignorance – not understanding the nature of cyclic existence and the law of cause and effect.

2 Greed – craving for the satisfaction of our senses by attaching ourselves to objects and people which we consider to be beautiful.

3 Anger – the opposite of humility and patience, and said to be the greatest barrier to enlightenment.

4 Pride – feeling superior to others.

5 Doubt – questioning the belief in cyclic existence and karma so that it becomes an obstacle to enlightenment.

6 The doctrine of delusion – holding on strongly to beliefs which bring about suffering to oneself and others.

Buddhists believe that these delusions lead people to make the divisions referred to by the Dalai Lama, because constantly clinging to things which make them feel *good* or *right* leads to the rejection of what makes them feel *bad*.

Buddhism teaches that the things which make people feel good are not good in themselves, but simply make them feel secure. They include close family and friends, home, town, country, culture, nationality, and colour. All forms of prejudice, including nationalism and racism, come from these delusions of the mind which glorify self by undermining others. Because they are negative feelings they cannot be the cause of happiness.

Equanimity

The practice of **equanimity** – setting ourselves equal with others – helps to overcome delusions such as greed, anger and pride, which build these invisible walls between people.

The first step towards seeing oneself as equal with others is to identify what everyone has in common. A Tibetan spiritual master, living and teaching in the West, wrote:

'All human beings have a wish in common. We wish to be happy and avoid suffering. Even newborn babies, animals and insects have this wish. It has been uppermost in our mind since beginningless time and is present even during our sleep. We spend our whole lives working very hard to fulfil this wish.'

(Geshe Kelsang Gyatso, *Universal Compassion*)

Buddhism teaches that the root cause of all people's delusions is the first delusion, **ignorance**, or not understanding the nature of samsara and the law of karma. Continually failing to understand why things happen feeds other delusions such as anger, and binds people to the Wheel of Life.

In his *Guide to the Bodhisattva's Way of Life*, Shantideva, an 8th century Buddhist master from India, said:

'First of all I should make an effort
To meditate on equalizing self and others.
I should protect all beings as I do myself
Because we are equal in wanting pleasure
And not wanting pain.'

Shantideva, an 8th century Buddhist

To equalize themselves with others, people have to balance the love they have for themselves with the love they have for others. This means developing as much care for the happiness of other people as for their own, and trying to remove the suffering of other people as well as their own.

'When we first attempt this meditation, doubts may arise. We may question the value of trying to remove the suffering of others, thinking, "No one else's suffering directly affects me. Each of us has to bear our own suffering, so why try to dispel the suffering of others?" While it is true that we do not have to experience others' suffering, it is still very important to try to help them. If we have a thorn in our foot, although our hand is not directly affected, it pulls out the thorn immediately. If we think of all

living beings as one body, one in wishing to be free from suffering, we will not hesitate to alleviate their sufferings.'
(*Universal Compassion*, Geshe Kelsang)

Lovingkindness

At the heart of all Buddhist practices is the attitude of lovingkindness towards all beings. By appreciating and respecting the human race as one entity, and practising equanimity to destroy the divisions they make, people can overcome all forms of separation and insecurity which give rise to prejudice and racism.

KEY IDEA

One of the steps on the Eightfold Noble Path to Enlightenment is **right action**. This means acting in a socially considerate way to others, and treating all beings equally.

If a group or nation generates hatred and violence through their insecurity, other people need to understand that returning this hatred and violence does not create harmony. According to Buddhist thought, by tolerance and understanding, people can gradually achieve universal unity.

FOR DISCUSSION

▶ HH the Dalai Lama says, 'Kindness, alone, is enough.' Discuss this point of view which maintains that all acts of aggression and hostility should be responded to with kindness.

FOR YOUR FOLDERS

▶ Buddhism says that all negativities create cause for suffering. Can you think of any occasion in your life when what a Buddhist would see as a negative thought or action brought positive results?

At the time of the Buddha

At the time of the Buddha, the role of women in society was essentially a domestic one. Women were not seen as necessarily *inferior* to men but *different*. Men and women generally agreed that the ideal woman was a good wife and mother. If a woman wanted to lead a spiritual life then she had to be single-minded although, according to historical records, female ascetics did exist.

A western Buddhist nun

When the Buddha began to teach, many more women chose spiritual paths because, unlike other spiritual teachers, the Buddha taught that women were as capable as men of reaching enlightenment. Although the Buddha taught that anyone who wished to *could* become enlightened, in Indian society there still continued a strong dominant male influence which limited women and prevented them from having equal status with men.

Modern research, mostly done by women, argues that the Buddha's teachings so clearly go beyond divisions and status that it is difficult to reconcile them with the rules for nuns – and the comments about women – that the Buddha is recorded as having made. Many Buddhist scholars argue that the Buddha's words have not been accurately recorded, and that the eight additional rules for nuns were a compromise which enabled women to lead a spiritual life, but complied with the Indian social system. Despite this unequal treatment, more and more women chose the monastic life, and although still subservient, were freed from worldly and wifely duties.

'The Buddha protected nuns from exploitation by monks, by saying that the nuns should not be called upon to sew, dye, or weave for the monks. Neither could the monks take for themselves donations made to the nuns. The mother of the famous monk Sumangala stated her freedom as a nun in this way:

O woman well set free! How free am I,
How thoroughly free from kitchen drudgery!
Me stained and squalid 'mong my cooking pots
My brutal husband ranked as even less
Than the sunshades he sits and weaves away.
Purged now of all my former lust and hate,
I dwell, musing at ease beneath the shade
of spreading boughs . . . O, but 'tis well with me!'
(Tsultrim Allione, *Women of Wisdom*)

> ## KEY IDEA
>
> Despite male hierarchy, the Buddha taught that women are as capable as men of becoming enlightened.

Modern attitudes

Buddhist teachers today recognize that western women no longer accept subservience, and recent teachings and books address women equally with men. Lay women and men are as capable of becoming enlightened as ordained women and men, but it is the monastic orders which are recognized as the most dedicated spiritual communities.

There are no boundaries to lay women's or nuns' spiritual practices, but certain advice is given to women which acknowledges their physical differences rather than their human potential. In Shantideva's 8th century text *A Guide to the Bodhisattva's Way of Life* (*Bodhisattvacharyavatara*), the dedication prayer includes the following line: 'May all the females throughout the universe who so desire be reborn in a male form.'

In Geshe Kelsang's guide to this text he explains this line as follows:

'Because of long-standing social inequities it has often been extremely difficult for women to break out of their expected roles and follow the spiritual path. Furthermore, women in solitary retreat face the danger of assault and other hindrances. Thus, for those women desirous of practising the dharma without such interferences, Shantideva extends his prayers.'
(Geshe Kelsang, *Meaningful to Behold*)

There are many examples of women in the past who have attained enlightenment. If respect for women increases within society, then, in terms of karma, there is every reason to have more and more women in respected roles such as spiritual teachers.

One example of a contemporary dedicated, female, Buddhist practitioner is Tenzin Palmo.

'Anila Tenzin Palmo is an Englishwoman who came to India in 1964. While living in Dalhousie she helped with theTibetan refugees and taught English to the Tulkus. Just after her 21st birthday, in 1964, she became a nun. After she served as secretary to her Lama, Khamtrul Rinpoche, for six years, he sent her to meditate in the mountainous region of Lahul in India where she lived for 18 years. She lived in a monastery for the first six years before moving into a cave and has spent most of the last 12 years engaged in several retreats there, recently completing a three year solitary retreat.'

(Thubten Pemo, 'Anila Tenzin Palmo', *Mandala*)

Tulku Recognized reincarnation of former spiritual teacher.

Sexlessness and Buddhahood

When a person becomes enlightened, there is no more division between male and female – just the perfect balance between the two.

KEY IDEA

Buddhas are neither male nor female, but take on male or female forms in order to communicate with sentient beings.

The princess described in the next column became known as Tara the Saviouress because of the limitless number of people she helped, and is now recognized as the **Buddha Tara** (Sanskrit), or **Kuan Lin** (Chinese). In Tibet and China she is possibly the most popular of Buddhist deities and is also known as the **Loving Mother**, the **Swift One**, and **Heroine.**

THE STORY OF TARA, THE BUDDHIST FEMALE DEITY

*'There was once a princess called **Moon of Wisdom-knowledge** who was an extremely devoted practitioner of the dharma. Finally, she produced the Thought of Enlightenment. At that time some monks urged her, "Because of these roots of virtue, if you pray in this body that you may become a man and perform the deeds according to the Teachings, then you will be thus transformed. Therefore that is what you should do." It is said there was much discussion. Finally, the princess spoke, saying:*

"Here there is no man, there is no woman, No self, no person, and no consciousness. Labelling 'male' or 'female' has no essence, But deceives the evil-minded world."

And she made the vow, "There are many who desire Enlightenment in a man's body, but none who work for the benefit of sentient beings in the body of a woman. Therefore, until samsara is empty, I shall work for the benefit of sentient beings in a woman's body."'

(From *In Praise of Tara* by Martin Willson, an English Buddhist monk.)

FOR YOUR FOLDERS

▶ Write a letter to your friend who has decided to become a Buddhist nun, trying to dissuade her from taking robes, because she will lose her 'freedom'. Then write her response.
▶ If you held Buddhist beliefs about reincarnation and enlightenment, would you like to be reborn as a male or a female in your next life? Give reasons.

Karma

Buddhists believe that until they realize the law of karma and exercise some control over their destiny, they are swept along from life to life, up and down, in confusion.

Buddhists are taught that self-control over unwholesome tendencies, or **mindfulness** – although difficult – can start in a very small way, and that the results can soon be seen.

A Lama and a Tibetan Geshe lead a 'puja' (prayer)

'Renunciation of violence must be born in the mind. Control of mind is something inborn. I am not talking here about the control of mind which is achieved in deep meditation. I am just talking about the kind of control which reduces anger, creates respect and concern for others, and allows a clearer realization that human beings are, basically, the same. . . To-day, you may be the type of person who is easily irritated over small things. If you become aware of this, realizing the consequences of your irritation, self-control will result.'

(HH the Dalai Lama, *Voices of Survival*)

KEY IDEA

Understanding karma enables us to learn through our own experience.

THE STORY OF GESHE BEN

There was once, living in Tibet, a robber who found it impossible to let any opportunity of stealing pass him by. However, one day, having thought about the teachings of the Buddha, he realized that his life of crime had to stop or he would come to no good. He became a monk and studied many holy texts, eventually earning himself the venerated title of **geshe**, or teacher, and a reputation as a good and learned man.

However, although he purified his past bad behaviour by sincerely regretting his actions in prayer and religious observances, he would still find himself caught out by his old habits.

When he passed a precious object, such as a statue, he would reach out to grab it with one hand but, immediately recognizing his bad intention, his other hand would grasp the first in an endeavour to control himself. At the same time he would call out to his friends to help him stop the thief.

The criminal mind

His Holiness the Dalai Lama also commented in the same article, about the human condition.

'Bad human beings think it is to their advantage to prevail over their fellow men . . . to use any method which seems expedient, no matter how cruel, in order to achieve this advantage. The advantage will not last; the methods used only create more problems, more suffering, more mistrust, more resentment, more division. The result is not good for anyone.'

(HH the Dalai Lama, *Voices of Survival*)

Although Buddhism says that crime will always be paid for with karmic consequences, it still recognizes the need to protect people from criminals, and at the same time protect criminals from creating more bad karma for themselves. A punishment which deliberately hurts or destroys another being implies that there is no other way that person can learn from their mistakes. In his article on Human Rights, James Belither, a Western Buddhist, says:

'Central to the Buddhist faith is the possibility of development. No matter how evilly someone

behaves they always have the possibility of correcting their behaviour. To deny that possibility of change by imposing the death penalty, for example, is to contradict the whole spirit of Buddhism.'

(James Belither, *Human Rights from a Buddhist Perspective*)

One story which illustrates how even the most evil murderers are capable of change is about the great Buddhist saint and poet of Tibet, **Milarepa**.

THE STORY OF MILAREPA

Milarepa lived in the 11th century. His youth was full of misfortunes and sorrows. His father died young and his uncle treated him badly. After he had suffered many years of servitude and humiliation, his mother persuaded him to take revenge on his cruel relatives. Milarepa found a teacher of black magic who agreed to divulge to him his sorcery, and with his sharp mind he quickly learned the sorcerer's tricks.

He returned to his home and coldly murdered even the infant relatives of his uncle, killing them by manifesting poisonous scorpions. He tore down their buildings with his magic powers, and eventually destroyed the whole of his native valley by conjuring up hailstorms.

Not long after this, however, he felt weighed down by his sins, and determined to lead a better life. He practised the dharma until, at last, with the help of his guru, and many years of meditation and penance, he became enlightened. He earned fame for his wisdom, compassion and great poetry and is regarded to this day as Tibet's greatest saint.

Guru Sanskrit term meaning a spiritual guide, or teacher.

Protection from evil

Buddhism teaches that understanding karma helps people to lessen their insecurity and fear within a violent society, because the only security from being harmed that anyone has is in not harming others.

Retaliation, revenge and punishment may make someone feel better temporarily, but eventually, if they have had the intention to harm another, the karmic cycle will continue.

Ajahn Sumedho, a Theravadin Buddhist Master, says:

'If you have the memory of murdering 999 people – that's just a horrendous memory now. Maybe you think, "That's getting off too easily; somebody who's killed 999 people should suffer a long time and be punished and tormented!" But it's not necessary that we go to any lengths to punish anyone because the punishment is the memory. As long as we remain ignorant, unenlightened, selfish beings, then we tend to create more karmic cycles. Our lack of forgiveness, lack of compassion, of trying to get even with "those evil criminals" – that's our karma: we have the karmic result of the miserable state of hatred.'

(Ajahn Sumedho, *Cittaviveka, Teachings from the Silent Mind*)

KEY IDEAS

Not harming others is our only security from not being harmed.

A bad person is someone who has not yet discovered their potential for good.

FOR DISCUSSION

▶ 'The fundamental difference between the Buddhist attitude to wrongdoing, and how society should deal with it, lies in the belief of karma.'

FOR YOUR FOLDERS

▶ Imagine you are a Buddhist who is applying for the post of governor of a high security prison which deals with society's worst offenders, like murderers and rapists. Write a letter of application explaining how your belief in Buddhism will assist you in the job if appointed.

13 POLITICS, AUTHORITY AND GOVERNMENT

Politics at the time of the Buddha

When the Buddha was alive, approximately 500 BCE, in northern India there was a simple society made up of small states which were democratic by nature. These were gradually conquered, and changed into larger, more complex states ruled by **rajas**, or kings.

The Buddha favoured republican methods of government, however, and recommended to his monks that regular councils based upon republican traditions would ensure the growth of the sangha.

While kings continued to rule the land the Buddhist attitude was to accept it, although this compromise obliged the Buddha to define the ideal king. In the **Anguttara Nikaya**, one of the Buddha's discourses, the Buddha tells his followers that a real king is one who 'rolls the Wheel of the Dharma'. When the Buddha first began to teach as an enlightened being, he was said to start the 'rolling of the Wheel of the Dharma', which means that he began to teach the truth about life to others. The wheel is still used as a symbol of the Buddhist spiritual path. The Buddha's view of an ideal ruler, then, is one who rules with the knowledge of the dharma, and when asked, 'Who is the ruler of the king?' he responds, 'It is dharma, O bhikkhu!'

KEY IDEA

A wise leader is one who is guided by the teachings of the dharma.

The humane qualities of wise leadership are repeatedly defined in the *Jataka Tales*, a collection of stories which the Buddha told about his former lives, when he came 'as a monkey amid the monkeys, as a deer amid the deer' and as 'their chief and their guide'. One example is as follows.

'O King, ... It is not your sword which makes you a king; it is love alone. Forget not that your life is but little to give if in giving you secure the happiness of your people. Rule them not through power because they are your subjects; nay, rule them through love because they are your children. In this way only you shall be king.'

(*The Monkey-Bridge*)

THE EMPEROR ASHOKA

One ruler who took the Buddha's advice was the Emperor Ashoka, who reigned in India in the 3rd century BCE.

As a prince, Ashoka was ruthless and ambitious. When his father died he planned to expand his empire, and invaded a neighbouring state where he and his armies massacred thousands of people. However, tormented by the memory of the bloodshed he had caused, he turned to Buddhism for moral guidance.

Ashoka's new respect for life led him to change many of his old habits. He stopped hunting, ordered that the minimum of animals be killed for food in his household, and spent his money on social improvements, not only in his land but also in his neighbours'. He encouraged moral values and had proclamations carved on rocks and pillars, many of which can still be seen all over India.

Through his influence, Buddhism spread throughout South Asia.

The Ashoka Pillar

Modern leadership

The Buddha taught repeatedly that the quality of love is the ultimate weapon against all problems and suffering. Today, contemporary Buddhist spiritual leaders continue to say that putting effort into developing our compassionate love is the most important thing we can do.

'All (of these) wrongs stem from our lack of human understanding, of mutual trust, and of mutual respect, based on kindness and love for all beings. This is why I feel there is only one way to achieve lasting, world peace, and that it's worthwhile for us to make the effort, even if it may not be attained during our own lifetimes.'
(HH the Dalai Lama)

Some people might say that believing love alone will make a successful government is naive, but this contradicts the simplicity of Buddhist belief.

Buddhism teaches that people reach personal perfection through gradual yet determined efforts to change. In the same way, it says, national, international and even universal problems can be solved by governments.

' to a large extent, our future is in the hands of the world leaders. It is, therefore, imperative that they have more frequent, person-to-person contact . . . Under an atmosphere of better understanding, there is hope for a general lessening of tensions, and a gradual cultivation of trust.'
(HH the Dalai Lama)

KEY IDEA

Success of governments also depends on developing the qualities taught in the dharma.

Although being motivated by love would be the prime consideration of the Buddhists' ideal government, unless used with wisdom it could be useless. The Noble Eightfold Path is divided into three parts, of which wisdom is the third.

Compassion alone, without the wisdom to see if it is really benefiting sentient beings, can still cause harm if used without discrimination. Using compassion with wisdom is sometimes referred to as **using skilful means**. Compassion used without wisdom is often referred to as **idiot compassion**.

Buddhism says, however, that wisdom should not be confused with knowledge or cleverness. There are many examples, in the past and present, of leaders whose great mental abilities, through

their selfishness and lack of compassion, have created enormous suffering.

'World peace will not result through external development. It does not depend upon reducing noise in the city or hiding in a cave. The only cause that can bring peace to universal beings is to change ourselves into others, to be attached to the comfort of others instead of our own, which we should renounce. The negative thought that cherishes ourself and not the other is the cause of all suffering and problems.'
(Lama Zopa Rinpoche, *The Wishfulfilling Golden Sun*)

Collective karma

Buddhism is a belief in **peace**: peace of mind, peace between people, peace in the world. There is no justification for war, in pure Buddhist thought, although decisions which cause suffering to a few people might be made if the leader has the wisdom to see that the action will prevent suffering to many.

Acts of nations motivated by greed and hostility create bad karma for all their citizens, and benevolent acts create good karma. The group creation of karma is called **collective karma**.

If a government has oppressed and exploited other nations in the past, then that country creates negative karma for its future and, similarly, its acts of compassion will bring future rewards.

FOR YOUR FOLDERS

▶ Imagine that a Buddhist political party is elected to govern the UK. Write down a list of all the issues they might tackle.
▶ Write a paragraph saying what you think the differences between cleverness and wisdom are, according to Buddhists.

TALKING POINTS

● It is not your sword that makes you a king, it is love alone;
● Compassion used without wisdom is idiot compassion.
Consider some practical examples.

31

14 CARE

Altruism

When asked which Buddhist belief can be of value to all people, HH the Dalai Lama said,

'. . . altruism or love and compassion, these I always consider key things – for individual cases or family level or national level or international level – for success and a happier environment.'

Buddhists say that meditating on love and compassion helps them to develop a caring attitude towards all beings.

In their practice of love and compassion, Buddhists try to meet every situation with an altruistic mind. Befriending an elderly neighbour and assisting with their wellbeing becomes as much second nature as saving an insect from drowning in a glass of cola.

> **Altruism** Unselfish regard or consideration for others.

> # KEY IDEA
> The mind which is motivated to help others transforms every situation into an opportunity for caring.

Right livelihood

Because of their belief in reincarnation and their view of death and dying as a preparation for the next life, some Buddhists choose to work with the terminally ill or the very old in institutions like AIDS centres and hospices. This is because they believe they can help people approach and prepare for their deaths with more acceptance and less fear. It is not always possible, though, to choose one's vocation.

'To live with right livelihood is to remain true to one's spiritual purpose while living in the world. . . How do you find out what your purpose is in life? As part of growing up we blunder about trying whatever comes to hand: academic life, business, sports, drugs, travel, sex, politics, relationships, having children. . . If we are fortunate we survive long enough to discover that on their own, or in combination, none of these things is a lasting refuge. Consequently, we look for something deeper and turn to meditation for an answer. Not everyone makes a good nurse or is suited to looking after the mentally handicapped, nor is everyone going to find Right Livelihood living in a commune, but some people may. All one can ever know for sure is that which it is good to do today.'
(Zen Master Daishin Morgan, *Right Livelihood*)

The power of the mind

1 POSITIVE THINKING

It is through the influence of Buddhist thought in the West that many 'alternative' therapies use **positive thinking** as a part of their treatment.

Buddhists say thinking positively about their condition can only benefit the sick person. By viewing their own suffering as just one small example in the suffering of the world, they can gain insights in their spiritual understanding.

Elea Redel is a Buddhist. She has suffered from rheumatoid arthritis for seven years, and is gradually losing the use of her body. Every movement brings pain. From *Mandala*, a journal for Buddhists, this article about her says:

'Elea says she has had to become friendly with her pain – accepting it without thinking it is good or bad; it is just the result of past actions. She has found there is no point in being upset with it; otherwise the pain is unbearable . . . Elea says her sickness has allowed her to better feel other people's suffering and understand the nature of suffering as pain is always with her. "In Buddhism we say may all people be happy, but when I was well I never really felt the suffering of others. Now I know how even a little pain affects an individual. When I see deformed beggars crawling along the road in India I feel for them and humanity. . ."'
(Owen Cole, 'To Wear Pain Like An Ornament', *Mandala*)

2 SELF-HEALING

Buddhism teaches that the power of the mind is so great that sometimes people can actually help heal themselves through meditation and concentration.

Suicide and euthanasia

Buddhism says that, because of karma, no one can escape pain and suffering by putting an end to this body. If the karma has not been fully extinguished then it will follow into a future life.

The karma involved in taking a decision to end a life also depends upon the motive. Rev. Chushin Passmore, Zen Master, makes this general comment on the difficult choices which we must make in life.

'When we truly listen to the heart in the stillness of meditation we can know for ourselves what best to do in any situation, however morally and emotionally fraught it seems . . . with meditation practice to support us, and the precepts to guide our actions, we are more likely to make wise decisions and fewer mistakes (even though these decisions may often go against current thinking in society at large).'

KEY IDEA

Because of karma, putting an end to life does not necessarily extinguish suffering.

Death and impermanence

'It is unsure whether tomorrow or the next life will come first.'

(The Buddha)

The awareness and acceptance of death as a natural part of life is an important aspect of the Buddhist teachings on **impermanence**, **suffering** and **karma**. Most people dismiss the thought of death, as if it could be avoided.

Buddhism says this view is unhealthy and unrealistic, and people should contemplate death and impermanence as a chance to value their precious human rebirths, and to understand the nature of samsara.

'At the hour of death, the king and the beggar are exactly equal in that no amount of relatives or possessions can affect or prevent death. But who is the richer at the time of death? If the beggar has created more merits, then although he looks materially poor he is really the rich man. From the Dharma point of view, the mind that has prepared itself for the journey into the next life has the real riches.'

(Lama Zopa Rinpoche, *The Wishfulfilling Golden Sun*)

KEY IDEA

We are all subject to change and no one or nothing can escape death and decay.

SOME BUDDHIST CARE AGENCIES

The Buddhist Hospice Trust
PO Box 51
Herne Bay
Kent CT6 6TP

Angulimala
Buddhist Prison Chaplaincy Organization
The Forest Hermitage
Lower Fulbrook
Warwick CV35 8AS

Charity Aid for India
186 Cowley Road
Oxford OX4 1OE

MEDITATION ON THE SUFFERING OF SENTIENT BEINGS

Close your eyes. Become very quiet and still. Concentrate on someone you know who you think is suffering. This might be because they are ill or unhappy. Try to imagine what it is like to be that person. Put yourself into a day in the life of that person. Try to generate compassion for that person.

Extend your feeling outwards to others. Imagine you are somewhere where you know there is great suffering, like a place of famine or war. Again, try to be inside one of these people, imagining what a day in their life must be like.

Again, generate compassion for these beings, and finally try to imagine how wonderful it would be to be able to relieve any being's pain.

The bodhisattva vow

When asked his reaction to being awarded the Nobel Prize for Peace, His Holiness the Dalai Lama responded with his favourite prayer from Shantideva, an acclaimed Buddhist teacher who lived in India during the 8th century CE.

'So long as space remains
So long as sentient beings' suffering is there
I will be there
To serve as much as I can.'

(Shantideva)

This brief recollection of the bodhisattva's vow embodies the Buddhist attitude to all life as they know it. So long as there is life on this planet its people must do all they can to care for it.

Engaged Buddhism

Buddhists today recognize that, more than at any other time since the Buddha lived on Earth, there is a need to move beyond prayer and meditation to act practically to help the world.

*'It is possible to meditate, to be peaceful and fully awake **while** helping others. When we hear the cries of the world we must be engaged.'*

(Thich Nhat Hanh)

This extract, along with the other extracts in this chapter, is from an article written by Thich Nhat Hanh, in a book called *The Path of Compassion, Contemporary Writings on Engaged Buddhism*, a collection of essays by Buddhists who believe that more Buddhists should become involved in social action.

The term which describes Buddhist social action is **Engaged Buddhism**. There are many examples of Buddhists working in the community and taking social and political action in the past. The present day Buddhists, concerned with the immediate endangerment of the world, have started using this term.

KEY IDEA

Engaged Buddhism seeks to use the philosophy of Buddhism for social awareness.

Collective karma

Buddhists see the environment they live in as being the result of **collective karma**. If they live in it, then it is their creation. If they want to continue living on Earth, then that, too, must be their creation.

'We have created a society in which the rich become richer and the poor become poorer, and in which man is so caught up in his own immediate problems that he cannot afford to be aware of what is going on with the rest of the human family.'

(Thich Nhat Hanh)

Social action intended to protect the environment, encourage respect for all races, creeds and cultures and to promote a healthy, safe and harmonious environment will have positive results in the future, be it in this or our future lifetimes, because of the law of karma.

Similarly, neglecting, destroying and polluting the planet will result in people living on a neglected and polluted planet.

To Buddhists, the wounded world in which they now live is proof that people have acted selfishly so, in order to protect the world, Buddhists would say that collectively, as members of the 'human family', everyone must now do all they can to heal it.

KEY IDEA

Everything that lives on Earth is interdependent and a result of collective karma.

Mental health

The Buddhist concept of mental health is a mind which is open. By learning to love and accept itself it becomes able to love and accept others. Although unique, it is able to accept its interdependence with the rest of the world, and it is a mind which, through turning inward, is able to look outward with compassion, equanimity and tolerance.

Buddhists believe that if everyone works towards having a healthy mind then they are less likely to create a sick environment and an unbalanced society.

'As a Buddhist monk, I, like psychiatrists, tend to look at the problem from the viewpoint of mental health. Buddhist meditation aims at creating harmony and equilibrium in the life of the individual. . .

Restoring mental health cannot be simply efforts to adjust man to the modern world with its galloping pace of economic growth. The world is ill. Adaptation to an ill environment cannot be the way to real mental health.'

(Thich Nhat Hanh)

KEY IDEA

Making our own minds healthy is a practical step towards the future health of our planet.

This simple prayer, written by Venerable Maha Ghosananda, sums up how Buddhists believe that working on our own minds will benefit the world. It is taken from *Paths of Compassion*.

A CAMBODIAN PRAYER

The suffering of Cambodia has been deep.
From this suffering comes great compassion.
Great compassion makes a peaceful heart.
A peaceful heart makes a peaceful person.
A peaceful person makes a peaceful family.
A peaceful family makes a peaceful community.
A peaceful community makes a peaceful nation.
A peaceful nation makes a peaceful world.
Amen.

Living in a pure land

It is a Buddhist belief that someone who has developed their mind to a state of great purity, because of their good karma, will be unable to experience much suffering.

As highly developed individuals they will enjoy the fruits of their endeavours and even the place they live in will be a **pure land** – beautiful, harmonious and pleasurable.

Sometimes it is possible to glimpse how a good state of mind affects someone's experience, by thinking about their present life. If a person is particularly happy about something then even the most dull environment and depressing weather can be transformed.

For some people who have created good karma, Buddhists say *this* world is a pure land. Buddhists say that, by practising Buddhist methods of self-improvement, people can transform an ordinary life on Earth into an extraordinarily happy experience.

THE CULTIVATION OF LOVINGKINDNESS

You will have sweet dreams, fall asleep easily, and awaken with a smile.
The gods and angels will love and protect you.
Men and women will love you.
Weapons won't be able to harm you.
People will welcome you wherever you go.
You'll have pleasant thoughts.
Your mind will become very quiet.
Animals will love you.
Your voice will become pleasant to listen to.
Your babies will be happy in the womb.
Your children will grow up happy.
If you fall off a cliff, a tree will always be there to catch you.
Your countenance will be serene and your eyes shiny.
You will become awakened.

TALKING POINTS

- A peaceful person helps to make a peaceful world.
- Adapting to a sick environment cannot be the way to real mental health.

THINGS TO DO

▶ Act a scene where a socially concerned non-Buddhist accuses a Buddhist of doing 'nothing except meditate'.

The human family

> ## KEY IDEA
> All human beings are born free and equal.

'Human beings are all fundamentally the same. We are made of human flesh, human bones, and human blood. What is more, our internal feelings – desires, hopes and ambitions – are the same: we all want to avoid suffering, and achieve happiness. And we all have an equal right to be happy. In other words, we belong to one big human family, which includes all of humankind on this planet.'
(HH the Dalai Lama)

His Holiness the Dalai Lama

Buddhism continually stresses the similarity of all human beings, to help people recognize the pointlessness of hostility. The Buddhist view of human suffering is that it is caused by people trying to find happiness through selfish actions. This attitude is called **self-cherishing** and is understood by Buddhists to be the cause of *all* suffering in samsara, not the cause of happiness.

Oppressive regimes in countries are the result of the self-cherishing of a group of people who try to protect their own interests by forcibly controlling anyone who does not share them. This fear of losing – or not getting – what they want for themselves results in the denial of the rights and needs of other people.

In his article on Human Rights, James Belither, a western student and teacher of Buddhism, writes:

'By denying human rights to its citizens, an oppressive government creates an atmosphere of corruption, fear and suspicion, which make social upheaval and conflict inevitable . . . If even one person oppresses another or is oppressed, this is a symptom of a moral disease which if allowed to grow will come to poison the whole society.'

The cure for self-cherishing is cherishing others. Buddhism says that if anyone wants to help themselves they should help others.

'The selfish man who is foolish thinks of nothing but himself and, therefore, the results are negative, for he arouses resentment, anger and mistrust in others. The selfish man who is wise, however, thinks of others, also, realizing that if he helps them, he is helping himself, for he will meet with a good response and achieve good results.'
(HH the Dalai Lama)

Respect for all people is at the heart of the United Nations Universal Declaration of Human Rights (see page 221). Respect for all people is also at the heart of Buddhism.

'Respect for the rights and dignity of others is not an impractical religious ideal, but the vital ingredient in the development of healthy, free and prosperous societies.'
(James Belither)

The practices of **cherishing others** and **good conduct** guide all Buddhists to strive for the rights and happiness of all beings above anything else.

'Generating one moment of love for one being is greater than making an ocean of offerings to a thousand Buddhas for a thousand ages.'
(The Buddha)

Only by respecting others can people have respect for themselves. Buddhists believe that being born human is a rare and precious opportunity to develop their spiritual potential, and this potential should not be denied to anyone.

'In the quest for peace, comfort and security, the methods applied by man are diverse and, sometimes, radically opposed to one another. All too frequently, the means adopted are cruel and revolting. Behaving in a way that is utterly unbecoming to his human status, man indulges in inhuman cruelties, torturing his fellow men as well as animals just for the sake of selfish gain. . . To be born human is a rare experience, and it is wise to use this golden opportunity as effectively as possible.'
(HH the Dalai Lama)

KEY IDEA

All humans are equal in their potential to become Buddha and equal in their right to be respected.

Living in harmony

Buddhism is not a religion which believes it can help people by conversion. In order to hear the teachings of the Buddha a person must first of all show interest. It is this interest which proves to the spiritual guide that the student is ready for the Buddhist spiritual path.

A stupa is a symbol of the enlightened mind. This design is known as the Stupa of Enlightenment which celebrates the Buddha's defeat of the forces of ignorance and confusion

This attitude shows that Buddhists believe that all humans should be respected for their varying thoughts and beliefs, and acknowledges that, whilst people are all similar in their wish to be happy, there are many different spiritual methods which can fulfil that wish. Everyone has the right to choose, without pressure or manipulation, their own way.

'Quality and justice derive from respect for others, the heart of all moral integrity, and it is the responsibility of all religions to secure and improve such rights rather than allow them to be corrupted by self-interest, and by limited identification with a particular class, caste, religious, national or ethnic grouping.'

(James Belither)

By generating attitudes which cherish others more than themselves, Buddhists can prevent themselves from becoming involved in actions which cause harm to others.

'It is of the utmost importance for us to ensure that Buddhism is always employed to realize the happiness and peace of man and not to convert others or to derive benefit from them.'

(HH the Dalai Lama)

'Do not harm others. Just as you feel affection on seeing a dearly beloved person, so you should extend lovingkindness to all creatures.'

(The Buddha)

KEY IDEA

Harmony is accepting our differences, not trying to make everyone the same.

TALKING POINT

- How would a Buddhist react to the view that respect for the rights and dignity of others is an impractical ideal?

FOR YOUR FOLDERS

▶ List some of the ways in which human beings can take away the rights of others, and then consider how Buddhists might try to respond in their thoughts and actions if they found themselves in any of these situations. Finally, try to decide how helpful their philosophy might be.

FOR DEBATE

▶ This house believes that humans can never be equal.

Buddhist men of peace, breaking down barriers

Two great Buddhist leaders have shown by their example that peace and harmony between different cultures is not a religious ideal but something which can be achieved through constant effort.

The Peace Pagoda at Milton Keynes

THE MOST VENERABLE NICHIDATSU FUJII

Nichidatsu Fujii was the founder of the Japanese Buddhist Order **Nipponzan Myohoji**. He died in his 100th year in 1985.

He and his followers would beat hand-drums and chant the prayer for peace *Namu Myo Ho Ren Ge Kyo*. During his travels to India, to regenerate interest in Buddhism, he met and became close to Mahatma Gandhi.

Throughout World War 2 he prayed and regularly fasted for its end and when it was over he turned especially to the teachings of Peace-Buddhism. His Order began constructing Peace Pagodas in Japan and soon these were being built all over the world as expressions of people's yearning for peace.

The Order have built Peace Pagodas in Milton Keynes and Battersea Park, encouraging cooperation between the faiths of Christianity and Buddhism which both have the teaching of non-violence at their base.

This message, adapted from his writings on the completion of the London Peace Pagoda, was given out of his concern that science and materialism were leading the world towards tragedy:

> *'Where is the solution to be discovered? It will not be found in today's scientifically oriented civilization. The non-violent movement of Mahatma Gandhi was an expression of this. Many people of the world are now looking to his non-violent movement as their hope of being freed from the threat posed by the civilization of science. The religious basis of the non-violent movement was laid as far back as more than 2500 years ago, seen in both Buddhism and Christianity, both religions being manifested in the form of the London Peace Pagoda.'*

HH THE DALAI LAMA

His Holiness Tenzin Gyatso is the 14th Tibetan Dalai Lama, the most well-known Buddhist leader on Earth, and the Nobel Peace Prize winner. He is the living example of Buddhism in practice, striving continually for peace in his country through non-violent methods. He uses his exile from his home land to generate interest in the Buddhist practices of peace and love between all beings.

In his meetings with other religious leaders he has always emphasized the common goal of all faiths and the need for unity amongst different religions:

> *'I always believe that it is much better to have a variety of religions, a variety of philosophies, rather than one single one. This is necessary because of the different mental dispositions of human beings. Each religion has certain unique ideas or techniques, and learning about them can only enrich one's own faith.'*

The techniques referred to by the Dalai Lama brought himself and Nichidatsu Fujii to their superior level of being human. Buddhism teaches that anyone who practises these methods can themselves reach the highest attainments of a human mind and body and experience inner peace and happiness.

Buddhist practices

THE NOBLE EIGHTFOLD PATH FOR SELF CONTROL

Buddhists use the guidance of the Noble Eightfold Path to control self-cherishing, and the aggression this attitude leads to.

'To begin with, of course, we must control the anger and hatred in ourselves, and as we learn to remain in peace, then we can demonstrate in society in a way that makes a real statement for world peace. If we ourselves remain always angry and then sing about world peace, it has little meaning.'

(HH the Dalai Lama)

MEDITATION FOR SELF AWARENESS

Buddhist practice emphasizes meditation as the primary method of changing our minds, because it is only through meditation that we can feel changing attitudes within ourselves. No matter how much we read or discuss, philosophizing does not actually change anything. It is only putting our good intentions into practice which can have an effect on ourselves and others. Thought must lead to feeling, feeling to intention, and intention to action.

TAKING REFUGE FOR INNER STRENGTH

Buddhists take refuge in the Buddha, the dharma and the sangha to release them from their reliance on external sources of help, like drugs, alcohol or another human being.

They believe that spiritual refuge in times of personal or large-scale human tragedy gives them the strength to help themselves and others.

Taking refuge is the gateway to becoming a Buddhist and each day Buddhists remind themselves in their daily prayers that there is no other reliable source of help in the world.

PRAYER FOR HELP

Tara is the Buddhist female deity who is most commonly prayed to in times of stress and adversity, because of her reputation of swiftly coming to the aid of beings in distress. A prayer to her is said to bring immediate release from fear and anxiety.

Request to Green Tara

*'And so I might become fully omniscient,
Please pacify quickly all obstacles, spirits,
Obstructions, epidemics, diseases and so
 forth,
The various causes of untimely death,
Bad dreams and omens, the eight fears
 and other afflictions,
And make it so that they no longer exist.'*

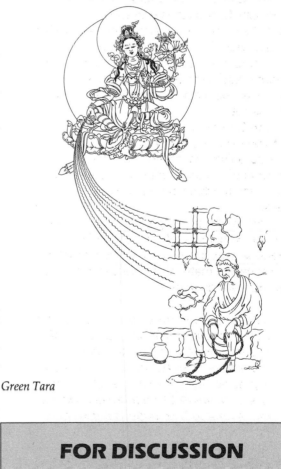

Green Tara

FOR DISCUSSION

▶ What do you think Buddhists mean by being a 'superior human being'? Does this view conflict with the Human Rights Declaration that all beings are born equal?

18 THE IDEAL SOCIETY

Using the dharma to govern

The Buddha's advice on wise government is to always use the **dharma** (see page 30). Whether this is through monarchy or democracy does not seem to matter as long as the dharma is the guiding force.

The ideal society for Buddhists, therefore, is one which is ruled by the universal power of the dharma. The dharma is *that which holds us back from suffering* or *spiritual teachings* (see page 19). Another interpretation is that it is 'the Truth'. Living in a society governed by the Truth means being guided by the ideals of spiritual, rather than material development.

In the Dighanikaya in the Pali canon, which is the earliest record of the Buddha's teachings, a discourse is given by the Buddha concerning the duties of a king.

The Buddha tells a story about a king who hands over his kingdom to his son so that he can devote the remainder of his own life to contemplation. The son experiences problems and runs to his father for help. The old king explains to his son that you cannot inherit the reward of good leadership, but must earn it, to which the son responds, 'What, then, Sir, is this noble duty of the Universal Monarch?' The King replies:

'That duty consists in one's support in honouring the Dharma, paying reverential homage to it, being one who reveres it, is a symbol and banner of it, one to whom the Dharma is the overlord, a righteous screen and protection in arranging for the family units, army, nobles, subordinates, Brahmans [the clergy], householders, country people and people of the market-towns, samanas, and brahmans [priests], animals and birds. Do not, my dear, in your kingdom set going or continue wrong action. Whoever in the kingdom should be without means, to him should be handed some.'
(H. Saddhatissa, *Buddhist Ethics*)

KEY IDEA

The ideal society has spiritual, rather than material, values.

Starting with the self

Buddhism says that faults exist in the world as a direct result of karma. The beings of this world have created not only their own *lives*, but their own *environment* through their actions, whether that be good or bad. What they see, and how they experience it, is a reflection of their own minds.

In a book called *The Questions of King Milinda*, which was written in Pali around the 4th century CE, the king questions the sage, Nagasena, about Buddhism. Likening a world of the dharma to a 'City of Righteousness', King Milinda asks Nagasena what one can buy in 'the shops' of 'The Blessed One'. Nagasena says:

'Long life, good health, beauty, rebirth in heaven, High birth, Nirvana – all are found for sale – There to be bought for karma, great or small – In the great Conqueror's world-famed bazaar. Come; show your faith, O brethren, as the price, Buy and enjoy such goods as you prefer!'

Buddhism teaches that it is knowledge of the dharma which enables us to take control of ourselves, our lives and the world around us. Once we start to put this knowledge into practical self-improvement then, when we look in our **karmic mirror** – our world – we will increasingly see the reflection of our own goodness: happiness, beauty and harmony.

KEY IDEA

Improving society begins with improving oneself.

Mandalas

A **mandala**, or **sacred circle** is a construction or picture which is used by some Buddhists to portray the Pure Land of the different holy beings, or **deities**. Mandalas use colours and geometric shapes to symbolize the particular energies and forces which individual Buddhists wish to develop in themselves, with the intention of eventually achieving rebirth in one of these perfect realms.

In their prayers, many Buddhists regularly make a symbolic **mandala offering** by visualizing a perfect environment populated and filled with everything wonderful they can imagine. Concentrating on a perfect world, and strengthening one's relationship with it and its deity, is said to create the cause for achieving rebirth in that pure land at the time of one's death.

Shambhala

Chögyam Trungpa Rinpoche, A Tibetan spiritual master who died in recent years, wrote a book called *Shambhala*. This book discusses in detail the legendary land of Shambhala, which may also have been the source of the legend of Shangri-la. Shambhala or Shangri-la perhaps best conjures up in the minds of all people who know anything about these legends, the hope of all people that somewhere in the world there exists a perfect society which is inhabited with perfect humans.

In the first chapter, entitled 'Creating an Enlightened Society', Trungpa Rinpoche writes:

> 'In Tibet, as well as many other Asian countries, there are stories about a legendary kingdom that was a source of learning and culture for present-day Asian societies. According to the legends, this was a place of peace and prosperity, governed by wise and compassionate rulers. The citizens were equally kind and learned, so that, in general, the kingdom was a model society. This place was called Shambhala.
>
> It is said that Buddhism played an important role in the development of the Shambhala society. . . After the king had received this instruction [i.e. from the Buddha], the stories say that all of the people of Shambhala began to practise meditation and to follow the Buddhist path of loving kindness and concern for all beings. In this way, not just the rulers but all of the subjects of the kingdom became highly developed people.
>
> Among the Tibetan people, there is a popular belief that the kingdom of Shambhala can still be found, hidden in a remote valley somewhere in the Himalayas. . .'
>
> (Chögyam Trungpa, *Shambhala*)

Buddhism teaches that spiritual goodness will bring its material rewards but that these will be secondary to the inner peace and tranquillity which spiritual development of itself brings.

Trungpa continues:

> 'While it is easy enough to dismiss the kingdom of Shambhala as pure fiction, it is also possible to see in this legend the expression of a deeply rooted and very real human desire for a good and fulfilling life.'

KEY IDEA

The ideals we have can be realized by the practice of a spiritual path.

In a book called *The Social Face of Buddhism*, Robert Thurman says in an article about creating good societies:

> 'The coming to Buddhahood is a social event, involving a whole field of sentient beings, whose collective existence must be developed to the point where the whole land is transformed, from an impure land of violence and exploitation and suffering into a pure land, a "Buddha land".'

In the opening prayers of *The Praise and Request to the Twenty-one Taras*, Mahayana Buddhists reflect on their belief that true happiness can only be achieved when every being is happy.

> 'May all sentient beings possess happiness and the cause of happiness;
> May all sentient beings be separated from suffering and the cause of suffering;
> May all sentient beings never be separated from the happiness that knows no suffering;
> May all sentient beings abide in equanimity, free from both feeling near or far and attachment or aversion.

FOR YOUR FOLDERS

► Find a picture of a mandala, then draw your own version. Choose your own shapes, patterns and colours.
► If you were a Buddhist and were to offer up an image of your perfect world, what would it be like? Describe it in your own words, or draw a picture of it.

FOR DISCUSSION

► How does the Buddhist vision of the ideal society conflict with those of a country like Britain?

Throughout their lives people are confronted with problems and issues that they have to cope with. Often they have to make personal decisions that affect not only themselves but others too. It is not always easy to know what is the right thing to do, and wrong decisions – whether they be in people's personal lives, socially or globally – can lead to even greater problems.

Christians, when looking for guidelines in their lives, see their main sources of inspiration as coming from:

- the life and teachings of Jesus Christ as expressed in the gospels
- the teachings of the Church
- their own individual conscience, taking into account the teachings of Jesus and the Church.

These sources give rise to Christian beliefs about humankind, the world and the universe. To Christians, life is not meaningless. Life in all its aspects has been created by the **Absolute** or **God**. Although life can be very painful and suffering can be immense, human beings are made in the image of God and *can* find redemption and salvation.

Christians believe that:

'God loved the world so much that he gave his only Son that everyone who has faith in him may not die but have eternal life.'

(John 3:16)

The world rejected his son (**Jesus**), and crucified him but Christians believe that Jesus was resurrected from the dead. Through his resurrection, humankind has been given the chance of new life. Life, then, is sacred and should be respected. Human beings are here for only a short time, and during that time they must try to develop as conscious beings, in order to fulfil the will of God. These beliefs lie behind Christian ethics, and influence the way that Christians see the world.

The three main sources of inspiration that Christians turn to are helpful as guidelines concerning personal, social and global issues.

The teachings of Jesus Christ

The teachings of **Jesus Christ**, the founder of Christianity, lie at the heart of Christian ethics. These are to be found in the four **gospels** which were written between 60 and 110 CE. The gospels tell of the life and work of Jesus Christ, and to Christians Jesus Christ represents the ideal person.

In his life, as portrayed in the gospels, Jesus teaches that human beings have the potential to bring about the Kingdom of Heaven on Earth. Jesus taught that men and women must learn to love one another:

'I give you a new commandment: love one another; as I have loved you, so you are to love one another.'

(John 13:34)

Jesus' teachings are challenging. They require self sacrifice and service. In fact they are so challenging and so demanding that few people in the world today, or in the past, have been able to follow them completely. In the gospels the teachings set an **ideal** – something people should try and aim for. Some of the following teachings show that this ideal requires that people change the way they think and act.

'Love your enemies.'

(Matthew 5:44)

'Love your neighbour as yourself.'

(Mark 12:31)

'If anyone hits you on the right cheek offer him the other as well.'

(Matthew 5:39)

'It is easier for a camel to pass through the eye of a needle, than for a rich man to enter the Kingdom of God.'

(Mark 10:25,26)

'Do not judge and you will not be judged.'

(Matthew 7:1)

'Always treat others as you would like them to treat you.'

(Matthew 7:12)

In the gospels, Jesus teaches that people need to be changed from within. This idea is often referred to in the gospels as being **reborn**. Gospel teachings are basically about human beings rising above the violence that characterizes their present existence and developing and evolving as human beings. They teach that people are capable of undergoing a definite inner development and change. This inner development requires that people become more understanding and aware of themselves, of others and of their relationship with God.

The teachings of the Church

Among Christians there are four different ways of using the word 'church':

- the whole company of Christians since the time of Jesus
- different groups or denominations
- the local Christian community
- a regular meeting in a purpose-built building. This building eventually became known as a church.

The Church is sometimes described as being the physical body of Jesus Christ, continuing his work in the world. In Christianity there are around 20 300 distinct **denominations** (branches). All these denominations belong to much larger groups or families; the **Roman Catholic Church**, the **Orthodox Churches** and the **Protestant Churches**. They each stress different things about Christian beliefs and because of this may have different views about certain moral issues. For instance, the Roman Catholic Church teaches that abortion is wrong whereas the Church of England accepts that in certain cases abortion is not wrong (see Section 23). Some Christians (e.g. the Society of Friends) might believe that all war is wrong whilst others (e.g. some Anglican members) may argue that in certain situations war is necessary (see Section 31). A Protestant church may look solely for authority to the **Bible**, whereas the Roman Catholic Church stresses the authority of the **Pope** and **tradition**. For every Christian their denomination will have its own teachings about moral issues, and these teachings will influence the individual's own responses. There may be intense argument among Christians about certain issues. Sometimes there is not universal agreement about what is right and wrong. Many Christians believe that they are guided by the **Holy Spirit**, the third element of the Holy Trinity. The Holy Spirit can be described as an invisible power that is given by God, which reveals his truth.

Individual conscience

Conscience has been defined as 'an inner sense that knows the difference between right and wrong.' This feeling, or inner sense seems to come quite often from an emotional response to a situation – something which says what is the right thing to do.

Christians believe that because human beings are spiritual beings, this small voice of conscience comes from a higher source, namely, God. They believe that because human beings are far from perfect they cannot act without God's help and that this help is called **grace**. Grace can be given on many levels, particularly regarding conscience, when something inside 'knows' what is right.

Christians believe **prayer** is an important way of becoming still inside, so that God can be heard. Through prayer and meditation, they believe, an answer to a particular problem may be given.

THINGS TO DO

▶ Look up the Sermon on the Mount (Matthew chapters 5, 6 and 7) in the New Testament. Write down some of the teachings given that you think are particularly challenging and difficult to do, e.g. 'Love your enemies'.

FOR YOUR FOLDERS

▶ Write down some of the problems that face people in their personal lives, as a society, and globally.
▶ Outline some Christian beliefs that influence the way Christians may tackle these problems.
▶ Read the quotes from the gospels, on page 42. In a world of violence, revenge, anger, selfishness, pride, poverty and injustice, what do you think might happen to this world if people really began to be 'reborn' and were able to apply these teachings to their lives?
▶ Explain why you think Christians might disagree about the right way to respond to a moral problem.

FOR DISCUSSION

▶ 'It's not true to say Christ's teachings are not valid in the world. The fact is they are not valid because the Church has never had the courage to put them into practice.'

One of the most difficult areas of life concerns relationships with other people. This area of human relationships is one that Jesus often spoke about in the gospels. His teachings are about human beings striving to become more conscious of their relationships with others and with God.

In Matthew 7:12 Jesus says, 'Treat others as you would like them to treat you.' This teaching has been called the **Golden Rule** by some Christians. It is a simple teaching but one that, when applied to human relationships, is very important for Christians.

To Christians the words of Jesus sum up the most important aspects of their faith:

'You shall love the Lord your God with all your heart, and with all your soul and with all your mind and with all your strength. The second [commandment] is this, "You shall love your neighbour as yourself." There is no other commandment greater than these.'

(Mark 12:28–31)

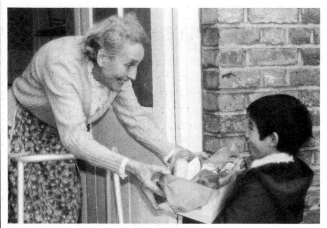

Treat others as you would like them to treat you (Matthew 7:12)

Christians will try to look to the teachings in the New Testament for guidance in their daily lives. The teachings set an ideal which, although difficult to live up to, provides guidelines about how people should try to treat their fellow women and men. Some of the most important and inspirational teachings are to be found in the **Sermon on the Mount** (Matthew chapters 5, 6 and 7). Here are just three examples:

'Love your enemies.'

(Matthew 5:44)

'You therefore must be perfect as your heavenly Father is perfect.'

(Matthew 5:48)

'Judge not, that you be not judged.'

(Matthew 7:1)

These and other teachings are basically concerned with people and their relationships. They teach the virtues of respect, concern, compassion, love, tolerance, honesty and selflessness. The life of Jesus is an inspiration to Christians, who believe that by his death he sacrificed his life for others.

'Greater love has no man than this, that a man lay down his life for his friends.'

(John 15:12–14)

TALKING POINT

● *'We must learn to live together as brothers and sisters or perish together as fools.'*

(Dr Martin Luther King)

GROUP WORK

▶ In groups of three, discuss a problem you have experienced in a relationship. Try to talk about the causes of this problem and how a Christian might suggest it could be resolved.

In his life and teachings Jesus consistently spoke about love:

'I give you a new commandment: love one another.'

(John 13:34)

'You shall love your neighbour as yourself.'

(Mark 12:31)

Love is a word that people often speak, sing or write about but it is not always an easy word to define or an easy thing to apply in daily life. In his Christmas Sermon, Dr Martin Luther King attempts to define what love means for Christians:

'There are three words for **love** in the Greek New Testament; one is the word eros. Eros is a sort of romantic love. There is and can always be something beautiful about eros. Some of the most beautiful love in all the world has been expressed this way.

Then the Greek language talks about philos, which is another word for love – a kind of intimate love between friends. This is the kind of love you have for those people that you get along with well, and those whom you like on this level you love because you are loved.

Then the Greek language has another word for love, and that is the word agape. Agape is more than romantic love, it is more than friendship. Agape is understanding, creative, redemptive goodwill to all people. Agape is an overflowing love that seeks nothing in return. Theologians would say that it is the love of God operating in the human heart. When you rise to love on this level, you love all men, not because you like them, not because their ways appeal to you, but you love them because God loves them. This is what Jesus meant when He said, "Love your enemies." And we're happy that He didn't say, "Like your enemies," because there are some people that we find it very difficult to like. Liking is an affectionate emotion, and we can't like anyone who would bomb our home. We can't like anyone who would exploit us. We can't like anyone who tramples over us with injustices. We can't like them. But Jesus reminds us that love is greater than liking. Love is understanding, creative, redemptive goodwill towards all people.'

Martin Luther King preaching his Christian sermon on love

Also, St Paul gives a beautiful description of what love is:

'Love is patient; love is kind and envies no one. Love is never boastful nor conceited, nor rude; never selfish, not quick to take offence. Love keeps no score of wrongs; does not gloat over other men's sins, but delights in the truth. There is nothing love cannot face; there is no limit to its faith, its hope, and its endurance. Love will never come to an end.'

(1 Corinthians 13:4–8)

New Testament Second part of the Bible which contains the gospels and the epistles.
Gospel One of four books which tell the life story and sayings of Jesus Christ.
Epistles Letters from early Christians, sent to the first churches.

Family life in the Bible

In the **Old Testament** there are specific references to the family, especially to people's responsibility to parents:

> 'Honour your father and your mother.'
>
> (Exodus 20:12)

> 'Listen to your father who gave you life and do not despise your mother when she is old.'
>
> (Proverbs 23:22)

There are very few references to the family in the New Testament, although in Luke Chapter 2 it says that Jesus disappeared for a while when he went to the temple, causing his parents concern. However, the general message of the New Testament is that people should work at their relationships and treat people with respect.

> **Old Testament** First part of the Bible, which tells about the relationship between God and his people, and how it developed.

The Church and the family

All Christian churches put great stress on the importance and value of the family. It is seen as an institution that is necessary for the stability of society, and one that is ordained by God.

> 'All members of the family, each according to his or her own gift, have the grace and responsibility of building day by day the communion of persons making the family a school of deeper humanity. This happens where there is care and love for the little ones, the sick, the aged; where there is mutual service every day; where there is a sharing of goods, of joys and sorrows.'
>
> (Pope John Paul II)

For Christians, children are seen as gifts from God. There is a need for unselfishness and self sacrifice in the family if people are to live together happily.

In the past, the Church has often had a negative approach to the rights of women and has been guilty of sexism (see Section 29). However, Churches today are concerned that women should have equal rights with men within the family. Nonetheless, it seems that the Roman Catholic Church has a rather different view of the role of women in society.

> 'While it must be recognized that women have the same rights as men to perform various public functions, society must be structured in such a way that wives and mothers are not, in practice, compelled to work outside the home.'
>
> (Pope John Paul II)

Today there are many pressures on family life and tension in the family can be caused by many things. In the past, sociologists often distinguished between two types of family:

'Unless you turn round and become like children, you will never enter the Kingdom of Heaven' (Matthew 18:3)

Family roles are changing

- **a nuclear family**, where husband and wife live alone with their children
- **the extended family**, which consists of several generations, possibly living in the same house, and having relatives living in the neighbourhood.

For Christians the rights of children should always be acknowledged. In the New Testament Jesus often refers to the importance of treating children properly:

'And they were bringing children to him, that he might touch them; and the disciples rebuked them. But when Jesus saw it he became indignant, and said to them, "Let the children come to me, do not hinder them; for to such belongs the Kingdom of God."'

(Mark 10:13–15)

'Fathers, do not exasperate your children, for fear they grow disheartened.'

(Colossians 3:21)

One aspect of life in Western society that is a cause for concern is the way that old people are treated. Often, when people get old they are seen as not being of value. If they are sick they are put into old people's homes; they have to live on very little income and provision of 'care' for the elderly means that they are often taken away from their family environment.

The Church of England outlines four principles in the provision of care for elderly people:

1 Care needs to be personal.
2 Elderly people and their families should retain as much choice as possible. (It must be recognized that the wishes of elderly people and their families may conflict.)
3 Elderly people should not be removed from their existing networks of relationships.
4 It should be made possible for elderly people to give as well as receive. This means, among other things, that they need to be guaranteed an adequate income.

(Church of England Board for Social Responsibility)

TALKING POINTS

- If we are all children of God then we are all united; we are all of one family.
- The close family unit may often be very inward looking and can be a breeding ground for prejudice, false information and psychological damage.

FOR DISCUSSION

▶ In theory, women have as many rights as men. In practice, however, women are often treated as second class citizens.

FOR YOUR FOLDERS

▶ What problems face the modern family today?
▶ Outline, in your own words, the teachings of Pope John Paul II on the family.
▶ What do you think the Christian attitude to the family is?
▶ What are the problems that face elderly people in our society? How can the Church help the elderly?

The Christian religion sets a high value on marriage. The joining of a husband and wife in **holy matrimony** is thought to reflect the union of Christ with his followers. Christians believe that, in their love for each other, married couples will experience and learn of God's love for his creation. In the gospels, Jesus taught that God's purpose was that marriage should be a lifelong and intimate union.

'In the beginning, at the Creation, God made them male and female. For this reason a man shall leave his father and mother, and be made one with his wife; and the two shall become one flesh.'

(Mark 10:6–8)

A Christian marriage ceremony

The Church has recognized that not everyone is called to marriage, and has at times given a high value to celibacy. Generally, Christians believe that there are three reasons for marriage:

- the right relationship for sexual intercourse
- the procreation of children
- the couple's mutual help and comfort in life.

In Britain, most Christians get married in a church service, although some may marry in a register office. Here are some extracts from a Roman Catholic marriage service which show some of the beliefs and practices of Christian marriage.

Priest: In the love of man and wife, God shows us a wonderful reflection of His own eternal love. Today N and N have dedicated themselves to one another in unending love. They will share with one another all that life brings. Let us ask God to bless them in the years ahead, and to be with them in all the circumstances of their marriage. . .

Priest: You have come together in this church so that the Lord may seal and strengthen your love in the presence of the church's minister and this community. Christ abundantly bless this love. He has already consecrated you in baptism and now he enriches and strengthens you by a special sacrament so that you may assume the duties of a marriage in mutual and lasting fidelity. . . Are you ready freely and without reservation to give yourselves to each other in marriage? . . .

Priest: Are you ready to love and honour each other as man and wife for the rest of your lives? . . . N, will you take N here present for your lawful wife (husband), according to the rite of our Holy Mother the Church?

Couple: I will.
I call upon these persons here present to witness that I, N, do take thee, N, to be my lawful wedded wife (husband), to have and to hold from this day forward, for better for worse, for richer for poorer, in sickness and in health, to love and to cherish, till death do us part.

Priest: What God has joined together, let no man put asunder.
(*The rings are blessed and exchanged*)
May the Lord bless this ring (these rings) which you give (to each other) as the sign of your love and fidelity.

(Roman Catholic Marriage Service)

THINGS TO DO

▶ Collect some other Christian marriage services and compare them with this one. Look at the marriage service in the Book of Common Prayer and the Alternative Service Book of the Church of England and compare them.

Some important biblical teachings on marriage

'In the beginning, at the creation, God made them male and female. For this reason a man shall leave his father and mother and be made one with his wife and the two shall become one flesh. It follows that they are no longer two individuals: they are one flesh. What God has joined together, man must not separate.'

(Jesus, in Mark 10:5–9)

'The husband must give the wife what is due to her, and the wife equally must give the husband his due. The wife cannot claim her body as her own; it is her husband's. Equally the husband cannot claim his body as his own; it is his wife's.'
(St Paul, in 1 Corinthians 7:3–5)

Divorce

If a couple finds that they cannot live together there are three main solutions:

Desertion – one partner simply leaves the other to live elsewhere.

Judicial separation – the courts grant a separation, meaning the couple are not allowed in any way to interfere in each other's lives, and then after a period of time one partner can apply for a divorce without the consent of the other.

Divorce – the marriage is officially declared by the courts to be at an end. After two years of living apart, and if both partners are willing, they may apply for a divorce.

Christian churches have different views on divorce. Since 1966 the Church of England has taught that divorce is acceptable. The Roman Catholic Church's teaching is that, in principle, a marriage cannot be dissolved.

A QUAKER VIEW

'No couple, marrying with any deep conviction of permanence, would willingly give up the struggle to overcome their difficulties and seek a way of escape. But where the difficulties involved in a marriage are, of their very nature, serving to drive a couple further apart in bitterness of mind and heart, or when they reduce them to an empty and conventional semblance of living together, then there can be little reason for keeping within the bonds of legal marriage two people between whom no spiritual marriage exists.'
(The Quaker Home Service, Society of Friends 1949)

A Roman Catholic view

The Roman Catholic Church teaches that a marriage between two baptized couples is a **sacrament** (a sacred ceremony) and cannot be dissolved. However, if the marriage involves one partner who is *not* baptized then the marriage can be dissolved under serious circumstances (i.e. if one partner converts to Catholicism but the other 'refuses to live peacefully with the new convert') (Code of Canon Law). Also, a marriage between two partners who are baptized can be dissolved if there is a just reason (Canon 1142), e.g. impotence or the inability to assume the obligations of marriage.

The Roman Catholic Church can also **annul** a marriage. An annulment is a declaration that the marriage bond did not exist. A marriage can be annulled if there is:

- a lack of **consent** (e.g. someone has been forced into marriage)
- a lack of **judgement** (e.g. if someone marries without being fully aware of what marriage entails)
- **inability** to carry out the duties of marriage (e.g. one partner may be mentally ill)
- a lack of **intention** (e.g. if one partner at the time of the marriage intends not to have children while the other wants to have children).

FOR DISCUSSION

▶ 'Before embarking on marriage couples should live together for at least a year.'
▶ 'Sex before marriage is acceptable.' Would being a Christian affect a person's view on this? If so, how and why?

FOR YOUR FOLDERS

▶ For Christians there are basically three reasons for marriage. In your own words explain what these are.
▶ Read the Roman Catholic marriage service, then list some Christian beliefs about marriage.
▶ Divorce is on the increase in Western society. List some reasons for this.
▶ Explain in your own words the following terms: desertion   judicial   annulment

Sexual ethics raise questions concerning sex outside marriage, homosexuality, modern medical research, birth control, celibacy and abortion.

FOR DISCUSSION

▶ After reading the appropriate quotations, discuss some of the key questions from a Christian viewpoint.

Here are some Christian views:

'Every sexual act must be within the framework of marriage.'
(Casti Conubii, Catholic Encyclical, Catholic Truth Society)

Loving relationships are important for Christians

'If two mature people who are not married are deeply in love and are committed to each other in heart, body and soul, then yes, I think sexual intercourse as an expression of this love is acceptable.'
(Anglican priest)

'If you do make a mistake, don't destroy the life . . . because also to that child God says: I have called you by your name, I have carved you in the palm of my hand: you are mine.'
(Mother Teresa, Roman Catholic nun)

'Although the foetus is to be specially respected and protected, nonetheless the life of the foetus is not absolutely sacrosanct if it endangers the life of the mother.'
(Church of England Board of Social Responsibility Report 1984)

Artificial insemination Putting male sperm – not necessarily taken from her husband or partner – into a female by artificial means.

'Artificial insemination violates the dignity of the person and the sanctity of marriage. It is contrary to God's Law . . . a third party becoming involved in a marriage is like "mechanical adultery".'
(John Hardon, Modern Catholic Dictionary, Robert Hall 1980)

'Those engaging in artificial insemination are involved in a positive affirmation of the family. It is therefore regarded as an acceptable practice.'
(Church of England Report, 'Human Fertilization and Embryology' 1984)

KEY QUESTION

Is homosexuality morally acceptable?

'Homosexual acts are disordered and can in no case be approved of.'
(Roman Catholic Declaration of Sexual Ethics 1975)

'Homosexual acts are not wrong, since the quality of any homosexual relationship is . . . to be assessed the same way as a heterosexual relationship. For homosexual men and women, permanent relationships characterized by love can be an appropriate and Christian way of expressing their sexuality.'
(Methodist discussion document 1979)

KEY QUESTION

Should Roman Catholic priests be celibate?

'Celibacy should be left to the free decision of the individual.'

(Hans Küng – Roman Catholic theologian)

'Only by being celibate can I give myself totally to God.'

(A Roman Catholic priest)

KEY QUESTION

Is the use of birth control morally acceptable?

'It is right and proper for parents to regulate the number of children they have and to space them out in the family, but not by means which artificially make it impossible for sexual intercourse to result in conception.'

(Catholic Truth Society)

'The Anglican view of contraception is that a couple may practise forms of contraception that are acceptable to both partners.'

(Church of England priest)

Anglican and **Church of England** are the same denomination. Anglican is used of the denomination outside England.

KEY QUESTION

Should doctors be allowed to do medical research on embryos?

'The human embryo has the right to proper respect. "Test tube babies" are indeed babies, and embryos cannot be manipulated, frozen or simply left to die without bringing into question the whole area of human rights. Human beings are not to be treated as means to an end.'

(The Catholic Truth Society 1985)

'We support the recommendation that research, under licence, be permitted on embryos up to 14 days old and agree that embryos should not be created purely for scientific research.'

(Anglican report 1984)

The responses that have been outlined are those of a variety of types of Christian church and a variety of views within those types. The Roman Catholic Church has very strict views on matters of sexual ethics. In the past this was true of most Protestant churches, but over the last 30 or 40 years these views have become more liberal.

Birth control

Most couples in modern society feel the need to control the number of children they have. There are many different types of **contraceptive** (methods by which couples can avoid an unwanted pregnancy). The Roman Catholic Church teaches that *all* artificial forms of contraception are wrong because the primary purpose of sexual intercourse is the begetting of children. The Roman Catholic Church, however, does not condemn **natural family planning** (NFP) which includes methods such as the woman becoming aware of her own fertile and infertile times by recording the natural signals of her body. The Roman Catholic Church's teachings continue to raise much controversy, especially among some priests and nuns in the developing world where overpopulation is an enormous problem.

The Anglican view and the view of most Protestant churches is that couples may practise forms of contraception that are acceptable to both partners.

FOR YOUR FOLDERS

▶ After reading all the different views, write down some of your own thoughts about these issues.
▶ Try to discover other Christian views on the issues discussed in this section.

FOR DISCUSSION

▶ How is it possible for Christians to hold such different views as those outlined in this section?

Christians believe that the human body is intended to house the spirit. Most Christian churches believe that to abuse the body and the mind is destructive and goes against God's purpose for humankind.

Alcohol

Alcohol, if abused, is extremely dangerous for individuals and society. Drinking alcohol to excess can cause personal problems, health problems, crime and death. Some Christians (e.g. Salvation Army members) never drink alcohol, and believe that the Church should do more to reduce alcohol abuse.

Other Christians believe that alcohol, used moderately and responsibly, can be one of the pleasures of life, and in the New Testament Jesus is sometimes seen drinking wine.

A METHODIST VIEW

'Alcohol can give pleasure and cause harm. It is used in celebration, socialization and relaxation; it can be enjoyed for its taste. It is also a significant factor in a range of personal and social problems, and can lead to accident, illness and death. . . All Methodists [should] consider seriously the claims of total abstinence, and make a personal commitment either to total abstinence or to responsible drinking.'

(*Through a Glass Darkly, Responsible Attitudes to Alcohol* 1987)

Smoking

A CHRISTIAN VIEWPOINT

'Christians hold that life is a gift from God and consequently place a high value on its preservation. The Christian ideal has been to refuse to expose life to actions or circumstances which carry with them high risks of harm. . . It has been shown that smoking renders the individual prone to illness and to premature death. It can therefore be argued that it is a denial of the goodness of created existence.'

(Church of England briefing)

Drugs

A CHRISTIAN APPROACH

Most Christian churches believe that to abuse the body and the mind with drugs is wrong. However, whilst condemning drug abuse, the churches would agree that many drug addicts and people with drug-related problems need care and help. Also, the question, 'Why do some people in our society resort to drugs?' needs to be considered seriously. One biblical reference that might be applied to drug abuse could be the following:

'Do you know that you are God's temple and that God's spirit dwells within you? If anyone destroys God's temple, God will destroy him. For God's temple is holy and that temple you are.'

(1 Corinthians 3:16,17)

This declaration by the Methodist Church in 1974 sums up the attitude of many modern Christian churches to drug abuse:

'Several guidelines help the Christian to determine his personal attitude to the non-medical use of drugs. Obviously he must face the serious scientific evidence about the harmful effect of drugs. His faith teaches him to use all things, including his money, responsibly. He seeks to meet problems and stresses by following Christ's teaching and living by his power. To Christ he offers the undiminished vigour of his body and mind. He loves his neighbour and therefore examines the probable effect of his behaviour, habits and example on that neighbour. He accepts his part in the responsibility of the Church in the work of education and rehabilitation.'

(Methodist Church 1974)

'Love your neighbour as yourself.'

(Matthew 22:39)

'Your body is a temple of the Holy Spirit.'

(1 Corinthians 6:19)

'And the earth brought forth grass and herb and God saw that it was good.'

(Genesis 1:12)

RASTAFARIANS

Many Rastafarians use **ganga** (marijuana) as part of their religious ritual, and as an aid to meditation. The Rastafarians say that God, who created all things, made the herb for human use and cite Genesis 2:16. Ras Sam Brown says, 'Ganga used moderately is not bad. We do not find ganga as a mental depressor, ganga sharpens your wits and keeps you intellectually balanced.'
(Ras Sam Brown and Leonard E. Barrett)

Ganga is part of the culture of Rastafarians

Fasting

Traditionally the ritual of fasting has been observed in the Christian Church. Christians would sometimes go without food and drink for long periods of time for the following reasons:

● to remember the time that Jesus went into the desert for 40 days and nights – Matthew chapter 4 – known as the temptation of Christ
● to practise self control and to spend time thinking about spiritual matters
● to clear the body of all its impurities to make it a more healthy place for the dwelling of the spirit
● during Lent as a preparation for the important festival of Easter.

Euthanasia

Euthanasia Gentle and easy death, the bringing about of this especially in cases of incurable and painful disease.

Human life is a gift from God

As with many other issues, there is not a universal Christian response as to whether, under certain circumstances, people should be allowed to take their own lives. However, in general, many Christians would apply the following principles to this issue:

● human life is a gift from God; it is sacred and has dignity
● death is an event in life, not necessarily the end of life
● better methods of caring for the dying should be developed (see **Hospice movement**, page 68).

FOR YOUR FOLDERS

▶ Write a few sentences describing Christian views on drugs, alcohol and smoking.
▶ Write down three reasons why Methodists are against drug abuse.
▶ What is your opinion about total abstention or moderate drinking as the best Christian approach?
▶ Why do some Christians fast today?
▶ *'Your body is a temple of the Holy Spirit.'*
(1 Corinthians 6:19)
Explain in your own words what you think these words mean. How might Christians apply them to the way they treat their bodies?
▶ 'We have a right to end our lives.' What arguments might Christians use in the discussion of this issue?

This is a world of great injustice and inequality. More people have died as a consequence of hunger in the past six years than have been killed in all the wars, revolutions and murders in the past 150 years. Every day, 35 000 people die as a result of hunger. In Britain, the division between those that 'have' and those that 'do not have' is growing greater.

The Christian Church is one of the richest institutions in the world and for many Christians the wealth of the Church is a cause for concern. The biblical teachings on wealth seem quite clear:

For many Christians, the wealth of the Church today is a cause for concern

'Good master, what must I do to win eternal life? And he said, "Go, sell everything you have and give to the poor and you will have riches in heaven."'
(Mark 10:17–21)

'You cannot serve God and money.'
(Matthew 6:24)

'The love of money is the root of all evil.'
(1 Timothy 6:6–10)

'It is easier for a camel to go through the eye of a needle than it is for a rich man to enter heaven.'
(Matthew 19:24)

The first Christian community in Jerusalem shared everything they had and gave to everyone who had need. The early Church taught its followers to renounce materialism and luxury and to care for the poor. St Paul, in his teaching, said:

'Command those who are rich in this present world not to be arrogant nor to put their hope in wealth which is so uncertain, but to put their hope in God who richly provides us with everything for our enjoyment.'
(1 Timothy 6:17)

Throughout the ages many Christians have followed the teachings of the New Testament and renounced all worldly gain. One of the vows of the **monastic order** (rules that monks and nuns have to follow when they decide to dedicate their lives to God) is the vow of poverty and this was seen as being an ideal by which Christians should try and live.

Christians believe that the means by which they obtain money should be fair. Many churches are opposed to such forms of obtaining money as gambling.

'Gambling appeals to chance and therefore cannot be reconciled with faith in God. Because we belong to one another we must live by love and mutual obligation. Gambling disregards moral responsibility and neighbourly concern.'
(*What Does Methodism Think?* 1980)

Christians are also against **usury** which is lending money, to be paid back at a high rate of interest. There are many occupations that Christians do not become involved in because they see it as a wrong way of obtaining money (for example, the arms trade, gambling, prostitution).

'The Church that is in solidarity with the poor can never be a
wealthy Church' (Archbishop Desmond Tutu)

THINKING POINTS

● 'As long as there is poverty in the world I
can never be rich, even if I have a million
dollars. I can never be what I ought to be
until you are what you ought to be.'
(Martin Luther King)

● 'A Church that is in solidarity with the poor
can never be a wealthy Church. It must
sell all in a sense to follow its Master. It
must use its wealth and resources for the
sake of the least of Christ's brethren.'
(Archbishop Desmond Tutu)

FOR YOUR FOLDERS

▶ The Church has enormous wealth
worldwide. Do you think it could do more
to help the world's poor? If so, what?
▶ 'If Christ's teaching, "Go, sell your
possessions, and give to the poor," was
followed by the world's Christians, then
we would have a wonderful, gentle
revolution on our hands.' Comment on
this.

TALKING POINT

● List some jobs that Christians would not
do for religious reasons.

The world in its ignorance crucified God's Son

To Christians, the problem of suffering and pain poses a serious question. How can a God who is supposed to be all loving and all powerful allow his creation to experience such suffering? If God is all powerful he must be able to prevent evil. But if God is both able and willing to prevent evil, then why does evil exist?

Christian responses to the problem of evil

- Suffering is part of life. It is a challenge for humankind as individuals to find inner strength, and as part of the world community to try to make the world a better place.
- One Christian way of dealing with suffering is to say that after death all the suffering of this world will be forgotten in the joy of a new life. 'For I reckon that the sufferings we now endure bear no comparison with the splendour as yet unrevealed which is in store for us.' (Romans 8:18)
- Jesus Christ, the Son of God, was tortured to death. Yet Christians believe that he rose from the dead. Out of darkness and death came light and hope.

- Suffering is caused by **sin** which results in selfishness and self-centredness. Sin is part of human nature and affects everyone. Sin does not mean simply doing something wrong, it is a whole attitude that leads people away from God.
- Suffering is part of life. It is only through suffering that people learn to grow as human beings. In a world without suffering there would be nothing to struggle for or against, nothing to strive for.
- Human beings have free will: they are free to choose between good and evil. Suffering is caused by ignorance and blindness. If people became more aware of the world they live in and more aware of themselves and others, then the world could be free of such things as wars, disease, violence, famine, cruelty, injustice, torture, mental illness, brutality, pollution, racism, oppression, etc.
- God suffers alongside people in the tragedies of the world.

Sin Turning away from God.

Traditionally Christian thinkers have said that there are two types of suffering:

- **moral** caused by human sin, ignorance and selfishness
- **natural** caused by natural phenomena like earthquakes, disease, floods, etc.

In their daily lives many Christians do not just accept the suffering in the world but believe that they can actively do something about it. These actions might include:

Prayer – One type of prayer is called **intercession**. To **intercede** means to *speak on behalf of somebody*. As well as asking for God's forgiveness the person praying may be aware of the needs of others. They may pray for the sick, the poor, the lonely, people who are close to them or for the whole world. Another type of prayer is called **supplication**, when a person prays for God's help in times of crisis.

Service – Some Christians may dedicate their whole life to serving others. This can take many forms, including working in hospices, working with the poor and disadvantaged. A person who has inspired others by her life of service is **Mother Teresa** who has spent her life working with the poor. She once said:

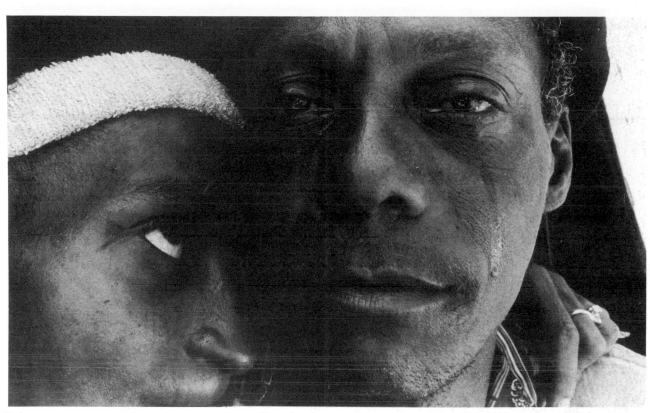

'I give you a new commandment: love one another as I have loved you' (Jesus, in John 13:34)

'What these people need even more than food and shelter is to be wanted. They understand that even if they only have a few hours left to live, they are loved. Make us worthy Lord, to serve those throughout the world who live and die poor and hungry.'

Action – The sheer scale of pain and suffering in the world has moved certain Christians to make a stand to try to change the conditions of those who suffer.

Camilo Torres, a Colombian Roman Catholic priest, became a freedom fighter to try to overthrow the corrupt Colombian government which oppressed their own people. Torres once said:

'Revolution is necessary to free the hungry, give drink to the thirsty, clothe the naked and procure a life of wellbeing for the needy majority. I believe that the revolutionary struggle is appropriate for the Christian. Only by revolution, by changing the concrete conditions of our country, can we enable men to practise love for each other.'

TALKING POINTS

- 'Through pain and suffering we learn.'
- 'In order to change the world we must firstly learn to change ourselves.'
  What do you think Christians might mean by these statements?

FOR YOUR FOLDERS

▶ Make a list of some examples of moral and natural suffering in the world today. What suffering could be avoided if people became more aware of themselves and others?

▶ What are your reactions to the Christian responses? Give reasons.

▶ Explain in your own words how some Christians have tried to work for a better world. Try to think of other famous Christians who have or who are working for a better world.

Work

What purpose does work serve? In a Church of England report in 1979, five purposes of work were outlined:

1 **Work is necessary** for human survival.
2 **Work is creative.**

> 'Through work humankind not only transforms nature, adapting it to its needs, but it also achieves fulfilment.'
>
> (Pope John Paul II)

3 **Work is painful**. Certain types of work can lead to all types of physical and psychological problems. This painful aspect of work is reflected in Genesis 3:17–19:

> 'You shall gain your bread by the sweat of your brow.'

Here work is seen as a punishment for disobeying God.

4 **Work is healthy.** Work brings people into relationships with other people. It helps them belong to a community by giving them a place, status, belonging and value.
5 **Work is good**. Work is a way of finding a meaning in life and of enriching people's lives. For a Christian it is regarded as a means of sharing with God and being creative in the world.

The Protestant work ethic

With the rise of the industrial revolution, many Protestant churches saw work as being a sort of religious duty. Hard work was seen as being a virtue. This became known as the **Protestant work ethic**. However, industrialists and capitalists often used this idea to exploit and oppress the people who worked for them. People worked for 15 hours a day for very little pay, and lived in absolute poverty. On Sundays they went to church where the minister would tell them they should not complain, they were doing God's will and that their reward would be in heaven. Even today the work ethic affects many people's lives and is especially hard for those who have been thrown out of work because of economic recession. The unemployed often feel that they are not wanted and that they are useless, and in the words of William Temple, the Archbishop of Canterbury between 1942 and 1944:

> 'Unemployment has the power to corrupt the soul of any man or woman.'

Vocation

A vocation is a **calling**, a job which someone does because they think they have a special ability to give service to other people . . . a special call from God. Many Christians believe that work should be a vocation, a calling, and that it should be a fulfilling and valuable thing. Some jobs that are especially recognized as vocations include the priesthood, nursing, working with the deprived and disabled, social work and working in areas of extreme poverty.

A METHODIST DEFINITION

> '**Vocation** Through the right use of his time, a Christian offers his life, gifts and effort to God. A sense of vocation means that we see what we do as an expression of our faith and a response to God's love for us. Ideally it should be possible to have a sense of vocation about the whole of life, but many must work in ways that do not allow the exercise of personal qualities. In these situations a sense of vocation is difficult or impossible to achieve. Those who work like this will want to take the opportunity of leisure to find activities in which a real sense of vocation is possible.'
>
> (What Does Methodism Think? 1980)

TALKING POINTS

- 'The Christian understanding of work as self fulfilment through the service of God and neighbour should help us to value our own work more highly and feel deeply for the unemployed. All of us should expect to remain workers all our lives so that even after we have retired we may spend whatever energy we have left in some form of service.'

  (John Stott)

- 'Whatever you do, work at it with all your heart as though you were working for the Lord and not for man.'

  (Colossians 3:23)

Christians at work in the community

Leisure

Leisure time is generally on the increase in the UK. Most Christians believe that leisure time should be used constructively so that people become rested and fulfilled.

> *'Leisure is good if used for the glory of God.'*
> (Methodist Conference 1974)

Traditionally, Sunday has been a day of rest in the UK. However, this is not so much the case today as, for example, more shops are opening on a Sunday:

> *'Every society needs a day of rest and "Recreation", such as the Christian Sunday has provided.'*
> (Church of England Board of Social Responsibility Report 1985)

FOR YOUR FOLDERS

▶ Give an outline of the five aspects of work given by the Church of England.
▶ In what ways might Christians' beliefs affect:
  (a) the type of job they do
  (b) their attitudes to work?
▶ What problems face the unemployed and how do you think the Church should try to help?
▶ Why might some Christians regard some jobs as vocations more than other forms of employment?

The State in its oppression of the people makes use again and again of the name of God

Throughout human history different people have been subjected to racism. **Racism** means treating people differently because of their racial origins.

During the last 400 years European countries invaded and colonized different parts of the world. Often these countries justified their oppression by saying it was in the cause of religion. People in Africa and India were seen as being inferior and little or no acknowledgement was made of their own cultures and religions. They were often seen as **heathens** and the white Church was seen as a symbol of salvation.

The churches, in the past, have not always spoken out against racism in society, but over the last few years there has been a growth in the Caribbean and West African Christian churches which helps to provide black communities with a sense of identity. Whether these churches are attached to mainstream denominations or to separate black denominations, the Christian message is seen to offer security against discrimination, especially in its teachings about equality and forgiveness.

Some black church leaders believe that black churches should develop their own **theology of protest**, clearly expressed in black theology which states, 'Our dignity as human beings is no longer at the mercy of the majority of blacks in the white mind.'

The growth of churches comprising Christian people from African and Caribbean backgrounds in Britain is seen by many as being the result of the way the 'white' churches have neglected racism and the black community in the past.

THINKING POINT

● *'The leadership of the Church is what I call "politely racist". It does not exercise vulgarity but it is extremely racist. Because of that, they are not able to listen to the black presence in their midst.'*

(Reverend Tony Ottey, Church of England Minister)

Christians believe that God created human beings in his image and likeness. This bond between the human person and the Creator provides the basis of human dignity. Christians believe that God is at the origin of humankind and that this makes all human beings equal before him. For Christians, the mystery of the birth of Christ as God's son shows that God wanted to unite all people.

ROMAN CATHOLIC TEACHING

'The Church's teaching on this matter is clear and straightforward. Every human being is made in the image of God. We are all brothers, and neighbours, of each other. There is no special merit in being good to members of your own family, your blood relations. To be good to people of your own religion, or nation, is to be expected, though behaviour often falls short of this expectation – the parable tells us how a priest passed by the man who had been robbed and beaten up in the street, and took no notice of him, though he had every duty to help him; it was a stranger, of another place and people, who helped the robbers' victim. The message is quite explicit: the stranger was the one who was the neighbour. And to love your neighbour as yourself is one of the two great, fundamental commandments. Charity, for the Christian, does not begin at home or end at home. Charity lies in what you do or allow to be done – not in how you think.

Racism is not the only kind of division, or form of selfishness, hindering human brotherhood. But in our time it is a particularly important one.'

(Catholic Truth Society)

A CHRISTIAN VIEW

'Every human being created in the image of God is a person for whom Christ died. Racism, which is the use of a person's racial origin to determine a person's value, is an assault on Christ's values, and a rejection of his sacrifice.'

(World Council of Churches 1980)

In Britain today racism is very much alive. In our inner cities racist attacks are on the increase. Attacks on Asians, Jews, Muslims, Hindus, Afro-Caribbean people and others are the results of ignorance. Organizations like the British Movement and the National Front are behind some of the attacks. Christians believe that racism awareness should begin at school and that young people should be made aware that 'black people' aren't responsible for unemployment, poor housing and poor services. They may be the victims of social injustice too. Young people should be aware that human beings, irrespective of race or creed, are basically the same and that, in the words of Martin Luther King, 'unless we learn to live together as brothers and sisters we will die together as fools'.

TALKING POINT

- 'The Christian religion was the single most effective means by which black people were distracted from their oppression.'
(John St John)

FOR DISCUSSION

▶ There is no doubt that Jesus came from the Middle East. In western Christian art he is almost always portrayed as a white man. What effect do you think this might have had over the centuries?

FOR YOUR FOLDERS

▶ Explain, in your own words, the meaning of racism.
▶ How have some Christians been guilty of racism in the past?
▶ Why do Christians believe that all people are equal?
▶ How far should the teaching 'love thy neighbour' be extended by white Christians to members of racial and religious minorities?

Throughout history men have held positions of power, wealth and decision-making. For the past 3000 years or so most people have lived in social structures conditioned by masculine attitudes and values.

Historical and religious writings over the last 3000 years illustrate the way that many societies have treated women.

I permit no woman to teach or to have authority over men, she is to keep silent.

(1 Timothy 2:12)

Women should remain at home, sit still, keep house and bear and bring up children.

(Martin Luther 1483–1546)

The souls of women are so small that some believe they have none at all.

(Samuel Butler 1612–1680)

Like all male-dominated institutions, the Church has been guilty of sexism. Women have had little power within the structure of the Church. God is always assumed to be a man and even today in most churches women are not allowed to become church leaders.

Over the last few years a new force has arisen in the Christian Church which is sometimes called **feminist theology**. Women are slowly beginning to make the Church think again about its male-dominated language and sexist attitudes.

THINKING POINT

● *'The women's movement has already made sizeable inroads into male supremacy, which, apart from inertia, employs ridicule as a means of counter-attack. Nowhere are males more firmly entrenched than in some of the Churches, particularly the Anglicans and Roman Catholics, though the as yet small group of Christian feminists is pressing them hard.*

A remarkable parallel to the gains of the women's movement are the changes in the life of nuns: the convents have suffered something approaching a mass exodus but those who remain have insisted on radical reforms, including discarding medieval dress for shorter skirts and a simple veil, taking university degrees, joining in political demonstrations, rebelling against the hierarchical powers of male prelates and mothers superior, and much else. These reforms contrast with the continuing refusal of the Roman Catholic and the bulk of (British) Anglican clergy to agree to women's ordination. Many Christian women are fed up with being expected to change the church flowers, polish the altar brass and make the tea and cakes for social events while they are refused the right to more than a token participation in their Church's services. Only a male is considered suitable to bless and administer the sacrament at Holy Communion, as if women were not "made in God's image" too. Feminists also argue that without female priests God's nature is not fully presented to the world.

The growing acceptance that God must have feminine as well as masculine characteristics – or that he/she is sexless – is tied up with the whole question of what is meant by gender, apart from biological differences. To what extent do these differences determine personality and ability? What relative parts are played by one's sex-linked genetic inheritance and what by nurture and upbringing (e.g. dolls or toy soldiers; identification with the parent of the same sex; expectations at school, in the media, etc.)? The answers to these questions are complex and disputed, but there are plenty of familiar, stereotyped characteristics, whatever their source or inevitability, which are associated with gender and which society normally accepts and, in practice, enforces. The male is associated with doing, controlling, achieving, and with being rational, decisive, ambitious compared with the female, who is associated with nurturing, comforting, submitting and being gentle, peaceful, irrational, intuitive.'

(John St John, *Religion and Social Justice*, Pergamon Press 1985)

Women priests

At the present time a debate is raging within the Anglican Church about whether it should allow women priests to be fully ordained. In Canada, New Zealand and the USA women can become priests but in Britain they can only become **deacons**. There are more than 1200 women priests in the Anglican Church worldwide and one woman bishop in the USA. These numbers are growing. In the following interview an American woman priest gives her opinion about this controversial subject.

'Surely, God the creator of everything is both male and female'

THINKING POINT

- 'At first I was rejected in my Church because I was black. Then I was rejected because I was a woman. The Church is controlled by men. It has been and still is guilty of sexism. There are many instances of women having considerable responsibility in the early Church. The gospels, let us not forget, were all written by men in a period of history when women had few rights, so when people tell me that all Christ's disciples were men I say, 'Of course it appears like that because the gospel writers were men living in a sexist world.' Christ, however, is recorded as being very close to a number of women and he tried to teach that everyone is equal. The language of the Church is sexist too. Why does it always convey a male God? Surely God, the creator of everything, is both male and female. As women we want to be consulted about attitudes in the Church and not be expected just to make cups of tea.'
(Reverend Nan Peete, author's interview)

FOR DISCUSSION

▶ Little boys are given guns for Christmas, little girls are given dolls. Sexism is therefore prevalent from the outset of a young person's life.

FOR YOUR FOLDERS

▶ List some examples of sexism that are still prevalent in society today.
▶ Why do many feminists still 'view the Church as an enemy', according to John St John?
▶ What do you think the arguments are for not allowing women priests?
▶ Why might Jesus' attitude to women be described as revolutionary?

Although the Church has been guilty of sexist attitudes, Jesus, as he is portrayed in the gospels, clearly did not discriminate against women. He taught in the Temple's court of women, showing that in his view women are just as intelligent as men. He included some women among his disciples, and after his resurrection revealed himself to a woman first. These incidents may not sound particularly remarkable today, but in Jesus' day his attitude can only be described as revolutionary. Christians believe that God created men and women to be equal.

Christians believe that, in the New Testament, Jesus' teachings were centred around forgiveness and compassion. Again, as in many of the New Testament teachings, Jesus sets out an ideal and, in a world in which many innocent people are victims of crime, these teachings can be seen as being unrealistic.

The question for Christians is how to implement the law and deal with people who break it in a just fashion. Generally, there are four aims of punishment. These are:

- to protect
- to deter (put others off)
- to reform
- to exact retribution.

This last aim can create problems for Christians, especially in the light of teachings such as:

'never pay back evil for evil'
(Romans 12:17)

'pass no judgement and you will not be judged'
(Matthew 7:1)

However, many Christians believe that punishment and forgiveness can go together. They lay great stress on looking at the motives and reasons for crime. Over the last 150 years many Christians have worked towards the idea of **reforming** criminals, as they see the theory of reform as most important. Many organizations that have been formed to improve our systems were initially set up by Christians. These include the **Howard League for Penal Reform** and **Radical Alternatives to Prison.**

Many Church men and women have consistently spoken out against the plight of prisoners in the UK and the dreadful conditions of our prisons. However, in the past the Church has often used the words of St Paul in Romans 13:1, 'Let every person be subject to the government authorities', to reinforce the state's punishment of the criminal.

Capital punishment

In 1970 in Britain, capital punishment was abolished. Like other members of society, Christians have different views on whether capital punishment should be brought back. However, there are certain ideas that Christians use to argue against its reintroduction.

AN ANGLICAN VIEWPOINT

In 1983 some of the speakers of the Church of England's General Synod made the following points:

- *'God is merciful and man shares in God's merciful nature.'*

- *'The taking of life as a penalty devalues human life.'*

- *'There is substantial doubt that capital punishment has any significant deterrent effect.'*

- *'The abolition of capital punishment gave prison chaplains a chance to work for the reform of all prisoners rather than just some of them.'*

(Report on Proceedings)

Many Christians are concerned about the conditions in our prisons

'Pass no judgement and you will not be judged' (Jesus, in Matthew 7:1)

'Jesus repudiated the law of talon, which demanded an eye for an eye and a tooth for a tooth. He taught us to love our enemies and do good to those who harm us. Although this does not mean that we should not punish at all, for we have seen that punishment can be good and just, it is a claim on us to temper the severity of punishment with a mercy which is born of love.'

(Catholic Truth Society)

Civil disobedience

In the past, and in some countries today, there are laws which Christians regard as being unjust and even immoral. For instance, in South Africa laws which oppress the black majority are seen by some Church leaders as needing to be changed and, in order to bring about this change, they indulge in a campaign of **civil disobedience**. The same was true in America up to the 1960s, when blacks were treated as second class citizens.

TALKING POINT

● 'The Church must say to worldly rulers, whose laws are at variance with the laws of God, "We had much rather obey God than man." (Acts 4:19).'

(Archbishop Desmond Tutu)

FOR YOUR FOLDERS

▶ How do you think Christians should respond to the problems of crime and punishment?
▶ How do you think the Christian Church can help criminals and the victims of crime?
▶ List some laws, either in Britain or in the world, which might be called unchristian.

Many Christians are concerned about inequalities in society

As the dominant religion in western Europe, Christianity has had a major influence on society and has itself been influenced by the continually changing world. Within the Christian Church there has been great debate about whether the Church should be involved in politics. Essentially, there are two schools of thought:
- the message of Christianity is basically a spiritual message and has nothing to do with the day to day running of society
- the teachings throughout the Bible stress things like justice and peace and Christians should be concerned and involved in the world in which they live.

Although many Christians in the past have used the teachings in the Bible to attack injustices, selected passages have often been used to justify unethical policies like religious wars and slavery. The self-interest and greed that seem to motivate a free capitalist market economy, as there is in western Europe, hardly fit in with the teachings of Jesus about selflessness and generosity. It can be argued, however, that Jesus' teachings were set against a world that was very different from today and so it is perhaps impossible to draw exact parallels with the modern world. However, many Christians would say that the teachings in the

gospels are relevant today because their message is eternal.

> 'The Church's primary role must be a spiritual one. I say this as a member of the Anglican Church.'
> (Patrick Jenkin, MP)

> 'I believe that the revolutionary struggle is appropriate for the Christian. Only by changing the concrete conditions of our country can we enable men to practise love for each other.'
> (Father Camilo Torres)

KEY QUESTION

Should a Christian become involved in politics?

War and peace

It seems that the world is never free from war. Throughout the ages Christians have discussed what their attitude to war should be.

Many Christians believe that there is such a thing as a **just war**. A just war is one in which Christians believe it is morally right to fight. For a war to be just it has to fulfil certain conditions:

- The war must only be started and controlled by the authority of the state as the ruler.

- There must be a just cause; those attacked are attacked because they deserve it.

- The war must be fought to promote good or avoid evil.

- Peace and justice must be restored afterwards.

- The war must be the last resort; all other possible ways of solving the problem must have been tried out.

- There must be 'proportionality' in the way the war is fought, for example innocent civilians should not be killed. Only enough force must be used to achieve the goals, no more.

Christianity also adopted the theory known as the **holy war**, which basically meant that God was on their side, particularly if the war was thought to protect the faith. However, in the past these theories have often been abused by both governments and churches. For instance, in the slaughter of World War 1, Christians on both British and German sides maintained that God was on their side. Christianity teaches the wisdom of peace, forgiveness and love, yet Christianity has followers who have interpreted these teachings to satisfy their own needs.

The teachings of Jesus in the gospels are clear, yet Christians have killed, and continue to kill, other people who are supposed, like them, to have been made in the image of God.

War is the cause of untold grief and suffering

PEACE TESTIMONY OF THE SOCIETY OF FRIENDS

'We utterly deny all outward wars and strife, and fightings with outward weapons, for any end, or under any pretence whatever; this is our testimony to the whole world. The Spirit of Christ by which we are guided is not changeable, so as once to command us from a thing as evil, and again to move unto it; and we certainly know, and testify to the world, that the Spirit of Christ, which leads us into all truth, will never move us to fight and war against any man with outward weapons, neither for the kingdom of Christ, nor for the kingdoms of the world.'
(from *A Declaration from the Harmless and Innocent People of God, called Quakers,* presented to Charles II, 1660)

THINGS TO DO

Copy out these quotes. Decide whether they answer 'yes' or 'no' to the **key question**.

▶ *'You shall love your neighbour as yourself.'* (Leviticus 19:18)

▶ *'You who oppress the poor and crush the destitute . . . the Lord has sworn by his holiness that your time is coming.'* (Amos 4:1–2)

▶ *'The Lord will answer . . . "Here I am" if you cease to pervert justice, to point the accusing finger and lay false charges. If you feed the hungry from your plenty and satisfy the needs of the wretched, then your light will rise like dawn out of darkness.'* (Isaiah 58:9–10)

▶ *'Pay the Emperor what belongs to the Emperor, and pay God what belongs to God.'* (Mark 12:13–17)

▶ *'He has sent me to proclaim liberty to the captives . . . set free the oppressed.'* (Luke 4:18)

▶ *'Every person must submit to the supreme authorities. There is no authority but by act of God. . .'* (Romans 13:1)

▶ *'I have come not to bring peace but a sword . . .'* (Matthew 10:34)

▶ *'My kingdom does not belong to this world.'* (John 18:36)

FOR YOUR FOLDERS

▶ Explain the theories of 'just' and 'holy' war.
▶ How have Christians justified these theories in the light of Jesus' teachings about forgiveness and love?
▶ Explain the beliefs of a pacifist.
▶ After looking at the eight biblical quotes, explain why some Christians think that they should be involved in politics while others are sure that they should not be.

Churches are involved in the struggle for justice

A theme that often occurs in the life and teaching of Jesus concerns helping people in need. Jesus is portrayed as healing the sick, showing concern for the poor, and teaching people to be tolerant of one another. Many of the stories in the New Testament concern the disadvantaged of society.

There are many organizations that have been set up by Christians who are concerned with trying to improve the quality of life for people. Many Christians work in these societies.

Some organizations

CHRISTIAN AID

'Christian faith provides the reason for caring. Christians believe that God loves the world and all that is in it. They believe that God became a human in Jesus and that in a real sense they can meet God in every human being.

In a practical sense Christian Aid is Christian because it was set up by the churches of the UK and Ireland to put into action the concern of Christians for those in need. This concern is for all, whatever their race or faith.'

(Christian Aid's Policy Statement)

CHURCH OF ENGLAND CHILDREN'S SOCIETY

This is an organization set up to help and improve the quality of life for children here and overseas.

THE HOSPICE MOVEMENT

In recent years the emphasis has moved from a debate about euthanasia to a concern for the care of those who are terminally ill. This has led to the growth of the Hospice Movement, which tries to help the dying spend their last few days in a loving and sympathetic environment so that they can die with dignity. One of its leaders, Dame Cicely Saunders, has written, 'We have to concern ourselves with the quality of life as well as with its length.'

L'ARCHE COMMUNITY

This was set up by Jean Vanier to help people with disabilities.

'People with a mental handicap who come to our communities are called to rise up in hope and to discover the beauty of their beings. Those who come to help are called to see what is most beautiful in their own hearts. And thus the body is formed. We discover we are linked together.

And because we are linked together, we learn to forgive each other for we can so easily hurt one another when we live together. We learn to celebrate the fact that we have been called together. Little by little, we become people of joy because we are people of prayer, people of covenant relationship.'

(Jean Vanier, *Resurgence 110*, May/June)

THE SAMARITANS

In 1953 Chad Varah, a Church of England priest, was appalled to discover that three suicides were taking place every day in London. He installed a telephone in his church and publicized the fact that anyone thinking of committing suicide could telephone him and talk to him. This was the start of the **Samaritans**. Today there are 174 centres and over 20 000 carefully selected and trained volunteers offering a 365-day 24-hour service (Christmas is their busiest time). They speak to 2 250 000 callers every year. The Samaritans:

● are not all Christians
● must not 'preach' if they are Christians
● must be good listeners, sympathetic and caring.

Charities

In the second half of the 19th century many social reformers, often Christians, began setting up homes and orphanages for the poor. The work of charities had begun. In 1905 the Liberal Party introduced a wide range of social services which later developed into the **welfare state**. The state became responsible for helping the poor. Today, because of government policies, more and more pressure is being put on charitable organizations as the number of poor increases. Poverty gives rise to a whole range of personal and social pressures and problems, such as drug addiction, alcohol abuse, crime, violence, prostitution and depression.

Christians have been pioneers in helping the poor and needy. In the 19th century the churches played a dominant part in the setting up of charities. An example of this was the **Dr Barnardo homes** for helping orphans. Today Christians work in many areas to alleviate the suffering of the poor and needy.

In 1985 the Church of England published a report called 'Faith in the City', which condemned the terrible poverty and bleak environments that millions of people have to endure in the urban priority areas. Also, in 1990, the Church of England published 'Faith in the Country', a report calling for more emphasis to be put on helping to look after those people who live in the country.

Down the centuries, Christian churches have taken Jesus' teachings about the underprivileged seriously. His position was clear:

'If you would be perfect go, sell what you possess and give to the poor and you will have treasure in Heaven.'

(Matthew 19:21)

'For when I was hungry you gave me food; when thirsty you gave me drink; when I was a stranger you took me into your home, when naked you clothed me; when I was ill you came to my help, when in prison you visited me.'

(Matthew 25:35–37)

In the extract on the right a Christian talks about what he believes the Church should do in Britain.

FOR YOUR FOLDERS

▶ How can the churches help the needy?
▶ Which organizations help?
▶ In your own words describe what Jesus' teachings about helping the needy mean.
▶ Explain in your own words what Billy Lucas says in the interview on the right.

THINKING POINT

● *'The Churches in Britain have enormous wealth. Indeed the Church represents one of the wealthiest sectors of society. Yet you can walk around any city in Britain today and find people who have to sleep on the streets while the church doors are locked. While young people are hassled on the streets by pimps, police officers and drug pushers, the churches lie silent like empty tombs. While the bishops live in palaces and the clergy in spacious vicarages, the poor live in rat infested damp hovels or on the street. The Church has lost its way. Jesus said, "Sell your possessions and give to the poor." The Church has its possessions. It locks them up at night while the poor struggle to live. Is this true Christianity? I don't think so. When Jesus saw the hypocrisy and the materialism of the Temple in Jerusalem, he turned the tables over. I have no doubt that he'd do the same thing in Britain today if he saw the state of the Church. Christianity to be true to its teaching, cannot compromise in any way. The Churches should be out there on the streets. The Churches should be demanding and protesting against what is going on in this country. The Churches should open their doors and keep them open, so that people can meet there, talk there, share their problems with others, sleep, dance, eat and drink in an atmosphere of tolerance and friendship. They should be places where people can learn how to become active and press for a better quality of life. But, alas, the Church in many places in Britain has become an empty tomb full of symbols that mean nothing to the people.'*
(Billy Lucas, Youth and Community worker, author's interview)

Christians believe that God created the Earth and that human beings are the responsible stewards or managers of creation. They believe that human beings should work wisely to protect what has been given to them, to work with nature and not against it.

Some Christians believe that some of the ideas in their religion have been deliberately abused in the pursuit of power and wealth. They argue that our present environmental crisis has a lot to do with Christian arrogance. In particular, they point to the idea that nature only exists to serve humanity, and that humanity as recorded in the Genesis account of creation has some sort of divine right to exploit nature. This has undoubtedly been true – the Earth is there to be used and exploited – and the churches have done very little to counter these destructive ideas. It has done little, either, to warn of the risks to the environment; *nor* to lead by example and show that a simple lifestyle is more in line with Jesus' teachings; *nor* to speak up and challenge the lifestyles of today's consumer-ridden and wasteful, unaware society.

Often people have blamed science alone for the desperate crisis the Earth now faces. To a certain extent this criticism is valid, but as 70 of the world's leading scientists wrote in 1983:

> 'We gave it away. We gave the power to people who didn't understand it and were not grown up enough or responsible enough to realize what they had.'

TALKING POINTS

- 'You appointed him ruler over everything you made; you placed him over all creation.'
  (Psalm 8:3–6)

- 'The dignity of nature as creation needs to be bound up with our responsibility for the preservation of life.'
  (World Council of Churches)

- 'It is tragic that our technological mastery is greater than our wisdom about ourselves.'
  (Pope John Paul II)

- ' "Because of what you have done," the Lord said, "the ground will be under a curse." '
  (Genesis 3:17)

- 'Nature is the art of God.'
  (Teilhard de Chardin)

'It is tragic that our technological mastery is greater than our wisdom about ourselves'

THINKING POINTS

- *'So God created man in His own image; in the image of God He created . . . them. God blessed them and said to them. "Be fruitful and increase, fill the Earth and subdue it, rule over . . . every living thing that moves upon the Earth." . . . So it was; and God saw all that He had made, and it was very good.'*

  (Genesis 1:27–29, 31)

- *'You appointed him ruler over everything you made; you placed him over all creation.'*

  (Psalm 8:6)

- *'A desacralized nature is in the power of humanity which is now able to destroy its own species and perhaps even all life on the Earth. Our own technological inventions and our social processes are threatening to get the upper hand, to become as overpowering as nature once was. What needs to be emphasized today, therefore, is the way that God and His creation are "related" rather than their "separateness". The dignity of nature as creation needs to be bound up with our responsibility for the preservation of life.'*

  (The World Council of Churches)

- *'I believe that the world is God's creation and therefore it is sacred. Human beings must act as responsible guardians and caring stewards. We must love the land and look after the Earth in its glorious diversity. We have no right to plunder, pollute, exploit, destroy, kill or in any way disrespect God's creation. Like in a family God is the Father and we are His children and all members of the family should live in harmony with each other. God's family includes the animal and natural world. If we are sensitive and caring we can live with nature rather than against nature. The advance of science and technology requires that human beings live with greater sensitivity than ever before since we are now equipped with extremely powerful and potentially destructive tools. This destructive impulse is not part of God. God is good and good only.'*

  (Simon Phipps, Bishop of Lincoln, *Resurgence* November/December 1986)

'. . . protecting the environment is not an option – it is an imperative that must be placed at the centre of economic and political decision making.'

  (David Gee, Director Friends of the Earth, 1991)

WHAT CHRISTIANS BELIEVE

- God created the Earth.
- God made humans his stewards and managers.
- God's world has been spoiled and exploited by greed, ignorance and selfishness.
- Humans should wisely protect what has been given to them. Humans should work with nature, not against it.
- Nature should never be exploited.

FOR YOUR FOLDERS

▶ Look at newspapers and watch the television to find out what environmental problems face people today. Find out what the churches are trying to do about them.

▶ Why is the Church not blameless over our ecological problems?

▶ How do you think the churches, governments and individuals can try to avert a massive environmental catastrophe?

▶ Explain in your own words what Christians believe about responsibility for Planet Earth.

▶ What are your local environmental issues? Try and find out if local churches are doing anything about them.

Christians believe that life has a purpose

This planet is part of an enormous universe. The Earth lies in a galaxy called the **Milky Way**. It is assumed that there are 100 *billion* galaxies, each containing some 10 *billion trillion* stars and planets. We know very little about the origins of the universe and about whether there is life on the other billions of planets.

Planet Earth orbits around the Sun. If we were any closer or any further away from the Sun then life on Earth as we know it would not be possible. Modern science suggests that planet Earth is a living organism. Scientists are beginning to see that the Earth is alive and astronauts have been able, for the first time in human history, to look at our planet from outer space. The experience of seeing this beautiful blue and white globe floating in the deep darkness of space moved them deeply and, as many of them have since declared, it was a profound spiritual experience.

Christians believe that the universe is not here as a result of chance but was created by God. They believe, therefore, that as our planet was created it is sacred. Christians also believe that:

'God created man in His own image; in the image of God He created . . . them. God blessed them and said to them, "Be fruitful and increase, fill the Earth and subdue it, rule over . . . every living thing that moves upon the Earth." So it was; and God saw all that He had made and it was very good.'
(Genesis 1:27–29,31)

Christians also believe that God:

'appointed him [humankind] ruler over everything.'
(Psalm 8:6)

In these two quotes there are many of the basic ideas that Christians have towards the planet.

- God created the planet.
- God created humankind in 'his own image' which means, among other things, that human beings have a responsibility to the planet.
- Human beings have been given the Earth to subdue and rule over it, i.e. to use it for their own purposes.

- The planet is sacred for God saw that it was 'very good'.
- Human beings are stewards of the planet, i.e. they are here to look after it and care for it.

Over the ages human beings have learnt to use the enormous power and scope of nature to their own advantage. In many ways they have learnt to 'subdue' nature. However, it is becoming increasingly clear that they have not been very good stewards and have failed to look after it. So much so, that many people think that they have polluted the planet to such an extent:

'that we have perhaps 15 years left. Fifteen springtimes. Five thousand days and nights. Five thousand glimmering dusks. Five thousand wakings. Unless we can change our minds and hearts and actions in time.'
(The Gaia Peace Atlas)

Christians are becoming increasingly aware of the damage that human beings have done and are doing to planet Earth. They are beginning to work within their churches and communities to highlight the dangers we all face.

World poverty

Amidst the beauty of planet Earth there is much suffering. Thirty-five thousand people die every day because of world hunger. The effect of world poverty is of real concern to Christians and many organizations and individuals work towards its alleviation. They are influenced by biblical references such as:

'The man with two shirts must share with him who has none and anyone who has food must do the same.'
Luke 3:11

KEY IDEAS

Christians believe in a God of love and justice revealed by Jesus Christ and who calls them to make a response of love: Christians set out to put such love into action.
Christians believe that Jesus Christ is to be found in our neighbours in need. Christians respond to Christ's presence in our neighbours.

KEY IDEAS

Christians believe that the coming of God's Kingdom is hindered by evil which must be fought in whatever form it appears. Christians are involved in this task of building God's Kingdom.

Animals

Humankind not only inflicts its suffering on itself, but also inflicts it upon others of God's creatures. The Christian Church has not always acknowledged the rights of animals in the past, but in the last 20 years there has been an increasing awareness that animals have rights too, as part of God's creation.

'Animals, as part of God's creation, have rights which must be respected.'
(Dr Donald Coggan, Archbishop of Canterbury in 1977 and President of the RSPCA)

'God has the right to have all his creatures treated with proper respect.'
(Cardinal Heenan, Catholic Archbishop)

'In the end, lack of respect for the life and wellbeing of an animal must bring with it a lowering of man's own self-respect. "In as much as ye do it to these the least of my little ones ye do it unto me".'
(Robert Runcie, Archbishop of Canterbury)

'Scientists must abandon laboratories and factories of death.'
(Pope John Paul II)

FOR YOUR FOLDERS

▶ 'All life is sacred.' What do you think this statement means?
▶ Explain what you think Christians mean by 'stewardship' and 'dominion'.
▶ *'In as much as you have done it unto one of the least of my brethren you have done it unto me.'* (Matthew 26:40) Consider this teaching with regard to our treatment of planet Earth.
▶ How do you think Christians can work towards relieving world poverty?

In December 1948 the United Nations produced its **Universal Declaration of Human Rights** (see pages 221–2). It states that all human beings have certain rights: the right to life, freedom, liberty, work, health care, housing, and education. The Universal Declaration was signed by the governments of countries all over the world.

All Christian churches believe that the Universal Declaration of Human Rights reflects many of the main principles of their religion. In the New Testament, Jesus teaches that human beings should learn to treat each other with respect and understanding. For example, one of the most famous parables that Jesus told is the parable of the Good Samaritan, which can be found in Luke chapter 10.

As well as being about helping somebody in need, the parable has a deeper meaning. Samaritans were despised by Jews and yet in Jesus' story the only person who helped the injured man was a Samaritan. This one example of Jesus' teachings shows that all human beings are to be respected, and for Christians the gospel stories offer many other examples of the rights of human beings (for example, 'You shall love your neighbour as yourself', Mark 12:31)

CHRISTIAN VIEWPOINTS

'Rights can be established on the basis of the doctrine of the image of God when we consider those human characteristics which are both distinctively human and shared with God.'
(Church of England report, 1977)

'Each individual man is truly a person. He has a nature that is endowed with intelligence and free will. As such he has rights and duties . . . these rights and duties are universal and inviolable.'
(Encyclical letter of Pope John XXIII, 1963)

For Christians, all people are children of God the creator – we are all made in the image of God. All are born equal in the sight of God. For Christians, human rights should not be violated in order that people can live in peace with each other.

Torture

Millions of people every day have their rights denied or violated. One of the most vicious violations of human rights is torture.

Although illegal under international law, torture is practised by over half the governments of the world. Torture is a crime against humanity. It is cruel and barbaric. One Christian organization concerned with the abolition of torture is **Action by Christians against Torture** (ACT).

ACT

ACT: What is it?
Action by Christians against Torture is a campaign sponsored by the Council of Churches in Britain and Ireland.
ACT's aim is 'to increase awareness in the churches, both nationally and locally, of the need, for reasons of Christian faith, to campaign against torture and to work for its abolition wherever and on whoever it is used.'

ACT: Why?
'Torture is a crime against God and humanity. ACT offers an opportunity for churches to campaign ecumenically against this evil and to support the victims of human rights abuse. Because our faith sets at its centre a symbol of torture: the cross. So we should be especially sensitive about torture and strive to make the resurrection promise a reality in people's lives by working to resist this intolerable evil.

Because we understand God to be the source of life, the upholder of justice, the origin of goodness. So we should affirm the things of life, and fight against all those of death – which includes torture.'
(Action by Christians against Torture)

TALKING POINT

● 'Freedom is never voluntarily given by the oppressor, it must be demanded by the oppressed.' (Martin Luther King)

THINKING POINT

- Throughout history there have been instances of Christians who have spoken out against injustices and oppression. The founder of Christianity himself on many occasions spoke out against the hypocrisy of the religious leaders of his time, and the government of the day had him crucified.

Liberation Theology

In South America a movement called **Liberation Theology** has emerged. These Christians believe that the gospels demand them to stand up and fight against poverty, exploitation, and lack of human rights. Liberation Theologians are inspired by the words of Jesus:

'He has sent me to bring good news to the poor, to proclaim liberty to the captives and to set free the oppressed.'

(Luke 4:18–19)

OSCAR ROMERO

Oscar Romero was Archbishop in El Salvador where the government has consistently violated human rights. Most of the people live in desperate poverty, and in order to keep power the government has brutally and cruelly crushed any opposition. Despite many threats against his life, Romero spoke out against the government in sermons. In 1980 he was gunned down by four masked men while he celebrated mass in his cathedral. His last words were, 'May Christ's sacrifice give us the courage to offer our own bodies for justice and peace.'

THINKING POINT

- "Anyone who has suffered torture remains tortured."

(Jean Amery)

DIETRICH BONHOEFFER

Dietrich Bonhoeffer was a German theologian who lived during the rise to power of Hitler's Nazi Party in Germany. The Nazis abandoned all human rights and began persecuting the Jews and other groups of people. 1941 saw the first mass deportation of Jews to concentration camps like Auschwitz and Belsen.

Bonhoeffer helped form the 'Confessing Church' which opposed the Nazis. He also became involved in helping groups of Jews escape the death camps.

In 1940 he joined the Abwehr, an organization that secretly worked to overthrow the Nazi state. Bonhoeffer believed that the true test of faith was helping the oppressed. To him the state did not represent justice so he decided to become a conspirator. Although he was a pacifist he was prepared to sacrifice not only himself, but also his principles to rid the world of the evils of Nazism. He was prepared to take part in an assassination of Hitler because he saw it as being the only course of action open to him. As a Christian, he would let God pass judgement. He himself did not see the murder of Hitler as being 'good', but rather as a practical necessity.

In 1942 Bonhoeffer was imprisoned. In 1945 he was executed for treason. In Canterbury Cathedral there is a chapel dedicated to martyrs of the 20th century – 'Dietrich Bonhoeffer' is the one German name there. Bishop Bell of Chichester said Bonhoeffer's death 'represents the resistance of the believing soul against injustice and cruelty.'

FOR YOUR FOLDERS

▶ Explain in your own words the Christian viewpoint of human rights.
▶ What is Liberation Theology?
▶ In your own words write a paragraph about Oscar Romero and one about Dietrich Bonhoeffer and their stand on human rights.

A statue of Christ in Rio de Janeiro

Christians only have to look at their newspapers or watch their televisions to realize that they live in a world torn by war, prejudice and ignorance. The world seems to be no better a place than it was 2000 years ago, at the time of Jesus, the founder of Christianity. War in the north, war in the south, war in the east, war in the west, war outside and war within. People only have to look to their own communities and their own families to experience the traumas of conflict and division. There seems to be little peace, either in the external or the internal world.

For over 2000 years Christianity has laid claim to be the world's most influential and superior creed, yet during those 2000 years the Church, corrupted by power, has dominated and subjugated millions of people.

The Western world is undergoing a spiritual crisis. Modern technology threatens to dominate people's lives, pollution threatens to end their lives. Many people have turned away from the promises of salvation through the Church, disillusioned.

2000 years ago a new message was given to humanity. The message of the New Testament is one of love. Jesus said, 'I give you a new commandment: love one another.' (John 13:34) This might sound a simple commandment but if people see themselves as being cells of God, ultimately joined together, then before they can hope for a world of peace they must learn how to walk the hard road of loving one another. Although humankind lives in a Global Village and has an increasing understanding of the world around them, they still find it difficult to live in peace with their neighbours.

> 'In order to be able to love and change the world for the better, we need to get in touch with love, and to be aware that human life, nature, our planet, the entire cosmos is essentially one and that behind it and sustaining it is another reality beyond our understanding . . . life on Earth is threatened. Love, if it is true to itself, must always be effective. It is the expression of love, the putting into practice what love demands which is all important.'
>
> (John St John, *Religion and Social Justice*, Pergamon Press 1985)

Many Christians believe that the essential message that Jesus gave humanity 2000 years ago has been lost in the trappings of the Christian religion. There are many teachings that have been lost through the mists of time but essentially Jesus asked people to look within themselves to find truth. The longest journey is the journey inwards and until people acquire knowledge about themselves and who they are then the world will continue to be torn apart by conflict and division. Until people find that still place of peace within they will continue to exert their selfishness, their ego and their ignorance upon a world which is potentially quite beautiful. There can be no peace until there is peace within. Jesus himself said, 'How blessed are the peace makers, God shall call them his sons.'

(Matthew 5:9)

Thomas Merton, one of the greatest Christian mystics of the 20th century, said:

> 'He who attempts to act and do things for others without deepening his own self understanding and capacity to love will not have anything to give others.'

Human beings have incredible potential. The manifestations of this can be seen in the technology that humankind has created, but there is a kind of duality in the human condition. Human beings can send signals out into the darkest and most distant areas of space yet they can create weapons of mass destruction. A child has the potential to become an Einstein or a Beethoven; or a child has the potential

'We need to be aware that human life, nature, our planet and the cosmos are essentially one'

to become a mass murderer. If people stop and look within they find that there is a whole universe; there is peace or there is the potential for war.

All religions and all ways have an essence, a kernel of truth, a mustard seed. If people look at the hidden inner meanings of the gospels they might find true salvation through the agonies of the cross, that is sometimes known as the search for self knowledge.

As humankind moves into a new millenium perhaps they have to abandon many of the mechanical and crystallized pre-judgements about what true Christianity is and go back to its roots, go back to that mustard seed.

> *'And this is another parable that he put before them: the kingdom of heaven is like a mustard seed which a man took and sowed in his field. As a seed mustard is smaller than any other; but when it has grown it is bigger than any garden plant; it becomes a tree, big enough for the birds to come and roost among its branches.'*
>
> (Matthew 13:31–32)

Christianity is one of the world's major religions. It is 2000 years old and millions of people from all cultures and with many different beliefs claim to be Christians. Sections 19–36 have only touched upon some of the ideas and moral values of this religion. However, even this superficial look at Christianity should give some ideas about its beliefs and values.

THINKING POINT

● *'Christian civilization has proved hollow to a terrifying degree; it is all veneer, but the inner man has remained untouched and therefore unchanged. Everything is to be found outside – in image and in word, in Church and in Bible – but never inside. Inside reign the archaic gods, supreme as of old . . .'*

(Jung, *Memories, Dreams and Reflections*, New York: Random House/Vintage, London: Fontana 1977)

FOR YOUR FOLDERS

Imagine you were a visitor from another planet who had to write a letter home explaining what Christianity is all about. In your letter you need to try to tackle the following questions:

▶ Outline some Christian beliefs that you have understood from sections 19–36.

▶ What personal, social and global problems face the people of planet Earth?

▶ How do Christians try and tackle these problems?

▶ How successful has Christianity been in making the teachings of the messenger, known as Jesus Christ, a reality on Earth?

On the move in an Indian city

Hinduism is a way of life. It relates to the religious, social, moral and political behaviour of about 83 per cent of the people of India. It is a living faith which has been constantly changing and developing since it began in India about 3500 years ago. It has no historical founder, and many sacred books, not just one. The oldest scriptures are called the **Veda**, and include **hymns** or songs to spirits controlling nature, rules for performing sacrifice, and philosophy about the mysteries of life and death. Hindus worship one god under different names and appearances, both male and female. They believe in the reincarnation of the soul or **atman**, which passes through many lives, not all human.

> *'Those who are born will surely die*
> *and the dead will be born again . . .'*
> (Bhagavad Gita 2:27)*

Hinduism is mainly practised in India but it is also found wherever Hindus have settled.

The Universal Moral Law

Hindus themselves call their faith **Sanatana-dharma** (the Universal Moral Law). Because it is universal it is applicable to *all* people. The core of Hindu moral law is **dharma** (moral duty, responsibility), and this will vary from person to person according to age, sex, social position, education and occupation.

Varna-ashrama-dharma is a term which explains that **dharma** is dependent on the social position (**varna**) into which individuals are born and their stage of life (**ashrama**).

> *'I have created the four varnas according to individual temperaments and work'*
> (Bhagavad Gita 4:13)

The varna-ashrama-dharma applies to the three upper classes (**varnas**) of Hindu society: **brahmins** (priests, professionals), **kshatriyas** (administrators, soldiers) and **vaishyas** (business people).

There is a fourth social division, the **shudras** who are artisans and landless farm labourers. They too have a dharma – the **sadharana-dharma** – which is a general code of behaviour, valid for all people regardless of their social status. It stresses the importance of truth, non-violence, honesty and respect for all living things.

> *'Better to do one's duty though imperfect, than another's task however well performed.*
> *Better to die following one's own dharma than to invite danger following another's dharma.'*
> (Bhagavad Gita 3:35)

'Truth alone, not falsehood, points to the path leading to God . . .'

(Mundaka Upanishad 3:1:6)

'The wise look impartially on a learned brahmin, a cow, an elephant, a dog and an outcaste.'

(Bhagavad Gita 5:18)

Community dharma

Originally the duties of the various varnas were related. A landowner was expected to pay his farmworkers enough. A ruler had a moral duty to reward the priests for carrying out rituals and celebrating festivals. These duties still are related in rural areas. Varna duties were designed to support the whole community.

Family dharma

Ideally, a Hindu's life is divided into four stages called **ashramas**. They are:

- **brahmacharya**, the student stage
- **grihastha**, the married householder stage
- **vanaprastha**, the retirement stage
- **sannyasa**, an optional renunciation stage.

Originally, the three upper varnas were expected to pass ritually through at least the first three stages, but in modern times only brahmins normally do this. Very few men become **sannyasins**. At each stage of life, Hindus are expected to follow a set of duties and responsibilities towards their immediate family members as well as themselves.

A brahmacharin's duties include diligent study, and showing respect to teachers and elders in the family. He may not have sex before marriage, nor take alcohol, drugs or tobacco.

A grihastha has a duty to get married, have children and educate them. He must support his wife, children, elderly parents and sick relatives. He must earn money honestly and spend it wisely. He must give to charity and offer hospitality. He must also perform rituals and celebrate festivals to continue the religious and cultural tradition.

A man's primary duty after retirement is to devote time to the study of scriptures, prayer and the training of his grandchildren. In this way he is preparing for the next existence.

'You must perform your bounden duty, for action is better than idleness . . .'

(Bhagavad Gita 3:8)

The performance of these various duties involves actions, and these actions result in **karma**. It is this karma, good or bad, which controls the form of the Hindu's next life. Dharma imposes three types of moral duty: to the world outside, to the immediate family, and to self.

Apad-dharma

Hindus believe that the rules of moral conduct of Sanatana-dharma, stated in the **Dharma-shastras** or law books, can be changed according to circumstances during times of distress or hardship. The ancient rulings of the law books have slowly been modified as society changed. Hindus consider that in the present age – **Kali Yuga** or the Black Age – ancient rules of morality are not generally valid or useful.

*Unless otherwise stated, all translations in sections 37–46, 49, 52 and 54 are by the author.

THINGS TO DO

▶ Hindu friends have described to you what they see as their dharma. Explain to them what you see as your dharma
(a) at school   (b) at home
(c) in a public place.

Varna A social class.
Karma The result of one's actions.

Ashrama A stage in life.
Dharma Social, moral or religious duty of an individual.

Sanatana-dharma The Universal Moral Law.
Varna-ashrama-dharma Set of duties of varnas and ashramas.
Sadharana-dharma Set of duties applicable to *all* people in society.
Apad-dharma (distress duty) – Responsibilities modified as a result of adversity or hardship.
Artisan Skilled manual worker, such as a mechanic or potter.

38 RELATIONSHIPS

Human respect

If a Hindu accidentally touches another human being with their foot, they must join palms and bow before that person, to beg forgiveness. The scriptures declare that every creature is a part of **Brahman**, the Supreme Spirit.

'Ishvara (the Lord) dwells in the hearts of all creatures, O Arjuna, causing them to revolve by His power, as if they were put into a machine.'
(Bhagavad Gita 18:61)

'A man commands respect through his education, religious actions, age, friends and wealth. Possessed of all these even a shudra* in his old age deserves respect.'
(Yajnavalkya 1:116)

(*artisan)

- As a result of the Hindu social divisions of varna or class, and **jati** or caste, people at the lower end of the social scale, because of the dirty and degrading nature of their occupation, do not always get the respect they deserve as human beings.
- As a rule, parents, grandparents and *all* elder relations are respected by the younger members in the family.
- Family priests and teachers receive respect for their learning and experience, although their work is sometimes made fun of by the younger generation.
- Respect is given and received within the same class and caste.

Friendship

A person's life is influenced by the elders in the extended family, by teachers, and by friendships. Friendships in Hindu society are formed in many ways:

- By living in the same village and belonging to the same caste.
- By living in the same block of flats in a large city.
- Through school, or by working in the same office, mill or factory.
- By attending the same temple in the neighbourhood.
- Through being members of a group singing devotional songs in a temple.
- By going on a **pilgrimage**, or religious journey.
- By attending the same college or club in a large city.

- By speaking the same language and living in the same region of India. India has 15 official languages as well as English. These are: Assamese, Bengali, Gujarati, Hindi, Kannada, Kashmiri, Malayalam, Marathi, Oriya, Punjabi, Sanskrit, Sindhi, Tamil, Telugu, Urdu.
- Through sports such as a local cricket or basketball team.

Friendship between the sexes is not acceptable in Hindu society. Boys and girls are kept apart. In cities, they may go to the cinema, or attend a sports club, or visit a disco *as a group*.

KEY IDEA
Lifelong friendships are generally formed between people speaking the same language and belonging to the same class or caste.

In India two men may be seen walking together with their arms around each other's shoulders, or they may embrace when they meet. This is an accepted gesture of friendship without any suggestion of homosexuality.

Caste barriers to friendship are breaking down in large industrial cities because people of different castes, through their education, their jobs and the amount they earn, can find themselves in the same **economic class.**

Love

'Love is a many splendoured thing' – so the song says. The word 'love' creates many different emotions in the hearts of different people.

KEY IDEA
Love is giving, receiving and forgiving.

Love affects men and women of all ages. A Hindu writer in the early 18th century classified love under 350 different headings; this number was later reduced to 20. There are 20 different Sanskrit words which describe love. Of these, eight deal with pure love and the rest describe sexual love. Some types of love are:

- **Love experienced through sight, sound, taste or touch** – *seeing* a sunrise or sunset, the Meenakshi temple tower at Madurai, south India; *listening* to Ravi Shankar's sitar music or Indian film songs; *tasting* rich food prepared for Diwali festival; *wearing* a silk sari.
- **Love of friends** – non-sexual affection between two people of the same sex.
- **Love of family** – love between a mother and child.
- **Spiritual love** as denoted by **bhakti** – complete surrender by a devotee to a personal deity: **Ishvara**.
- **Sexual love** – see Section 41 on sexuality.

In a family, love between a mother and a child is based on pure affection. Love between a father and a son or daughter is made up of both respect and affection. Informal love is usually found between cousins. A married woman and her husband's younger brother may have a light-hearted – but non-sexual – affectionate relationship.

Relationships

A relationship is a link or connection between two or more people. Relationships can also include other living creatures, such as dogs or cats. Any relationship between individuals is based on varied ideas or emotions. Hindu moral values are based upon the following key ideals.

- A mother's concern for her children's safety, physical well-being, emotional development, education and marriage is based on pure love.

KEY IDEA

'A son may be born (or become) wicked, but there is no wicked mother.'
(From a prayer to Mother Goddess)

- A father has authority in the family; a son generally respects that authority, even when his ideas are different from those of his father because of the generation gap.
- A relationship between two men or two women in Hindu society need not be sexual, but could be based on mutual respect and friendship.
- A husband's relationship with his wife includes a sexual element. In many Hindu families the wife submits her own personality to her husband's.

- A young boy and girl can rarely have a relationship based on mutual love leading to marriage.

In large cities, young people in rich and westernized Hindu families get opportunities to meet. They may learn about each other's likes, dislikes and interests, fall in love and marry, *if* the families approve. Even in these circumstances, though, there is very little premarital sex.

KEY IDEAS

Unequal caste or class and family backgrounds create problems in relationships. All relationships are monitored by society.

Because of the accepted separation of the sexes, even a truly platonic relationship between a man and a woman is assumed to be sexual by Hindu society.

Brahman The Supreme Spirit in Hinduism without form, quality or gender.
Ishvara An aspect of Brahman worshipped by an individual as a personal deity in the form of an image.
Bhakti Complete devotion to God.
Varna A social category or group of individuals in Hindu society.
Jati (caste) An occupational group engaged in a particular type of job within the varna category.
Extended family Family including grandparents, aunts, uncles and cousins.
Platonic relationship A relationship based on friendship, without sexual involvement.

FOR YOUR FOLDERS

▶ How do varna and jati influence human respect and relationship?
▶ Hindus say caste loyalties, local temples, pilgrimage, language and living in the same village create lifelong friendships. Explain how this can be.
▶ For young Hindu men and women, falling in love does not always lead to marriage. Why do you think this is?

A Hindu **extended family** includes people of three or four generations, all living together. The women cook for everyone and the money earned by the men is shared. The older men and women decide how the money is spent, taking account of what everyone needs. Families give stability to Hindu society and provide security for their members. The family also controls the sexual behaviour of its members, including those who are married.

In a Hindu family, property passes from father to son and the older or senior men make the decisions, although the older women do have considerable influence. Such a system is called **patriarchal** or **patrilineal.**

In Hindu villages, the family is an important economic unit because it provides a stable workforce, which is held together by family ties. In larger cities or **urban** areas, the family provides workers for business. The diagram at the bottom of the page shows how an **extended** Hindu family is made up.

Women can marry into or out of the family, and are called **mobile members.** Men in the father's family are **permanent** members. Some members of the mother's family take important parts in religious ceremonies for the eldest and second sons, and daughters.

The **nuclear** family is made up mainly of the mother, father and sons and daughters, as shown in this diagram.

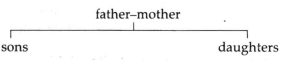

```
              father–mother
       ┌────────────┴────────────┐
     sons                     daughters
```

An urban nuclear family does not forget its duties and responsibilities to the extended family. It may include a grandparent or the unmarried sister of the father. The family provides support for its elderly, sick, disabled and less well-off members. Sometimes it will also take care of the adult unmarried women.

Family relationships

Relationships within the family are very close, and each member has responsibilities for the others. For example, an elder brother should make sure that his brothers and sisters go to school and, later on, make good marriages. In return for this concern they should respect his decisions. A daughter should help her mother, and look after her brothers and their needs.

The family relationship names are shown in the chart. They tell exactly whether an individual is young or old, or related through mother or father. It is their position in the family which controls their duties and responsibilites.

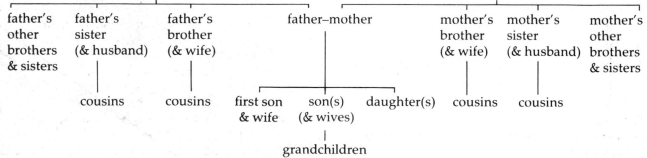

FAMILY RELATIONSHIPS

Family position	Hindi
Paternal grandfather	Dada
Paternal grandmother	Dadi
Maternal grandfather	Nana
Maternal grandmother	Nani
Father	Bap, Pita
Mother	Ma, Mata
Brother	Bhai, Bhayya
Sister	Didi, Behen
Father's brother	Chacha
Father's brother's wife	Chachi
Mother's brother	Mama
Mother's brother's wife	Mami
Mother's sister	Mausi, Massi
Mother's sister's husband	Mausa
Father's sister	Phuphi
Father's sister's husband	Phua, Bhua
Friend	Mitra, Doast

In Hindu society, single-parent families are very rare and are most likely to result from the death of one partner. Hindus normally practise **monogamy**, which means a man has only one wife. This is approved by secular law as well as by the Dharma-shastras (ancient Hindu law books). Hindus' conduct and behaviour is controlled by dharma, which provides guidelines for the rights and duties of all members of the family.

KEY IDEA

The duties of each member of the family ensure that the rights of the others are protected.

Religious duties of family members

Grandparents
- Study of scriptures.
- Religious and moral instruction of grandchildren by retelling stories from Hindu myths and legends.

Parents
- Ensuring the continuance of the family name through sons.
- Offering daily worship to the family deities.
- Celebrating festivals and performing 'rites of passage' rituals to preserve the religious traditions.
- Earning money honestly.
- Providing necessities and some extras for the family.
- Providing shelter, clothing, food, education and moral training for children.
- Caring for aged parents, unmarried daughters and the less well-off members of the family.
- Offering hospitality to guests.
- Charitable giving.

Children
- Showing respect and obedience to parents, grandparents and all older relations.
- Studying hard and respecting teachers.
- Avoiding food and drink that may cause harm to themselves or to others.
- Avoiding selfish actions which will bring suffering and disrepute on the family.

FOR YOUR FOLDERS

- ▶ Draw your own family tree and compare it to those on page 82.
- ▶ How does your family differ from the Hindu extended family described on page 82?
- ▶ Why do Hindus consider that personal duties protect the rights of other members of a family?

FOR DISCUSSION

- ▶ Young Hindus' duty of obedience to their elders affects their personal freedom of thought and actions.
- ▶ Young Hindus rebel against their family structure because they think it discourages their initiative.
- ▶ Why are Indian languages rich in words for family relationships?

Marriage

For a Hindu man marriage is a religious duty. It is more of a samskara or **sacrament** than a contract. It is an important tradition for women and it is the only samskara permitted to **shudras**, the artisan class.

Some religious rituals can be performed only by a married couple.

Arranged marriages are the most common for Hindus. They are arranged by the elders in the family. The elders consider carefully the horoscopes of the young people, and the social, financial and religious status of both families.

Love marriages are possible but less common in Hindu society. If the young people choose their own partners, the choice is only approved by parents and other elder relatives if the families are of equal social standing. In her new home a bride has to look after her parents-in-law and other senior relatives. If there is a vast difference between the family traditions, she will experience great difficulties with regard to religious rituals and food.

The social and ritual status of the couple are of great significance.

Matrimonial advertisements in newspapers, like the one on the right, play an important part in arranged marriages.

WESTERN INDIAN BRAHMIN family seek a bride for their son, 27, B Com, studying law. The girl should be a graduate, tall, fair-skinned, brought up in the Hindu tradition. Apply with a photo and horoscope.

All Hindu marriages have to be registered. For Hindus, monogamy is normal. This means they each have only one partner.

'A woman should be respected and given pleasure by her husband, brother, father, parents-in-law, husband's younger brother and other relatives with ornaments, clothes and food.'

(Yajnavalkya 82)

'A woman should keep the house tidy, do the housework expertly, be contented, be economical in housekeeping, bow before her parents-in-law and show devotion to her husband.'

(Yajnavalkya 83)

IMPORTANT RITUALS IN THE WEDDING CEREMONY

- Giving of the daughter in marriage.
- Worship of the family deities.
- Songs of blessing.
- Offering of **ghee** (clarified butter) and grain to the sacred fire, with prayers for health, prosperity, sons and a long married life.
- Taking seven steps before the sacred fire.
- Giving of the marriage necklace to the bride.
- Promise by the bridegroom to look after the bride and to follow his **dharma** (religious duty), **artha** (earning money honestly) and **kama** (enjoyment of sexual and other pleasures) *with moderation.*

A bride and groom offer roasted rice to Agni (fire)

It used to be common for a bride's parents to give a **dowry** to the bridegroom's parents. This was the daughter's natural inheritance from her father's property. The size of the dowry affected the bride's status in her new home.

A law abolishing dowry came into force in India in October 1985. Many parents are still expected to give money to the bridegroom's parents as 'wedding gifts' on their daughter's marriage. If their parents do not give anything, or if they do not give enough, the mental cruelty inflicted on young brides can be so severe that they commit suicide.

> 'The need for action is no longer disputed. According to the police, 2755 women died of burns in Delhi alone in the five years from 1979 to 1983. An overwhelming majority were married, and of these, 1402 were aged 18 to 25.'
> (*The Guardian* 3 October 1985)

Divorce

In Hindu law, based on the Dharma-shastras, marriage was for life. High class or caste Hindus could not divorce their spouses, but divorce or separation was practised among the lower castes in rural areas.

Since the **Hindu Marriage Act 1955**, marriages can be ended by divorce but traditional Hindus do not accept the idea. Divorce is not common in Hindu society and it can be a social stigma. Re-marriage after divorce is difficult. Some people advertise in newspapers for new partners.

Samskara Rituals performed at various stages of growth and development of an individual.
Shudra A member of the fourth social category or varna. An artisan such as a potter, a washerman, a barber.
Artha Earning money by honest effort.
Kama Enjoyment of the good things in life.
Dowry Money given by a bride's family to the bridegroom's family at marriage. The practice of dowry is now illegal in India.

WOMEN HAVE LITTLE FREEDOM TO CHOOSE THEIR MARRIAGE PARTNERS

○ Poonam (22) was 'shown' to many prospective husbands who rejected her. Her sisters Kamini (20) and Alka (18) refused to be paraded in the marriage market. All three sisters hanged themselves in Kanpur.
○ Basanti (14), daughter of a washerman in Calcutta, attempted suicide after many rejections. One boy agreed to marry her for 12 000 rupees but later said that Basanti was too short.
○ Sudha works in a bank in Bombay on a four-figure salary. She was rejected by six boys because she is not slim or beautiful. Sudha's mother said, '. . . if you want your children to be married in the same caste and community, then this sort of thing is inevitable.'

(Based on Svati Chakravarty and Ruchira Gupta, 'Humiliation in the marriage market', *The Sunday Observer* (Bombay), 6 March 1988)

FOR YOUR FOLDER

▶ Why are the caste and family traditions of a bride and groom still important in a Hindu marriage?
▶ The Hindu tradition is that love after marriage produces more lasting happiness. Do you think this is true? Give reasons.
▶ How can a Hindu arranged marriage affect a bride's life in her husband's family?

Every human being has male and female characteristics in their personality. The dominant traits determine a person's sexuality, either masculine or feminine.

Sexuality is expressed through behaviour, the sexual drive, clothes, food, drink, cosmetics, sport, work and hobbies.

Hindu scriptures and society approve only of sex within marriage.

'In powerful (beings) I am their strength free from desire (kama) and attachment; and in (all) beings I am the desire (kama) which is not contrary to morality (dharma).'
(Bhagavad Gita 7:11)

Homosexuality

Some men and women are inclined to express their sexuality through a loving relationship with a partner of their own sex.

Male **homosexuality** and its female counterpart, **lesbianism**, exist in Hindu society, but both these forms of sexual expression are regarded as socially unacceptable.

Heterosexuality

This form of sexual behaviour has scriptural approval since every Hindu male has a religious duty to marry and produce sons.

Although premarital and extramarital sex occur in society, they are rarely talked about and never approved of.

Celibacy

Traditionally, a Hindu's life is divided into four stages or **ashramas**, and these apply to the three upper **varnas** (or classes), which are **brahmins** (priests, professionals), **kshatriyas** (administrators, soldiers), and **vaishyas** (business people). The four ashramas are **brahmacharya** (student stage), **grihastha** (married householder stage), **vanaprastha** (retirement), and **sannyasa** (renunciation).

A student, whether following the western type of education or the traditional Sanskrit education is, by definition, celibate. For Hindus marriage does not take place until their studies are completed and they have found employment. Among other things, the scriptures advise a student not to have sex, therefore a **brahmacharin** is also a virgin. Since girls have equal opportunities for education they also fall into this category while they are students.

Premarital sex is strongly discouraged. Parents watch their children carefully and, as a result, most young Hindus have no sexual experience before marriage.

Some Hindu men, on completing their traditional Sanskrit education, skip the next two ashramas and go on to become **sannyasins**, therefore remaining celibate.

Chastity

Chastity is the state of being sexually pure, i.e. not indulging in unlawful sexual intercourse. A chaste wife, devoted to her husband is a **pativrata**.

Birth control

A hundred years ago life expectancy in India was very low, medical science was not very advanced, and many children died before they were five years old. These factors influenced Hindu attitudes and many couples had six, eight or even ten children, in the hope that three or four would survive. Birth control was not practised, even by the few who were well educated.

Because of modern medical advances and improved nutrition, the Indian life span increased. Fewer deaths occurred and the population began to grow. In 1991 it was about 844 million.

Hindus have no objection to birth control on religious grounds and they have supported the Indian government scheme of birth control. For the vast majority of Hindus in India, however, modern methods of birth control are too expensive to buy and too tricky to understand. The **condom** is widely used by people with plenty of money, but for the vast majority of the poor, the effective method is female sterilization and male vasectomy.

Abortion

Abortion is legal in India if it is carried out in government clinics. Hindus (83 per cent of the total population) clearly support abortion, both as a method of ending unwanted pregnancies and, indirectly, as a method of birth control. An estimated 5 million abortions take place in India every year. Birth control clinics are always trying to increase their effectiveness to save women from abortions.

Modern medical research

FERTILITY AND INFERTILITY

Many childless Hindu couples long to have a son. If modern medical methods can fulfil their wishes, they have no religious objection to 'test-tube' babies.

However, the idea of artificial insemination by **donor** is difficult for Hindus to accept. This is because of the importance of definite *male* ancestry for inheritance, and the need to establish caste and family background at marriage. The identity of donors is unknown and this would be unacceptable to a Hindu family. Furthermore, Hindu personal law allows adoption from relatives in cases of infertility, which takes away any doubts about inheritance.

AMNIOCENTESIS

Amniocentesis is a scientific method for detecting abnormalities in the foetus. One form of the test also discloses the sex of a foetus. Since 1986 it has been widely used in India by both rich and poor, mainly to find out the baby's sex.

A small quantity of the fluid around the foetus is taken from the womb using a special kind of needle. This is called **amniotic fluid**. Analysis of the chromosomes in the fluid helps to identify the sex of the foetus, as well as any genetic problems. The test can give almost perfectly accurate results.

Bombay and Delhi are major centres for this test, but hospitals and private clinics in small towns and cities in eight states offer the service as well. It costs between 200 and 500 rupees (about £7–£15). Because it is so cheap, even poor families can afford the test. A recent survey in the Bombay slums showed that many women had abortions after learning that their foetuses were female.

In Hindu society, sons are the main support for the family; girls are seen as a drain on resources. First there is the expense of their upbringing and education, then there are large dowry payments on marriage (even though dowry is illegal!). Parents argue that it is better to spend 500 rupees avoiding a girl's birth rather than spend thousands on her marriage.

TRANSPLANTS

The sale of human organs for transplant is illegal in the UK and most of Europe. In India, there are some government hospitals where kidney transplants are carried out. In most cases the patient and the donor are Hindus, although they may be unrelated and unknown to each other. There is no 'sale' as such but a rich patient may give a 'reward' to the poor donor. If transplants save lives, Hindu ethics raise no objection to modern medical research. At the same time, in Bombay there is a dangerous market in kidneys for sale which are offered by poor Indians from the slums to rich foreigners.

SUPPORTING LIFE

Life-support machines are very expensive and are available only in large city hospitals. The people who benefit belong to a tiny wealthy minority. Hindus, however, have no religious objection to their use.

Brahmin A priest, a professional, a member of the first varna.
Kshatiya A soldier and administrator, a member of the second varna.
Vaishya A businessman, a farmer, a member of the third varna.
Ashrama A stage in an individual's life.
Brahmacharya The student stage.
Grihastha The married householder stage.
Vanaprastha The retirement stage.
Sannyasa A stage in life when worldly ties are given up to meditate upon God.
Pativrata A faithful and devoted wife.
Sannyasin A person who has given up all worldly attachments.
Amniotic fluid The fluid surrounding the foetus inside the mother's womb.

FOR YOUR FOLDERS

► Why is homosexuality unacceptable to most Hindus?
► How do Hindus justify aborting female foetuses after sex-determination tests?
► If Hindus believe that all life is sacred, why is abortion legal in India?
► Why is chastity so important in the Hindu family?

Drugs

Modern medicine uses drugs to fight disease and suffering. Drugs change the body chemistry and affect the natural balance of a healthy body. Used properly, drugs like aspirin and penicillin bring benefits. Others can cause all sorts of harm, they can increase suffering and affect individuals and society. In some cases, where medicines are scarce and expensive, dangerous drugs can be helpful. Drugs such as opium can relieve pain. Years ago, opium was used rarely and in very small quantities. Now it is grown and processed (mostly into heroin) for profit because of western demand.

Nowadays illegal drugs are transported quickly from the source to the consumer, by means of air travel. Young people everywhere may experiment with drugs for 'fun' but if they get addicted to them, these same drugs lead to self-degradation, crime and premature death. The dangerous drugs are known as **speed**, **grass** (also called pot, dope or hash), **smack** and **acid**. Hindu society, in general, does not tolerate these dangerous drugs, but there are exceptions.

Drugs have been used for occult and ritual purposes by certain groups in Hinduism to bring on trances and visions. Many **sadhus** still use them. Most of the commonly used drugs in India are derived from the **hemp** or cannabis plant. They include **hashish** (the tender leaves), **bhang** (a drink made from hemp leaves) **ganja** (a narcotic, made from dried leaves, and smoked) and **charus** (the resinous extract from the stalk of the hemp plant).

Opium was brought into India in the 14th century CE, probably from Persia, and was used in Indian medicine. For many centuries an aromatic **smoke roll**, like a cigar made with cardamom, saffron and sandalwood, was used to cure coughs, asthma, sore eyes and headaches. This was replaced by tobacco after 1600 CE. Tobacco has no medical benefits. **Cheroots**, **bidis** and **hookah**, along with cigarettes, are widely used.

Smoking in the presence of elders in the family shows a lack of respect. This leads to firm control of the habit in homes. Partly for this reason, and partly because of the low cost compared to cigarettes, **chewing tobacco** is widely used in Hindu society, especially in the rural areas. In India, smoking is banned on public transport and in cinemas, theatres and temples.

The use of traditional drugs, in moderation, by some people for religious rituals seems to be tolerated in Hindu society. The ancient lawgiver Manu warns against wilful addiction.

'He [man] must not get wilfully addicted to any object or substance of self-gratification; he must try to overcome such dependence through will-power.'

(Manu 4:16)

Alcohol

The pre-Aryans and Dravidians, who lived in ancient India, commonly drank distilled spirits and fermented preparations. So, too, did the Aryans who came in about 1500 BCE. These ancient brews are mentioned in Hindu literature. The famous **soma** of the **Rig Veda** (the earliest scriptures) was an intoxicating drink made from a plant which has been forgotten. At the **Soma Sacrifice ritual** the host, the priests and the guests all drank it freely.

Use of alcoholic drinks in moderation is tolerated in modern Hindu society. However, at all Indian government functions, at home and abroad, only soft drinks are served.

All Indian manufactured spirits and beers carry government approval when served in 'permit' bars. They are also treated with religious toleration by Hindus. **Tadi**, made from the sap of the palmyra tree, is a strong intoxicant widely used in the coastal regions.

Fasting

Fasting in Hinduism does not necessarily mean going without food. Only those who are physically fit go on a complete fast on religious occasions such as the birth festivals of the gods Rama and Krishna. Others are allowed to eat certain foods when they are observing a fast. It is mainly women who undertake fasts as religious acts. In the villages, women work hard in the fields. Elsewhere, they do heavy work on building projects and in factories. In small towns, women in middle-class families face laborious housework – cooking, fetching water, cleaning the house and washing clothes.

FASTING FOOD

Any dish made with rice, wheat, millet and pulses is not allowed. Permissible foods include milk, peanuts, fresh fruit, dates, almonds, sage, yoghurt, sweet potatoes, coconuts and ghee (clarified butter).

A strict vegetarian diet in India is high in starch (rice, flat bread), but the fasting food is comparatively high in proteins and very nourishing. When women observe religious fasts, the fasting food enables them to have a regular intake of nourishing food. This gives them energy for their hard work.

Some men also undertake regular fasts once a week, once a fortnight, or once a month on days dedicated to a particular deity, as a spiritual discipline. The scriptures strongly discourage complete fasting, since the body is weakened though lack of food.

In the Bhagavad Gita, Krishna (God) says:

*'O Arjuna, he who overeats or observes a complete fast, who sleeps too much or is (always) awake cannot succeed in yoga.
Yoga destroys suffering (brings happiness) for him who is moderate in eating, leisure activities, work, sleep and wakefulness.'*

(Bhagavad Gita 6:16, 17)

Severe self-discipline (tapas)

Many Hindus seeking **spiritual enlightenment** give up worldly possessions and attachment to the things of this life. It is not advocated by all schools of Indian thought, though. Giving up worldly things completely is called **tapas**, which means *heat* or *ardour*.

TAPAS

Tapas is practised by some **sadhus** (holy men) and **yogis** (men disciplined in yoga). The genuine **tapaswin** carries out his tapas in forest retreats.

● Some stand in water, immersed up to their waists or necks.
● Some sit or stand still on the same spot for years.
● Some always remain standing.
● Some sleep only on bare earth.
● Some keep their bodies bent.
● Some never cut their nails and they keep their fists permanently closed.
● Women may practise tapas but instances are very rare.

Such severe forms of self-discipline are not encouraged by the scriptures since they torture the body and spirit.

KEY IDEA

Tapas is a lesser path to God.

In the Bhagavad Gita, Lord Krishna says:

'A man of action is superior to a tapaswin, or a follower of the path of knowledge, or one who blindly performs orthodox rituals; therefore, O Arjuna, be a man of action.'

(Bhagavad Gita 6:46)

'No one can see me, as you have seen me, merely by knowing the vedas, by severe self-discipline (tapas), by giving to charity or by performing sacrifice.'

(Bhagavad Gita 11:53)

Yoga A system of Hindu philosophy which aims to free an individual from pain and suffering, leading the inner-self towards **Brahman** by means of physical exercises and meditation. Yoga must be learned from a teacher to avoid any physical harm.

FOR YOUR FOLDERS

► Why are traditional drugs derived from the hemp plant tolerated in some Hindu groups?
► There are social factors which control smoking in Hindu society. Work out what these are.
► Some early Hindu texts advise on the use of alcohol. Do you think what they say is useful or valid? Give reasons.
► What limits does the Hindu holy book, the Bhagavad Gita, put on fasting and severe self-discipline? Does its teaching apply today in cases of extreme dieting leading to anorexia? Explain your answer.

FOR DISCUSSION

► Hindu tolerance of drugs and alcohol encourages young people to experiment with addictive substances.

What is wealth?

What does anyone understand by the word 'wealth'? How can it be measured? The Aryans, who settled in India in about 1500 BCE, measured it by the number of cattle they owned. As Hindu society became more settled, people's ideas about what they meant by wealth, or **artha**, changed. If someone owned a lot of land, and had plenty of gold, silver and precious stones, they would be considered wealthy. Alternatively, someone who had plenty of food and clothes, and somewhere comfortable to live might also be thought of as wealthy.

Wealthy people were often expected to have good qualities, such as generosity and kindness, because they were well off. In fact, many of them used their wealth to gain power over people with authority in their society.

> 'A man of wealth is considered (by society) respectable, a pandit (scholar), a critical judge of fine arts, an orator and handsome. But, in reality, it is his wealth (gold) that attracts these compliments and not the man himself.
> (Bhartrihari Niti Shatak, 8th century, CE)

Being wealthy does bring power, and rich men may not always give others the respect they deserve.

> 'Men of advanced age and experience, men of self-control and fortitude, men of great learning – these men wait like mere servants at the door of a man of great wealth.'
> (Chanakya, quoted by Sharngadhara, 14th century CE)

Kautilya (Chanakya), who lived around 300 BCE and was the author of the **Artha-shastra**, considered that fame and power were wealth. Although ordinary people were encouraged to try to become wealthy, some philosophers thought that money was the root of all evil. Ramakrishna (1836–86), a Hindu mystic, never touched money in his life. It was said that touching gold, iron or copper, even accidentally, caused him physical pain.

Coined money

Money in the form of coins was first used in India in 300 BCE. The skill of making coins was learnt from the Greeks. Coins from the 1st century BCE had carvings of local rulers on them. The Sanskrit word rupa means *picture*. In the 5th century CE, coins with images of important people on them were called **rupaka**, which later became **rupee**. In Hindu kingdoms in south India, between the 9th and 17th centuries CE, gold coins were used. **Demand drafts** were commonly used by Hindu merchants in the 16th century. These were like letters of credit, or cheques. In India today, symbols of wealth that are commonly used are coins, bank notes, cheques and credit cards.

The four aims of human life

Since about 800 BCE, Hindus have believed that there are four basic aims in life, for everyone. These are:
- **dharma** – morality, religious and social duty
- **artha** – gaining wealth by lawful means
- **kama** – enjoyment of the good life
- **moksha** – freedom or liberation.

Discussions about the second aim, artha, are included in various dharma-shastras, and in the Mahabharata and the Artha-shastra. The Artha-shastra takes artha to mean gaining wealth, power and influence by using money and political power properly.

Artha

Hindu law encourages people to earn money honestly and lawfully. In this way, a man can provide for his wife, children and extended family. The first aim of life, dharma, has to be followed all through this life, even when a Hindu is earning money and enjoying the benefits. Honest effort is emphasized, and the method of earning money must be honourable and not harm anyone else. Gaining wealth dishonestly would taint the money and the person earning it, and affect his livelihood badly. The same applies to the third aim, kama. Enjoyment must be moderate, not excessive. Manu, the lawgiver, offers the following advice to householders, but it is helpful for everyone.

> 'A (brahmin) householder should (normally) earn his livelihood and maintain his family in a way that clashes very little with other people's interests, except in times of distress.'
> (Manusmriti 4:2)

> 'He should earn a living for a simple existence by his (varna) occupations which are not hard to follow

and which do not bring his (varna's) social status into disrepute.'

(Manu 4:3)

'A brahmin should not use unlawful means for his livelihood; he should maintain his family through a profession which is honest, straightforward, pure and worthy of a brahmin.'

(Manu 4:11)

'He who seeks happiness must strive for contentment and self-control; happiness arises from contentment, uncontrolled pursuit of wealth will result in unhappiness.'

(Manu 4:12)

'Whether he is well-off or in distress, he must not pursue wealth through degrading and harmful activities, nor through forbidden occupations (for his varna), nor through accepting presents from others (bribery).'

(Manu 4:15)

Hindus put definite limits on artha, as well as dharma and kama. At the marriage ceremony, the bridegroom promises to his father-in-law three times that he will always pursue dharma, artha and kama in moderation ('. . . *dharmé ch arthé ch kamé ch naticharami*').

For Kautilya, the author of the Artha-shastra, artha means gaining wealth, power and influence by using money and political power properly. He considers artha to be the main aim in life and teaches that moral, aesthetic and spiritual aims follow on from a right attitude to wealth.

The Artha-shastra includes teachings about accounts, coinage, trade and commerce, the armed forces, weights and measures, agriculture, law, government and administration, taxation and economic development in a kingdom. Kautilya sees wealth as power.

The Mahabharata says that dharma depends on artha. Becoming wealthy should lead to generosity and compassion, a desire to keep religious ceremonies, pleasure, courage, self-confidence, learning and joy. Artha cannot be gained without following the rules of dharma.

KEY IDEA

Artha is not to be pursued by ignoring the rules of dharma.

Dishonest wealth

In Hindu society in modern India, wealth is not distributed evenly. At the top end of the scale, there are very wealthy people who can afford to spend as much as they want to. In contrast, there are poor people who live in such poverty that a banana or a biscuit would be a luxury, just for a feast day. This extreme poverty drives people to try to gain money by any means they can, often dishonestly. Even people who are not so badly off sometimes try to improve their position by turning to crime. This goes totally against Hindu teachings and ethics.

Although most people still earn their money honestly, greed for money is a social evil which is spreading among the Hindu society. It is made worse by the increased advertising and availability of luxury consumer goods. Money obtained illegally, for example by smuggling or bribery, is called **kalapaisa**, which literally means black money.

FOR YOUR FOLDERS

▶ What limits does Manu, the lawgiver, put on earning a living?
▶ How would these affect the activities of a Hindu worker today?
▶ How do the Mahabharata and the Artha-shastra, the ancient Hindu texts, view artha or wealth?

Manu Ancient Hindu lawgiver who compiled the Manu-smriti. (The code of Manu containing rules of behaviour based on custom and convention.) The code lays down moral and ethical principles for the guidance of all four varnas and deals with many topics, including duties of students, householders, women, retired persons, sannyasins, and kings; civil and criminal law; the four aims of life; the nature of good and evil, and spiritual liberation.
Dharma Religious or social duty.
Artha Earning money by honest effort; wealth.
Kama Enjoying the good things in life.
Moksha Spiritual liberation; release from the cycle of birth, death and rebirth.

Evil

Hinduism recognizes two kinds of evil. These are **natural** evil and **moral** evil.

Natural evil

Samsara, the cycle of birth, death and re-birth is a **natural** evil, since the individual life-force or **atman** has to go through death and re-birth many times over.

Hindus believe that death is evil, and creatures such as wild beasts and snakes that cause death are also evil. Diseases such as smallpox and cholera are considered evil. Hindus believe they are sent by angry village gods to punish people for committing **paapa**, the sin of omission. Paapa may be failing to make the correct offerings to the gods according to local custom. Hindus also believe that all gods are forms of the Supreme Spirit, **Brahman**. This means that Brahman, in the form of the gods who send smallpox or cholera, is capable of doing evil. Brahman is all good, all powerful, yet some parts of Brahman's creation are evil; this is a seemingly unresolvable paradox.

Moral evil

Hindus believe that some human beings have a tendency towards evil. Their actions result in **moral evil**, such as adultery, incest, theft, telling lies, murder, and causing injury or suffering to others.

Many Hindus believe in ghosts and evil spirits. These are the souls of human beings who have died prematurely or in tragic circumstances, such as women in childbirth, or people who were drowned or killed in accidents. If there is a sudden illness in a Hindu family, or a domestic animal is ill, villagers make offerings to these ghosts at a cross-roads or near a stream to remove the evil influence.

Moral evil, or the tendency towards evil, is explained by the law of **karma**. It is karma – the result of actions – which causes people's tendency towards evil and motivates evil acts. In the **puranas** or myths, some demons are said to have obtained their evil power by performing good actions, for example by devotion to **Shiva**. **Vishnu**, the Preserver God, in his **avatars** (incarnations) kills – thus committing an evil act – the wicked demons Ravana and Hiranyakashipu, to bring about the greater good. Even a demon is not considered totally evil.

NARASIMHA, THE MAN-LION AVATAR OF VISHNU

Hiranyakashipu was an ambitious demon who worshipped Shiva for many years and thus obtained his greatest desire.

'O Lord of the Universe, protect me from death from Gods, man or beast; in the sky, in water and on earth; inside as well as outside any building; during day or night; and from all conventional weapons of my enemies.'
'So be it.' said Shiva.

The demon became all-powerful, conquering Heaven and Earth. Gods appealed to Vishnu to destroy the demon and restore order. Hiranyakashipu had a son called Pralhad who was a loyal follower of Vishnu. The demon punished his son time and again for this devotion, so Pralhad prayed to Vishnu for help. Vishnu decided to reincarnate himself on Earth.

During a heated quarrel with his son, the demon asked Pralhad where he might find Vishnu.

'Vishnu is everywhere, father, even in this pillar,' replied Pralhad. The demon kicked the pillar near the entrance to the palace.

The pillar split vertically and Vishnu emerged as Narasimha, a powerful being, half man, half lion. He was neither inside nor outside the building; the time was just after sunset, neither day nor night. Narasimha grabbed the demon and placed him across his lap so that the demon was not in the sky, not in water, not on earth. Narasimha used his powerful claws to tear the demon to death. Vishnu had defeated all five conditions of Shiva's boon and delivered Heaven and Earth from oppression.

Suffering

KEY IDEA

All life is suffering; death is suffering.

Hindus believe that all suffering results from people's actions. Creation has some fault in it which causes suffering. Later Hindu texts, the **Puranas** (3rd century BCE to 1000 CE), suggest that suffering arises from **paapa** – sinful action – not only in this present life, but in previous lives as well.

The Hindu belief in the re-incarnation of the soul is based on the law of karma. A soul's next existence is decided by karma – the result of good and bad actions – in a previous life or lives. Bad karma can be improved by good actions.

If a creature – human, animal or bird – has suffering in its present existence, its karma is held responsible. Good life is the result of good karma; suffering is caused by bad or evil actions. It is not the fault of God or another creature; each living being is responsible for its own suffering.

Response to suffering

This law of karma can lead to indifference to others' suffering in Hindu society, unless it is balanced by awareness of the unity of all creation and therefore the dharma of caring for other living creatures. Suffering is sometimes seen as the just reward for sinful actions in a previous existence; it is blamed on karma or **daiva** (fate). Millions of people suffer shortages of food, shelter and medical help. Animals, too, suffer a lack of proper care. The responsibility for this is *mistakenly* blamed on karma.

Nevertheless, there *are* numerous examples of concerned Hindus who think they are responsible for relieving the suffering around them. There are also many schools and colleges which are not funded by the central or the state governments, but by donations from caring Hindus in society. These institutions tackle social problems by educating the students and helping them to become self-sufficient and find employment.

Traditional Hindus worship Brahman individually or as a family, not as a congregation. As a result individual worshippers do not get the chance to see other people's problems or needs. In the sectarian Hindu organizations, where congregational worship is normal, members worshipping together can see people's physical and economic conditions and offer help where needed.

> ## KEY IDEA
> Paapa denotes physical and moral lack of goodness.

Orthodox Hindus believe that five great sins are:

- the killing of a learned brahmin
- drinking alcohol, particularly spirits
- stealing gold
- disrespect to a teacher and his wife
- wilful abortion. (This prohibition is largely ignored in modern India – see page 86.)

> ## KEY IDEAS
> Sinful actions result in suffering.
> Re-birth is full of pain and suffering.

Krishna (God) says in the Bhagavad Gita:

'Great souls who have become one with Me have reached the highest goal. They do not undergo re-birth, a condition which is impermanent and full of pain and suffering.'

(Bhagavad Gita 8:15)

'The result of a virtuous action is pure joy; actions done out of passion bring pain and suffering; ignorance arises from actions motivated by "dark" intentions.'

(Bhagavad Gita 14:16)

> ## KEY IDEA
> Hindus believe that the universe is made up of good and evil forces.

> ## FOR YOUR FOLDERS
> ▶ The law of karma attempts to explain evil tendencies in human beings. Do you find it convincing? For example, can good actions have evil consequences? Give reasons.
> ▶ How do some Hindus respond to others' suffering?
> ▶ Explain the Hindu idea of paapa.

> **Paradox** Statement which seems to contradict itself.

Work

In Hindu society, physical or manual work is considered less dignified than office work. People doing manual work have a lower status in society than those doing office work.

In India, 83 per cent of the population are Hindus. They are at various stages of education and development. The ranges are wide:

- from landless labourers to atomic scientists
- from drivers of bullock carts to intercontinental jet pilots
- from roadside market traders to lawyers, judges, doctors, engineers and college lecturers
- from railway station porters and rickshaw drivers to office clerks in their millions.

Ritual pollution and work

The Hindu idea of purity is mainly concerned with religious or **ritual purity**. Physical cleanliness contributes towards ritual purity, but they are not considered to be the same.

In Hinduism, pollution means *ritual* impurity, and has little or nothing to do with *actual* physical or chemical contamination. Pollution is caused in many ways. Menstruation makes a woman physically impure for four days, and she is not allowed to have physical contact with anyone during that time. The birth of a child puts both the mother and her baby into a state of ritual pollution, and no one but the midwife is allowed to touch either of them. A death in a family puts all the adult members, including boys who have received the sacred thread (see page 98) into a state of ritual pollution for ten days, and no one is allowed to have any physical contact with them.

The rules about short-term ritual impurity were probably set out to prevent infection or contamination going into or out of a household. All of them are removed when the impure person has a **ritual bath** at the end of the stated time.

These beliefs about ritual pollution affect the status of people whose work involves any of the tasks which cause pollution. For example, traditional village midwives are of low caste, because they are continually coming into contact with mothers and their newly born babies.

Ritual pollution is also caused by physical contact with dead animals, human excreta and other dirt, funeral materials, alcohol and also handling or eating meat or fish. This kind of pollution, which is connected with a person's livelihood, is **permanent**. Therefore, leather workers, night-soil removers and cremation ground attendants are always polluted, even though they may bathe and put on clean clothes. Their 'pollution' is passed on through touch. Even water, or food cooked in water, can pass this ritual pollution from a person of low caste to someone of higher caste.

Hindus believe that a brahmin remains ritually pure, whatever happens. He may get sprayed with muddy water by a passing vehicle, but he still remains pure because of his spiritual state. The degree of ritual pollution increases as people move down the varna or caste scale. Those at the bottom are always impure.

Untouchables

In the past, people who did the dirty or polluting jobs were put outside the caste system, into a fifth group. Hindus in all the other castes avoided touching them, or even getting into their shadows, for fear of becoming polluted. These people were called **untouchables**. Mahatma Gandhi called them **harijans**, which means children of God, but they called themselves **dalit**, which means oppressed.

'Untouchability' was abolished by law in India in 1950. The Indian government introduced a policy of reserving places in schools and colleges, and jobs in the public sector, for dalits. This has improved their social and economic position slightly, but instead of removing discrimination on the grounds of caste, it has strengthened the idea in the minds of some Hindus.

POSITIVE DISCRIMINATION

Special laws give dalits opportunities for education and jobs are reserved for them in government departments. This means that a certain number of posts at all levels must be given to applicants who are dalits.

KEY IDEA

Traditionally, different classes and castes worked at particular jobs suited to their talents and temperaments.

In the Bhagavad Gita Krishna (God) says:

'Do the work allocated to you according to your dharma, for work is better than idleness.'
(Bhagavad Gita 3:8)

'A man engaged in the performance of his duties leads his soul towards liberation.'
(Bhagavad Gita 18:45)

'When a man worships the Highest God (Brahman), the creator of this universe, through his work according to his dharma, he finds liberation from the cycle of re-births.'
(Bhagavad Gita 18:46)

Work in modern cities

In the villages, the work people do depends mainly on their caste. In the cities and industrial centres, because of equal opportunities in education and training, members of all castes may do jobs which are not their traditional occupations. For example, a farmer's daughter may become a teacher and a mechanic's son may become a minister in the State government; a leather worker's son may become a station master or a bank executive and a Brahmin's son may become a pilot or a foreman in a factory.

Leisure

Leisure and pleasure, or **kama,** make up one of the four main aims of Hindu life (see page 90). Hindus believe each person should keep a balance between work and enjoyment. Hindus should enjoy life, like everyone else. The ways they enjoy life can be as varied as they might be in any other society. There are typically Indian sports, as well as international ones. India gave polo to Britian and, in return, took cricket as one of its national games. All except two of the Indian cricket team which visited Britain in 1990 were Hindus.

Bombay, in Western India, has now the largest film industry. It is known as the 'Bollywood' of Asia! Films are the most popular national entertainment in India. Many are based on stories of Hindu gods and heroes. In Britain Hindus enjoy Hindi videos at home, and video hire shops provide a living for many British Hindus. Sports centres in Britain are popular among Hindu boys, who enjoy swimming, badminton, squash and athletics.

In Indian villages, celebrations of Hindu festivals are times of leisure and enjoyment for all. There are also regional festivals such as **Ganesha** (in Western India), **Durga Puja** (in Bengal) and **Rama-Leela** (in

North India). These are celebrated as public festivals with worship, folksongs and dances, dramatic performances, processions of images of the deities, or gods, through towns and villages, and special food.

Villagers hold annual fairs or **jatras** to honour the guardian deity of their village. They are held after the harvest is safely gathered in.

The Big Wheel at a village fair in India

FOR DISCUSSION

▶ Work is either ritually clean or polluting.
▶ Doing your work as a duty is the simplest form of worship.

FOR YOUR FOLDERS

▶ How do the ideas of ritual purity and pollution affect a Hindu's work and life?
▶ What factors bring about temporary or short-term pollution?
▶ Certain occupations are considered permanently polluting by Hindus. What justifications are there for this attitude?
▶ Do certain jobs lead to a lower social status in Britain as they do in Hindu society in India? What are they? Give reasons.

Racism in early India

The **Aryans** were fair-skinned nomadic fighters. They settled in India in about 1500 BCE, after conquering the original, dark-skinned inhabitants, whom they included in the Aryan society as artisans and manual workers. It was the Aryans who introduced the system of varna, which is still an important feature of Hindu society today.

Varna is a Sanskrit word which means *colour*. The class divisions were based on the colour of people's skin, and were a form of racism. These divisions gave Aryans higher social standing than the darker skinned lower castes. Over the centuries there has been intermarriage between people descended from the Aryans and those descended from the original inhabitants. Many other people have also settled in India, so there is no such thing as Aryan racial purity any more. However, the varna system is still very strong. There is religious support for it in the Bhagavad Gita (Chapter 4, see page 95) and in the Rig Veda, Book 10, Hymn 90.

> 'When the Primal Man was divided
> the brahmin (priest) arose from his mouth,
> the kshatriya (soldier) from his arms,
> the vaishya (merchant) from his thighs and
> the shudra (artisan) from his feet.'
>
> (Purusha hymn)

Prejudice

Within the varna system, groups developed according to the kind of work the people did. The skills of each trade were kept secret within families, with sons learning from their fathers and following the same occupation. At first, it was possible for someone to change from one occupation to another. Later, though, as families became more exclusive it was very difficult for anyone to change from one type of work to another. Many kinds of skill became **hereditary**, being passed only from father to sons, and caste rules stopped people from different groups eating together. They certainly could not marry outside their own group.

In the last 90 years, caste barriers have been broken down in the large cities and people are more free to mix socially. In the villages, though, people of lower caste still suffer because of prejudice against them. Even today it is better to choose marriage partners from the same caste or varna. The varna system emphasizes differences between human beings and encourages discrimination and prejudice. Because it has support in the Hindu

scriptures, it is taken as perfectly acceptable by many people. The laws which provide the dalit (see page 94) with places in schools and colleges, and with jobs, have improved the quality of life for many people; but in villages and rural areas the old system is still very strong. Nonetheless, pressure for the abolition of 'untouchability' and improved opportunities for the dalits came mainly from within the Hindu community, and from members of the higher castes.

Brahmins, the highest varna, make up less than 2 per cent of the Hindu population of India. They are the focus of extreme prejudice from the lower castes, including the dalits. (There are about 150 million dalits in India.)

There is also prejudice between the light-skinned inhabitants of northern India and the dark-skinned people of south India, which works both ways. The regional languages – Hindi in the north and Tamil in the south – also cause some prejudice.

Religious prejudice

There is prejudice between Hindus and Muslims in India, because of their different religious beliefs.

In the UK, Hindus do not suffer religious prejudice but they do experience racial prejudice, just like other ethnic groups.

In the past, orthodox Hindus considered Europeans to have the same status as shudras, the artisans and manual workers. After the British colonized India in the 18th century they were, grudgingly, seen as the ruling caste. Their behaviour was exactly the same as it was in any other caste, in terms of mixing socially, eating and marriage. There was racism, on both sides, between the 'ruling British' and the 'ruled Indians' right up to Indian Independence in 1947.

During their rule in India, the British established 'European only' clubs at various centres of administration. Hindu brahmins most certainly never invited the British into their homes, because of the pollution they would cause. Since 1947 very many Europeans have lived and worked in India, and social mixing has been possible to a limited extent in large cities.

The position of dalits in modern India

In spite of the 'reserved' places for dalits in schools and colleges, very few young dalits are able to take full advantage of their opportunities. A large number of boys and girls do not go beyond the primary level of schooling because they have to earn money to help the family.

JANI, A CASE STUDY

Jani, a former untouchable but now registered as a scheduled caste woman, came to Bombay from her village with her two teenage sons and a younger daughter. Jani is a widow and she cleans toilets and washrooms in a large block of flats. She and her three children live in one room provided by her employer, who also gives her food on the days of Hindu festivals. Both boys work for the Bombay Municipal Authority as garbage collectors – there are 120 000 altogether – and earn 400 rupees each per month. Their sister goes to a secondary school and hopes to attend college. Jani and her sons follow their traditional caste occupation, but now they live in a better home, and are paid cash wages.

Working on another's land

KEY IDEA

The varna is a large group of people linked by kinship ties, ritual practices, eating habits and cultural values. Within each varna there are many occupational groups called jati or castes.

DEVIDASS, A CASE STUDY

Devidass is a dalit farmer from a village in Bihar, north India. His small mud-brick house is outside the village boundary. The most powerful landowners in the village are from the khatri caste. They are rich and they have influence, not only in their village but at the bank in the nearest town. The poor farmers, not all dalit, do not get loans from the bank because of 'official' rules, so they borrow from Ramsingh, a rich landowner, who charges 48 per cent interest. Devidass was forced to borrow money privately to buy seed and fertilizer.

That was five years ago. His crop failed so he sold half his land to pay off the loan and the interest. He can barely make ends meet from his small field, so he, his wife and two daughters have to work for the richer landlords at half the normal rate of pay. Devidass and his wife worry about their daughters' honour because the richer landowners consider them fair game. Devidass is determined not to get into debt again, because if he failed to pay back the money he would be a bondman, like some other dalits, and would have to work without getting any cash until the loan was written off.

FOR DISCUSSION

▶ Laws can control and change human behaviour but they cannot remove human prejudices

FOR YOUR FOLDERS

▶ Was the varna division in early Hindu society racist in origin? Is it sanctioned by any religious text? Explain your answers.
▶ What evidence is there, if any, that the policy of 'reserved jobs' for dalits has improved their social status in Hindu society?

Attitudes to women

Historically and traditionally, the Hindu society and religion have been dominated by men. In the last 100 years, though, women have begun to have more influence in how things are done.

The ancient law book of Manu, written in about 300 CE, says that a woman does not need to have money of her own, since she is supported by her father before marriage, by her husband after marriage and by her sons in her old age. This teaching was accepted and followed right up to this century. However, a Hindu law book does not have the same authority as 'revealed scripture', so Manu's ideas have been gradually updated.

Although the position of women is changing slightly, these rules are still in operation:

- Only men may act as priests at religious rituals.
- Only boys of the three upper varnas are supposed to experience all 16 life-cycle rituals.
- Only sons may perform funeral rites and annual remembrance ceremonies.
- Only boys of the three upper varnas go through the **sacred thread** or initiation ceremony, which allows them to represent the family at religious rituals. At this ceremony offerings are made to the sacred fire, prayers are offered to the Sun and the boy is given a sacred thread to wear at religious rituals.

Ghee is offered to Agni (fire) at a sacred thread ceremony

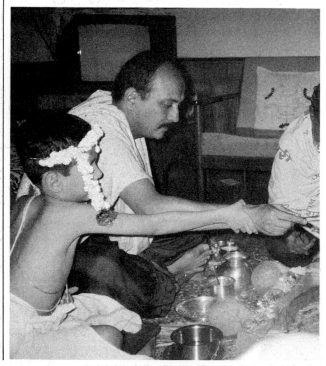

- When a marriage is being arranged, a young man may get the chance to select a partner from a number of possible brides.
- A young woman is unlikely to be allowed to refuse the first proposal.
- Boys get better care, food and education since they are 'insurance' for the parents' old age.

An independent secondary school at Puné (western India) provides equal opportunities for boys and girls in education and in social and religious activities. The woman teacher in charge of social studies expressed her views in conversation.

'We try to involve our pupils in the society around us. Our girls don't just learn from books. They go to live in a village for two weeks in their holidays and experience the harshness of conditions, see the changes and help the women to read and write. They take part in the religious festivals of Ganesha each year. In their first year at school they experience a simplified initiation ceremony. They don't actually wear the sacred thread but all the rituals and prayers are explained to them. I am sure the experience gives them spiritual strength to study the modern 'scriptures' such as physics, chemistry, biology and computer science. I think girls need the thread ceremony just as boys do.'

Widowhood in Hindu society

In the past, young widows from high caste Hindu families burned themselves on their husbands' funeral pyres. This was known as **suttee** or **sati**. Sometimes they were forced to do this against their will. Ram Mohan Roy (1772–1833), a Hindu religious reformer, protested and agitated very strongly against the practice. The custom was abolished by law in 1829, but the widows were forbidden to re-marry by Hindu customary law. The **Hindu Widows' Re-marriage Act, 1856**, removed the *religious* prohibition, but society did not accept this change until the 1940s. Widows had no education, no money and no social standing. This forced them to remain as unpaid housemaids in their husbands' families.

Women in society

Nowadays, women in Hindu families are less restricted than they were in previous generations. The modern mother-in-law is more likely to be a friend than a threat to the new bride.

STATISTICS

The following figures show how the situation has improved, for men and women, over the last years.

Literacy (people able to read and write):

	1971 census	**1981 census**
men	39.52%	46.89%
women	18.70%	24.82%

Employment: In 1981, of the total regular workforce

men	177.55 million
women	44.17 million

Growth in literacy of women, by percentage:

1951	**1961**	**1971**	**1981**
7.9	13.0	18.7	24.8

Because of the increased opportunities in education and employment, Hindu women are becoming aware of their own potential and abilities and are taking advantage of the openings available to them.

In the villages and rural areas, daughters-in-law of rich Hindu farmers will no longer be expected to work in the fields. Dowry is illegal, but money gifts from the bride's father are still expected when a Hindu girl is married (see page 85).

Hindu women benefit from the equal opportunities written into the Indian Constitution. All jobs are open to both men and women. This means that Hindu women who take up the opportunities for better education can go into a wide variety of professions. In the cities, many educated Hindu women are financially independent and hold well-paid jobs. According to Hindu law, women are now allowed to own property in their own right. Young Hindu women are not so submissive as their mothers and grandmothers were.

ONE COUPLE'S FIGHT AGAINST INJUSTICE

Professor D.K.Karve (1858–1962) started the Widow Re-Marriage Association in 1894 and established a Hindu Widows' Home in Puné in 1896. After the death of his first wife, Professor Karve married a widow, Godubai Joshi, in 1893. She was named Anandi after marriage. This marriage was disapproved of by brahmins in western India and the Karves were persecuted for many years. Widows living at the Hindu Widows' Home were educated to make them self-sufficient members of society. The money needed for their education was raised by Professor Karve through donations for many years. This small effort became the Indian Women's University in 1916. The Widow Re-marriage Association was disbanded in 1958.

THINKING POINT

● A Hindu woman can be a consultant physician, a university professor, an architect, an engineer or prime minister, but she cannot officiate as a priest in the home or in the temple.

FOR DISCUSSION

► Greater educational opportunities for women are bound to affect the Hindu family.

FOR YOUR FOLDERS

► How does traditional Hinduism limit a woman's religious experience and participation in Hindu society?
► How did Hindu society in India treat a widow who re-married at the beginning of the 20th century?
► In what different ways has the position of Hindu women gradually improved in the last 60 years?

Crime

In Hindu tradition, 'law' as it is understood in the West cannot be separated from the wider idea of dharma. The areas covered by dharma include:

- self-control
- religious and social duty
- charity and mercy
- **achara**, the rules and customs in religious ceremonies and everyday life
- **sukrita**, good conduct and behaviour
- **paapa**, anti-social behaviour, crime or sin.

The major Dharma-shastras were compiled between 200 BCE and 1100 CE. They set out the rules of acceptable behaviour for all varnas and castes and give guidelines on suitable **danda** (punishment) and correction for crimes. The normal definition of a crime is an act which is against the law, but Hindus see crime as a sin, or an act against dharma and the natural order of creation.

In ancient India, the system of punishment for wrongdoers was not laid down by any particular body. Kings and their judges were guided by the recommendations in the Dharma-shastras. There were other books they could use, such as the Artha-shastra (written in about 300 BCE); dramatic and prose writings; the Puranas and the Mahabharata, as well as the writings of some foreign travellers.

Crimes, and their punishments according to ancient Hindu texts, are given on the next page.

The present Indian law affecting all Indians is based on English Common Law, as well as the **Indian Penal Code 1896** (revised 1961).

The Hindu view of punishment

In Hindu society, a crime was seen as an act against the common rules of decency and morality. Punishment was viewed as part of the wrongdoer's karma.

The Vedas and Upanishads, the most holy scriptures of Hinduism, view crime as sin against the natural laws of all creation. The Dharma-shastras, the Puranas and the Mahabharata say that a king – or in modern times, the state – has a duty to protect his subjects and punish offenders, so that people can carry out the duties associated with their position and stage in life, and follow their aims of dharma, artha and kama (see pages 90–91). A king must control the sinful (those committing **paapa**) by suitable punishment (**danda**), or else he must kill them. Justice is necessary to protect society. Danda has three components.

- **retribution**, which means the criminal pays for what they have done
- **restraint**, which prevents the criminal from doing it again
- **reformation**, which changes the behaviour of the criminal.

Capital punishment

The death penalty for murder and treason still exists in modern India, in spite of the principle of **ahimsa** (non-violence). The death penalty is society's response to violence carried out against its members and its laws, and most Hindus see it as justified.

Crime	Punishment
Theft	Fines, to death sentence, according to the gravity of the crime Brahmins are exempt from capital punishment
House breaking	Corporal punishment, to death
Kidnapping ● a woman ● a maiden ● a man	 ● Confiscation of property, or death ● Corporal punishment, or death ● Highest fine, or death
Highway robbery	Possibly corporal punishment and fines
Forgery of documents	Fine or death Heavy fines for altering a charter of land grants
Adulteration of goods (giving short measure or watering down) rice, butter, molasses, medicines	Fines – tradesmen to be considered as thieves
Gambling	Branding and banishment
Adultery with ● woman of own caste ● woman of lowest caste ● woman of superior caste ● Adultery by a woman	Fines: ● highest fine ● moderate fine ● capital punishment Disfigurement or abandonment
Rape of ● any woman ● a brahmin woman	Mutilation: ● two fingers cut off ● death
Incest by men Incest by women	Castration Disfigurement or abandomnent
Abduction	Woman generally not considered guilty. If she had sex willingly, she was punished by death
Defamation	Generally a fine: a small fine for a brahmin, higher fines for other varnas. For a shudra – corporal punishment
Assault	Fine imposed according to caste; higher fine for low caste offender
Murder Manslaughter Conspiracy to murder	Death sentence Confiscation of property All culprits sentenced alike
A brahmin causing abortion, killing a brahmin woman or a chaste woman	Condemned to death
Offences against the State Treason	Death sentence A brahmin was drowned for treason

49 POLITICS, AUTHORITY AND GOVERNMENT

Religion and politics

The political values of the early Hindu states in India cannot be separated from their religious and moral views. The ancient scriptures have a lot to say about politics, law and government, as well as dharma, artha, kama and moksha (see pages 90–91).

Politics and government

In Hindu India, there are different names for the various aspects of politics and political science:

- **Rajadharma**, the duties of kings
- **Danda-niti**, laws and legal science
- **Niti-shastra**, the understanding and application of wisdom
- **Artha-shastra**, the understanding and application of political science.

There are important guidelines about Hindu policy and government in these important books:

- The **Mahabharata** (300 BCE – 300 CE)
- The **Artha-shastra** (300 BCE – 100 CE?)
- The **Shukraniti** (date uncertain, possibly 800 CE)

The Hindu texts written after about 1000 CE have little to add to these three books.

Young Shivaji (1627–80) is encouraged by his mother to found a Hindu kingdom in western India

The Hindu state

THE NATURE AND AIMS OF THE HINDU STATE

In Hindu India, from 300 BCE, most states were monarchies, ruled by kings. The king had power and authority over ministers and provincial governors. The duty of the state (and therefore the king) was to protect the people and allow them to follow their dharma. The state used laws to control any anti-social behaviour.

Hindus who have studied political history from about 300 BCE say that the aims of the Hindu state were to encourage dharma, artha and kama. This meant encouraging:

- virtue and morality
- trade, industry and agriculture
- the enjoyment of music and dancing.

FUNCTIONS OF THE STATE

For a long time the Hindu state in ancient India carried out those functions which are necessary for an orderly society. It defended its territory against aggression from outside, it protected people and their property, it maintained law and order and administered justice.

The Mahabharata and the Artha-shastra teach that the activities of the state should influence the whole of human life; state government has a duty to encourage righteous conduct. It should maintain rest-houses, charity halls and hospitals, and help in times of disasters such as floods and famine. It should also aim to develop the resources of the kingdom and control criminal and anti-social actions. The state also has the right to interfere in religious and social matters.

The Golden Age of Kingship

Monarchy was the most common form of government. The right to be king was generally hereditary and the eldest son, unless he was unfit, would inherit the crown. The king was believed to possess divine authority so long as he was good, pious and just, and was only answerable to God. The king was the upholder of law, a master and servant of the people. As a trustee of the kingdom's wealth, he should not use the wealth of the royal treasury for his own personal benefit. The king had to dedicate his life to service and the welfare of his people. This was his dharma, which went with his caste. A tyrant could not hold power for long.

Royal pomp and pageantry gradually increased during the first eight centuries CE. The king became the real head of state, controlling the treasury and the army, and planning foreign policy for war and peace. He chose his ministers and presided over them in council. Taxes were usually set according to local laws, but the king could increase or decrease them. He could alter customary law by his own decrees, and was the supreme judicial authority. He settled all appeals in person, or through his chief judge, or through the village councils, called **panchayats**. The personal qualities of the king affected the kingdom, for better or for worse.

Modern India

Since Independence in 1947, India has been a secular state. This means that no one religion is favoured above any other. Nevertheless, Hindu values can be seen to operate at some levels and in certain areas. One example is the doctrine of **ahimsa** or non-violence. This was followed by Mahatma Gandhi during his opposition to the British Raj.

The ethics of pacifism

Ahimsa is the avoidance of physical or mental harm to other creatures, and **satya** is truth or truthfulness. These are two important virtues of Hindu ethics. For over 30 years from 1915 the pacifist doctrine of non-violence and non-cooperation was used as a political weapon by a Hindu leader of India, Mahatma Gandhi, against British rule in India. In spite of Gandhi's efforts, however, hundreds of thousands of Indians gave up their decision to gain independence by non-violent means and formed a militant force. The non-violent struggle of Gandhi unintentionally produced much suffering and bloodshed, but considering the huge resources of the British government in India, and the unarmed civil disobedience of the Indians based on ahimsa, it cannot be denied that Indian Independence came about through mainly non-violent means.

Just war

Hindus believe that the use of force is acceptable in defence of a **just cause**. This would include invasion by enemy forces, wrongful seizure of power and legal authority, and exploitation and oppression of the people.

THE KAURAVAS AND THE SONS OF KING PANDU

In the central story of the Mahabharata, the royal cousins, the Kauravas and the sons of King Pandu, quarrelled over the kingdom. The Kuru princes refused their cousins' claim to a half share in the kingdom. The God Krishna tried conciliation on behalf of the Pandu princes but failed. Both sides got ready for battle, but Arjuna, the third son of Pandu, refused to kill his kinsmen to gain a kingdom, and laid down his weapons. On the battlefield, Krishna advised Arjuna that fighting in the cause of **dharma-yuddha**, a just war, is the duty of a soldier.

In the Bhagavad Gita, Krishna (God) says,

'Having regard to your duty, you should not hesitate, because for a warrior (kshatriya) there is nothing greater than a just war (dharma-yuddha).

But if you do not fight in this just war, you will neglect your varna (duty), harm your reputation and commit the sin of omission.'

(Bhagavad Gita 2:31, 33)

FOR DISCUSSION
▶ Is it possible to live according to the ahimsa ideal in the modern world?

FOR YOUR FOLDERS
▶ What were the important functions and duties of the state mentioned in early Hindu texts?
▶ Is the Hindu idea of dharma-yuddha (just war) sensible in the modern world?

Hindu attitudes to misfortune

Hindus blame an individual's suffering on **karma** (see pages 92–93). The needy in society go through some form of suffering so, Hindus believe, they pay the price in this life for evil actions done in a previous existence. An orphan's karma is responsible for the death of the parents. The poor may have caused someone to starve in a previous life. The disabled, the mentally handicapped and the mentally ill may have inflicted cruelty on someone in a previous existence. This argument is generally put forward by many Hindus to defend their indifference and lack of compassion for the needy.

BABA AMTÉ

There *are* many Hindus who have dedicated their lives to the service of the needy and the afflicted. One such person is Baba Amté. In his youth he worked with Mahatma Gandhi. So that he could experience the utter humiliation felt by sweepers and scavengers, Baba Amté worked as a sweeper, clearing away human excrement. One day, when he was taking his basket to a dump, he noticed a leper. Leprosy was feared and thought to be highly infectious. Baba decided to serve the lepers. He went to medical school in Calcutta and learned about the disease. On his return he started a leprosy clinic at Warora near Nagpur. Now there are clinics in the surrounding villages. After treatment, lepers are trained in different jobs and now they are responsible for running their entire community. Baba Amté's dedication has given hundreds of lepers dignity, hope and a new lease of life.

Charity

In spite of the general influence of the law of karma, Hindus from all walks of life give to charity. **Dana** or giving is a virtue in Hindu ethics. It stores up good karma for the giver. There is no welfare state in India, no DSS and no government agency to help the needy. Those who are able to spare cash, food or clothes *do* give to the needy in their immediate area. Before their midday meal, many families give food to at least one person in need. Beggars are given cash at railway stations, bus stations and outside temples.

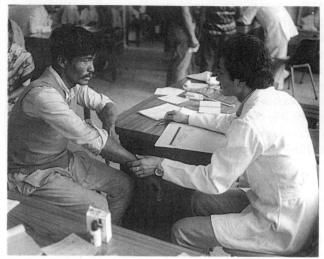

Leprosy clinic at Warora, near Nagpur

Old age

Old age is thought by Hindus to be the result of good actions. To enjoy a long life, surrounded by sons, grandsons and other relations, is a reward for previous godly living. In Hindu society old people enjoy great honour and are looked after by their families. Many elderly men remain as heads of their families until they die.

The care of the elderly

Charity begins at home, so all the less well-off members of the family are taken care of first. A tiny proportion of the elderly live in old people's homes. It is the **religious duty** of a man to care for his parents in their old age. A Hindu's status in society is lowered if his elderly parents are living in an old people's home. He is considered cruel and heartless to inflict such a lonely life on the parents who gave him the gift of life, took care of him, educated him and found him a suitable wife.

The generation gap

In some families in the cities, where living space is small and the son and daughter-in-law may both have full-time jobs, elderly parents can be both a help and a hindrance. They are probably set in their ways, they may need constant attention, and hold old-fashioned views on life, which they will speak out frequently.

Grandparents teach their grandchildren the family traditions and shower affection on them. If they have always lived in a village or a small town, they will find it difficult to adjust to the pace of city life. They tend to complain about the shortage of water, the traffic noise, the vast crowds and the lack of open space. However, in spite of differences of opinion, elderly parents are rarely neglected in Hindu homes.

Hospices

There are hospitals and nursing homes where the incurably sick are looked after, but they are very expensive and the average Hindu family cannot afford them. Generally speaking, any members of the family who may be suffering from cancer or a stroke are usually looked after at home. Even then, the medical expenses can be a huge burden on the family budget.

Euthanasia

In Hindu ethics, the taking of another person's life is not only a crime but a great sin. In theory, putting an end to another's suffering by mercy killing is not acceptable but, in practice, especially in the villages, substances such as opium are probably used for this purpose. It is never acknowledged officially.

Suicide

Taking one's own life is quite another matter. Suicide was widely practised in Hindu society in India. It was considered to be an act of religious merit. Faithful wives burnt themselves on their husbands' funeral pyres; they were honoured for their virtue and constancy. **Suttee** or **sati**, as the practice was called, was abolished in 1829 by Lord William Bentinck after sustained agitation against the practice by many Hindus, led by Ram Mohan Roy.

Over the centuries, many Hindus have fasted and starved themselves to death. This was probably the most common method of suicide. In fact, although Mahatma Gandhi did not commit suicide, several times he threatened to fast until death, to gain his political desires. Some Hindus drown themselves in the holy river Ganges, or in other sacred rivers of India as a religious act.

Both the holy books, the Ramayana and the Mahabharata, mention suicide by drowning or by starvation. In modern India many Hindu women commit suicide to escape from an unhappy marriage by jumping into a well, or setting themselves on fire. Some Hindus burn themselves to death publicly as a political protest; others offer their lives to a deity in return for answering prayers or fulfilling requests. In this way, suicide can become a religious act, and an acceptable sacrifice. If it is used as a means of escape from suffering it is not approved of. It is said to be the result of karma, an unavoidable but sad end to life.

KEY IDEAS

A life of suffering and want is the result of karma.
Suicide as a religious act is acceptable in Hinduism.

THINGS TO DO

▶ Write a letter of about 200 words to a Hindu pen-friend in India explaining why some elderly people in Britain prefer to live in sheltered accommodation or old people's homes even when their sons could look after them in their own homes. Include these points in the letter: British family structure, personal freedom, housing, National Health Service, state pensions for men and women, views of your own grandparents or elderly people you know.

FOR YOUR FOLDERS

▶ Describe briefly how Baba Amté brought hope, dignity and a new lease of life to lepers in central India.
▶ How do Hindus connect misfortune and karma?
▶ In what way can suicide be a religious act in Hinduism?

Creation

The earliest Hindu scripture, the Rig Veda (book 10, hymn 129) deals with the creation of the universe, the nature of the Supreme Spirit and its relation to the material world. The power of creation, preservation and destruction arises from a single deity who is given many names:

- **Prajapati**, the Lord of Creatures
- **Vishwakarman**, the World-maker
- **Brahman**, the Supreme Spirit of Hinduism.

The later holy books also hold that the universe was created by God.

Ahimsa principles in worship

Since the early Vedic Age (1500–1200 BCE) Hindus have followed the ethic of **ahimsa** which means they avoid harming other living things, including creatures, plants and trees. Hindus still try to avoid harming fellow creatures since ahimsa is an important part of Hinduism today.

Hindu worship includes respect and concern for mountains and rivers as well as animals, birds, plants and trees. Animals and birds such as the bull, tiger, mouse, peacock, the divine eagle and swan are used as vehicles (**vahana**) for riding on by various deities of Hinduism and so they are sacred. Similar reverence is shown to medicinal plants, and holy trees like the **banyan** and **pipal** – Indian fig trees – are revered by many Hindus.

When human beings interfere with nature for profit, it often upsets the natural balance and affects the environment. In spite of the protection given to other living things through Hindu worship, and active protests and demonstrations by Hindus in some parts of India, some thoughtless felling of trees has occurred.

LOSS OF FOREST COVER AS A PERCENTAGE OF THE GEOGRAPHICAL AREA

In 1972–75 forest cover was 16.84%; in 1980–82 it was 14.10%. Over ten years the loss of forest cover is therefore 2.74%.

The story of Sunderlal Bahuguna illustrates what some Hindus, inspired by ahimsa, are doing to prevent damage to forests in the Himalayan foot-hills in Uttar Pradesh.

SUNDERLAL BAHUGUNA

Sunderlal Bahuguna, a concerned Hindu, has started two movements. One is to stop the construction of a high dam at Tehri, which will flood land already under cultivation. The other is the Chipko movement which aims to prevent further felling of the dense forests in the Himalayas. He argues that high dams, which are full in the monsoons, actually cause rivers like the Ganges to flood, as the flood-gates have to be opened when further rainfall occurs after the monsoon season. He suggests that if the deep gorges which already exist in the upper reaches of the mountain are used, the resulting water power generated by natural drops of about 900 m could be used to generate electricity; such projects would be environment-friendly and profitable.

The Chipko movement is against deforestation.

Sunderlal Bahuguna argues that dense forests would keep moisture in the upper reaches of the Himalayas for a longer period and the rivers would have a steady supply of water throughout the year. The forests would also support human and wild life by providing seasonal fruit and nuts, honey, fodder and fuel. He has many followers who would plant new trees on the terrace land if the secular government agrees to pump water from the deep gorges up to the higher ground. Conservation of forests will check floods, prevent soil erosion and provide more oxygen.

(Sunderlal Bahuguna 'The Good Earth', *Illustrated Weekly of India* (Bombay) 24–30 June, 1990.

Human irresponsibility

Irresponsible behaviour by human beings creates pollution of the environment everywhere, and India is no exception.

Narmada Valley project

If the project is completed, it will benefit millions of people in Gujarat, Madhya Pradesh and Maharashtra. There is oppositon from Hindu villagers who live in the area to be flooded because they have to move, and compensation for the arable land that will be flooded has not been properly worked out. Groups concerned with the protection of wildlife, many of them led by Hindus, have also raised objections, because many animals and their habitat will be destroyed if the project continues.

What are Hindus doing about the damage to the environment?

Hindus make up 83 per cent of the Indian population, and Hindu values affect many areas of Indian society. Whatever plans are made by the secular government, eight out of ten of the people affected are Hindus. Many schemes and projects for conservation, and many protests and demonstrations against destruction of the environment, have come about because of pressure from Hindus. Many Hindus, whether they are private citizens or government officials at least partly responsible for the government's industrial planning, are aware of the damage caused to the environment as a result of this type of development.

Politicians in New Delhi and in the state capitals are constantly reminded of environmental issues, and a real effort is being made to improve the environment.

Shelter in Calcutta

Secular Non-religious

KEY IDEA

By considering mountains, rivers, animals, birds, plants and trees as sacred, Hindu worship patterns create environmental awareness.

FOR YOUR FOLDERS

► Explain how ahimsa and other Hindu beliefs emphasize the sanctity of God's creation.
► Can the construction of reservoirs by flooding whole valleys be justified in view of the Hindu concept of ahimsa? Give reasons.

Planet Earth

Hindus believe that the whole universe was created by God. It is given in trust to people for their enjoyment. All creation – oceans, mountains, human beings, animals, birds, plants, forests, lakes, rivers – is a part of the Creator God and therefore deserves reverence. Hindus respect Indian fig trees, cows, monkeys, snakes, elephants, peacocks, the divine eagles; and the rivers Ganges, Jumna, Krishna and Kaveri. In the Bhagavad Gita, Krishna says,

> 'Now see, O Arjuna, in my body the entire Universe – movable and immovable – and whatever else you wish to see.'
> (Bhagavad Gita 11:7)

Because this Earth is sacred, Hindus offer worship to the plot of land where they plan to build a house. Devout Hindus say a prayer to Goddess Earth every morning:

> 'O Goddess Earth, the consort of Vishnu, you whose garments are the oceans and whose ornaments are the hills and mountain ranges, please forgive me as I walk on you this day.'
> (A Hindu prayer)

The Hindu view of animals

The ancient Hindu lawgiver, Manu, is quite clear in his teachings about kindness to animals.

> 'By controlling his senses, by curbing emotions, and by destroying hatred; By avoiding any harm to animals or to nature, a man will come to be fit and ready for everlasting life.'
> (D.G. Butler, *Many Lights*)

The Aryans, who were pastoral people, held cows in special esteem, because they gave milk and produced bullocks for work in the fields. Cow hide was used for footwear and battle drums. The animals' usefulness turned into **sacredness** in the early centuries CE, when they began to be worshipped. The cow figures prominently in the mythology of the god Krishna. In the 4th century CE, killing a cow was considered a sin. Over the years the cow became a divine animal and today it is revered deeply by devout Hindus. Killing cows is banned in secular India. There are thousands of retirement homes, called **gowshalas**, for elderly animals, mainly cows.

Mahatma Gandhi founded an organization in 1942 for the care of cows and spoke strongly against slaughtering them. Acharya Vinoba Bhave, the Hindu social reformer and a disciple of Gandhi, was respected by both the government and ordinary people of India for his work on land re-allocation to peasant farmers. He supported Gandhi's view:

> 'Cows should be treated by us with a sense of gratitude. In Indian socialism, they occupy an equal place with the humans. Therefore, cows must be respected, as we do to our own mothers.'
> (D.N. Khurody, *Dairying in India*)

A large majority of Hindus are vegetarians because of their strong belief in ahimsa (see page 106). In Hindu society, butchers are of low caste because handling meat is a polluting occupation.

Hindus consider the tiger to be a sacred animal since it is the vehicle of the Goddess Durga; the peacock is sacred because it is the vehicle of Saraswati, the Goddess of Learning and the Arts. In south India, temple elephants are given much reverence since they carry the image of the deity in procession during the annual festivals. Tigers, peacocks and elephants are among protected animals in India.

Pandit Nehru, the first Prime Minister of India, grew up in a Hindu home. He put into words the Hindu view when he supported the preservation of forests and sanctuaries for wild life:

> 'In spite of our culture and civilization in many ways man continues to be not only wild but more dangerous than any of the so-called wild animals. . . We talk in one language and act in another way. . . The cow is one of the treasures of India and should be protected . . . our forests are essential for us from many points of view. Let us preserve them. . . We must try to preserve whatever is left of our forests and the wild life that inhabits them.'
> (Jawaharlal Nehru: 'Foreword' in E.P. Gee, *The Wildlife of India*)

Poverty

A typical Hindu view of poverty is expressed by the hero of an ancient Sanskrit play – *The Clay Cart* – from the early centuries CE. Charudatta, the hero, rejects poverty in no uncertain terms when he says,

> 'If I were to choose between death and poverty I would prefer death, because it is a short, sharp pain while poverty is a lingering agony.'

India's poverty stems from two main causes:

- nearly 200 years' colonial exploitation by European powers
- an explosive growth in population coupled with insufficient food production.

Out of the present (1991) population of 844 million, over 300 million are hungry. Hinduism views poverty as evil, firstly because it prevents a householder from performing his dharma of looking after his wife, children and elderly relatives; secondly, because the lack of surplus money stops him from fulfilling the third aim in life, kama, and enjoying the good things that life has to offer.

FOR YOUR FOLDERS

▶ If you believed, as Hindus do, that all created things exist in God and are part of the creative force that is God, how would this affect your interaction with
  (a) your parents
  (b) your friends
  (c) people you dislike
  (d) people from another country
  (e) animals
  (f) plants?

THE RURAL DEVELOPMENT PROGRAMME

- **Improving the village environment** by persuading villagers to maintain roads, dispose of rubbish, and plant more trees.
- **Improving farming methods** by providing good quality seeds – millet and rice, by supplementing local organic fertilizers with some chemical fertilizers, by providing small tractors, and by training villagers to conserve the water of local streams and dig wells near their fields.
- **Reducing poverty** by providing training and paid employment to some village youths in Jnana Prabodhini's engineering workshop. This workshop is based at Shivapur. It was donated by a large engineering firm in Poona to manufacture accessories for their diesel engines. This workshop creates an income for Jnana Prabodhini and at the same time provides many families with ready cash.

Recently Jnana Prabodhini has started another school at Solapur, and gradually its 1000 dedicated teachers and social workers are reducing poverty and illiteracy.

A HINDU EXPERIMENT IN EDUCATION AND RURAL DEVELOPMENT

An educational institution named **Jnana Prabodhini** (The Awareness of Knowledge) was started in Poona, western India, in August 1962 by a group of Hindu teachers. They had no school building and no money but great faith in their objectives. Extra tuition for gifted boys and girls was given in various schools until suitable rooms were found to hold classes. Bank loans and private donations from Hindus solved the problem of the school building. To make Jnana Prabodhini self-sufficient and non-political they started a factory making electrical capacitors. The profits from this provided an income for the school. The rural development programme, begun in 1968, is aimed at improving about 20 villages not far from Poona.

Jnana Prabodhini school for gifted boys and girls selects pupils from rural and urban primary schools. Pupils are taught in English but the Hindu cultural heritage and at least three Indian languages are taught as well, along with other school subjects.

The pupils are trained to tackle poverty and illiteracy, and many of them have dedicated their lives to Jnana Prabodhini work after their university education. The school is based on the Hindu idea of working for the welfare of all. It is open to gifted boys and girls of all castes and religions. Pupils from poor homes receive free education. The Jnana Prabodhini institute is working towards national awareness of Hindu values. It is teaching a mix of the humanities, science and technology, coupled with the Hindu values of truth, ahimsa, compassion, purity, and a spirit of sacrifice.

The UN Declaration of Human Rights

Hinduism is in agreement with the UN Declaration of Human Rights (see page 221) with the following changes to some clauses, shown in italics, to show how *practice* may differ in India.

1   All human beings are born free, have equal human dignity *but possess different talents and capacities to do different jobs.*

3   *All life is sacred and everyone has the right to be free from violence (ahimsa).*

10 All trials should be public in a court of law *or before a village panchayat.*

12 *A family has a right to privacy in personal affairs, and each individual has a right to protect his or her reputation.*

16 *All Hindu men and women have a duty to marry and have children, especially sons.*
Since 1955 both men and women have equal rights in divorce.

18 *An individual's freedom of thought, expression of opinion, conscience and religious activity are governed by his or her dharma and family tradition.*
An individual's right to attend religious meetings and join religious associations is largely determined by his or her varna and jati (caste) loyalties and duties.

23 All have the right to work under just conditions of employment *but many dalits (disadvantaged) are exploited in rural India.*
There should be equal pay for equal work.
This works well in government offices and professions in the cities, but women and dalits working as farm labourers are paid lower wages than others from higher and clean castes.
The right to form and join a trades union is often governed by the advice of other caste members.

26 All have the right to an education *but very few dalits go beyond the primary level and very few individuals from the 4th varna (shudra) study the Sanskrit scriptures.*

27 *All have a right to share in the cultural life of the community according to their varying traditions.*

29 *The duties (dharma) of each individual, if carried out faithfully, will protect the rights and freedoms of others in society.*

In spite of the formal declaration of human rights, many millions of people in India do not enjoy a standard of living adequate for their health and well-being, housing, medical care, unemployment and old age.

The Indian Constitution

Although the Indian Constitution is not based on Hindu ethics, it affects the 83 per cent of the population who are Hindu. Some aspects of the Constitution conflict with traditional Hindu ideas, but Hinduism has developed over 3500 years, always adapting to the changing times. In theory, there is full acceptance by Hindus of the Constitution. The Constitution specifically lists the fundamental rights of all citizens.

● **The right to equality** This means equality before the law, equality of opportunity in public employment, and social equality. All citizens get equal protection of the law without discrimination on grounds of religion, race, caste, sex or place of birth.

● **The right to freedom** This secures freedom of speech and expression, freedom of peaceful assembly, association, movement and residence, freedom of owning, holding and selling property and the right to follow any profession, trade, occupation or business. These rights are subject to certain restrictions imposed by the government.

● **The right against exploitation** This prohibits forced or bonded labour, child labour, and other forms of exploitation.

● **The right to freedom of religion** This provides freedom of conscience to all citizens, particularly to the minorities, and freedom to profess, practise and spread a religious faith. In this section of the Constitution the word 'Hindu' includes Hindus, Sikhs, Jains and Buddhists.

● **Cultural and educational rights** These protect the minorities and are based on religion, culture, community, language and script.

● **The right to property** Every citizen has a right to obtain, hold and sell property, and this right cannot be set aside by arbitrary decisions of government agencies.

● **The fundamental rights of all citizens** These are fully protected by the courts.

● **Constitutional remedies** Every citizen has a right to constitutional remedies through the courts of law if fundamental rights are threatened or infringed by any person or institution.

Hindus' jobs are limited by caste

Caste and human rights

The traditional varna and caste system in Hindu society is gradually breaking down in large cities. However, it still affects the basic human rights of many Hindus, especially in rural areas. For instance, many dalits are not free to live where they wish, as their homes are deliberately situated away from those of high caste Hindus, and in many villages they live just outside the village boundary. Hindus are not really free to marry anyone they like, since caste and family tradition still control the choice of a marriage partner in most cases.

In a village, priests, farmers, shopkeepers, barbers, carpenters, washermen, potters, rope-makers, leather workers and other castes normally do their traditional jobs and depend on each other's services. Although, to a large extent, job opportunities are restricted by caste in the villages, the dependence between them does provide a degree of job security, since inter-caste services continue from father to son, generation to generation.

In the cities, however, jobs in government departments and offices are open to all men and women, whatever their castes. Job-training opportunities are also secure for youngsters if they wish to follow their fathers' occupations. Because of wider opportunities for education and work in the cities, the economic cooperation between castes in rural areas is gradually becoming less important as sons working in factories and government departments in towns provide economic security for their families in the villages. The old dependence of individual caste families on each other's skills and abilities is lessening; young men learn new trades and professions in the cities, and they are paid in cash. They gain independence and freedom of choice, but lose the personal and family security of the long-established village and its castes, which work together to support the community.

It is interesting that in the new secular India a number of educational and occupational privileges are reserved for dalits and tribal people in an attempt to make up for the discrimination in the past. The secular government is thus using religious criteria to allocate privilege to some sectors of the community and to discriminate against others.

KEY IDEAS

It is estimated that there are 2 million bonded labourers in India, many of them in Bihar. They are compelled to work for others for non-payment of debt. Men are paid four rupees per day and women three rupees per day, until the debts are paid off.
From the 1981 census 23.51 per cent of the total population are underprivileged castes or tribes.

FOR DISCUSSION

▶ There are many countries where the UN Declaration of Human Rights has not fully succeeded in persuading people to improve the quality of life. Why not?

FOR YOUR FOLDERS

▶ In daily life, how could a modern Hindu live according to the demands of the UN Declaration of Human Rights?
▶ Do you think the Human Rights that the caste system upholds are of greater or less importance to the individual than those it limits?

Past Hindu attitudes to foreigners

In the 8th century Arabs brought Islam to India. This was the beginning of a conflict between Muslims and Hindus which continued throughout many centuries of Islamic rule. It was caused by basic differences in religious beliefs, philosophies and practices.

In the 16th century European merchants, particularly the Portuguese and the British, who came by the sea routes, were known as **firangis** (foreigners) and considered as shudras by the orthodox Hindus. When the British became rulers, they retained their separate cultural identity and were not absorbed into Hindu society.

International relations

India is a secular state. It has no official state religion, although 83 per cent of the population are Hindus. India's international relations are entirely a secular matter, and the values of the country's majority religion, Hinduism, are not regarded as relevant to it.

The ideal Hindu society

Mahatma Gandhi first read John Ruskin's book *Unto This Last* in 1904, while he was in South Africa. Later, Gandhiji published an adaptation of Ruskin's work and called it *Sarvodaya* – welfare of all. The word 'sarvodaya' occurs in an ancient Jain scripture. The concept of welfare for all is found in a Hindu prayer:

'May all be happy here;
May all be free from disease.
May all be righteous
and without suffering.'

Mahatma Gandhi maintained that:

- the good of the individual is included in the welfare of all people
- all types of work have the same dignity and all persons have the right to earn a living from their work
- a life of labour is worth living.
  The Bhagavad Gita provides scriptural authority for this:

'. . . those who are sinless, have true wisdom and work for the welfare of all their fellow beings attain liberation.' (Bhagavad Gita 5:25)

'Those who possess self-control and an impartial attitude, and work for the welfare of all beings also reach me'

(Bhagavad Gita 12:4)

Vinoba Bhave, a disciple of Gandhi, founded the non-political **Sarvodaya-Samaj** (Society for the Welfare of All) in 1948. If the Sarvodaya ideal is to work, politicians will need to introduce laws to remove inequalities in society and establish truly democratic values in government. People's attitudes have to change; they have to base their lives firmly on dharma (moral and social duty), satya (truth) and ahimsa (non-violence).

Vinoba Bhave

An ideal society based on the values of Hinduism would come about if all citizens practised:

- Universal goodwill
- Tolerance of other faiths
- Spirituality
- Dignity of labour
- Social mixing and eating together to remove caste barriers
- Freedom of belief (a fundamental concept of Hinduism)
- Service to others (jana seva)
- Basic education for all children
- Equality in all matters important to life as a dignified human being
- Truth, non-violence, self-control and absence of greed
- Their personal dharma faithfully, to protect other people's rights
- Rituals with understanding of and respect for their significance.

FOR DISCUSSION

▶ Explain the Hindu view that 'Man engrossed in the material world becomes de-humanized but a spiritual man tends to behave more justly towards all creatures.' Do you agree?

FOR YOUR FOLDERS

▶ How easy do you think it is for a practising Hindu to live in a secular state?
▶ In your opinion, is Vinoba Bhave's ideal state based on Hindu values a practical proposition in the modern world? Give reasons.

Sarvodaya Welfare for all.
Dharma Social or moral duty.
Satya Truth.
Ahimsa Non-violence.

The principles of Hinduism

The three important principles of Hinduism – dharma, satya and ahimsa – support the desirable elements in the present society. If followed closely, they will lead to new ideas and practices in Hinduism itself, and bring about democratic values for all people.

DHARMA

Dharma (duty) should be the guide:

- in preserving the present democracy
- in protecting fundamental rights listed in the UN Charter and the Indian Constitution
- in population control and food production
- in giving equal opportunities to and providing basic amenities for all
- in letting women experience the thread ceremony to enable them to train as priests
- in removing exploitation of the dalits by imposing heavy fines on the rich landowners.

SATYA

Satya (truth) should be the motive in the practice of Hinduism and the tolerance of all other faiths.

AHIMSA

Ahimsa (non-violence) should be practised in thought, word and deed:

- to encourage more social mixing of all castes
- to ensure that industrial development goes hand in hand with village development without destroying the natural environment.

Such a society will continue the tradition of continual development in Hinduism and make it meaningful for the 21st century and beyond.

Who are Muslims?

Muslims are people who have become aware, at some point in their lives, of the reality of the existence of God, and have committed themselves to submission to God's will as expressed in the revelations given to the Prophet Muhammad (peace be upon him) known as the **Qur'an**.

This awareness leads to a deepened consciousness of the importance of the gift of human life, and the responsibility that goes with it. Like a dry and curled up desert plant suddenly being given the drop of moisture that will make it spread out its leaves and sink its roots, and flourish – the human being suddenly becomes aware of the great thirst, the great dependence, and joy in being at one with the Creator.

It is traditional to call God 'He' – Allah always describes Himself using the male pronoun. Muslims do not accept that God can be compared with the human race, and prefer to use the name **Allah** in place of the word 'god' which can be made plural or taken as being female.

TAQWA

Once this awareness (known as **taqwa**) has begun in a person, life is never the same again. However, the moment of belief is only the beginning of a long journey. The Muslim suddenly sees that everything in life, every ambition, every object, every possession, is not quite what it had seemed before. Every part of themselves and the planet on which they live is a gift, something which might not ever have existed if Allah had not willed it to. Similarly, when its time comes, every part of it will cease to be because Allah wills it so. There is no longer any meaning to fear, or ambition, or ownership, or pride. The human role is not to own or to have, but simply to be.

SHARIAH

There is only one aim or ambition which continues to make any sense – and that is to accept, or **submit**. This is the meaning of the word 'Muslim'. So Muslims aim to live out the will of Allah so far as is humanly possible, in whatever circumstances they find themselves in life. The road of life is known in Islam as **shariah** – the way. Muslims believe they must search for it, and follow it through all life's tests and temptations, difficulties and tragedies, consciously considering *in every situation* what the will of Allah would be for them and others at any given moment.

Muslim life is guided by the Qur'an

The will of Allah

Islam is not just a matter of ritual – prayers or fasting or feasts. It is the conscious bringing of *every* moment of the day, *every* decision, *every* detail of the Muslim's thoughts and actions, into deliberate line with what they accept as being the will of Allah.

How is the will of Allah known? The Muslim bases all decisions on the revealed words of the **Holy Qur'an**, the messages that were delivered, over a period of 23 years, to the inspired prophet **Muhammad**. Not one word in the Qur'an is believed by Muslims to be the thought or teaching of Muhammad himself – although he is revered above all human beings as one of the most perfect of

Allah's messengers. Other messengers were Abraham, Moses, Jesus and, in fact, at least 24000 prophets. Jesus is especially revered by many Muslims, for he was the great miracle-worker. Muhammad's ministry was not based on any miracles other than the receiving of the Qur'an – but that in itself is regarded as a very great miracle. Muhammad is so important to Muslims because he was the **last** prophet, the **seal** of all that was revealed to the prophets before him.

> 'Muhammad is . . . the Apostle of God and the Seal of the prophets.'
>
> (surah 33:40)

Muslims believe that if the pure teachings of the earlier prophets had not been altered and changed by those who later wrote about them, it would be easily seen that the revealed message was the same.

The human spirit

Islam teaches that every human being is a creation of the one God, and all are born equal. Sadly, the worth of individuals, as they grow into adults, becomes spoiled as they fall away from the standards set for humanity by the Creator. Natural reason enables any person, whose mind is not damaged, to see the evidence for the existence of God, but no one is forced to accept it or act upon it. It is purely a matter of choice.

This does not mean that Allah loves the deliberate wrongdoer any less. Many human parents know only too well just how much they can love a child who is making terrible mistakes in life. It does mean, though, that they are building up for themselves a pattern of inevitable consequences. Muslims believe the universe is based on justice, tempered with mercy. The human spirit, created deliberately in this way by Allah who is the Lord of Compassion, is generous. As soon as any person truly repents of wrongdoing, Muslims are prepared to forgive and to put things right, so far as is possible. Allah has far greater compassion than any human being does.

Some people seem determined to bring about their own doom, in spite of the desperate efforts of those who love them. In the same way, the future for some people will be permanent death, because of their absolute refusal to accept the love and mercy of Allah, or to live in a way acceptable to him.

> 'Nobody knows what they will earn tomorrow, nor does anyone know in what land they are to die.

> Only God has full knowledge, and is acquainted with all things.'
>
> (surah 31:34)

> 'We shall most certainly try you with fear and hunger and with the loss of goods or lives or the fruits of your toil. But give encouragement to those who patiently persevere, and, when calamity befalls them, say, "Behold, to God we belong, and to Him do we return." '
>
> (surah 2:155–156)

> 'Or do you think that you shall enter the Garden without such trials as came to those who passed away before you?'
>
> (surah 2:214)

> 'Revile not destiny, for, behold, – I am Destiny.'
>
> (Hadith)

FOR YOUR FOLDER

- Explain in your own words the following terms.
  Allah   shariah   Qur'an   prophet   compassion
- What is meant by Islam? What does submission involve, for a Muslim?
- Why does the Muslim regard the planet and every part of life on it as a gift?
- How does taqwa alter a person's attitude to life?
- Why do Muslims believe Muhammad's revelation and mission were necessary? Why is he known as 'the Seal'?

THINGS TO DO

- Choose one of the passages quoted on these pages and copy it out carefully, giving it a decorative border. What does the passage you have chosen mean? Why did you choose it?

The South East Essex College of Arts & Technology
Carnarvon Road   Southend on Sea   Essex   SS2 6LS
Tel: Southend (0702) 220400   Fax: Southend (0702) 432320

Muslims believe that, whether they are aware of it or not, *all* human beings are creations of Allah, and are loved by him. Therefore there are certain basic rights which should be shared by the *whole* of humanity, and which should be observed in society, whether the people are Muslims or not. These human rights have been granted by Allah, and not by any ruler or government, and it is the duty of Muslims to protect them *actively*. Failure to do so results in loss of human rights, which can lead to tyranny.

> 'As you are, so you will have rulers over you.'
>
> (Hadith)

The security of life

Muslims believe that human life is sacred, and should not be ended without justification. It is not permissible in Islam to oppress women, children, old people, the sick or the wounded, or indeed, any person.

The right to the basic necessities of life

The Earth is a wealthy place, and there is enough for all. No human being should go in need while others are able to waste what they have. The needs of any suffering person must be attended to. The hungry should be fed, the naked clothed, and the wounded or diseased treated, whether they are Muslim or not, and whether they are friends or enemies.

The sanctity and security of private life, and honour

To any Muslim the home is a private refuge. No person should enter another's home, or spy on it, without consent. It should be a safe place for all who live in it. No one has the right to abuse, or defame, or insult, or threaten. The honour and chastity of all women is to be respected.

Honour is important, and ridicule is never fun, especially when there is arrogance or selfishness or malice behind it. Muslims believe that we may laugh *with* people, to share in the happiness of life but we must never laugh *at* people, or cause them distress.

> 'Do not laugh at one another, nor defame one another, nor be sarcastic to each other, nor call each other by offensive names. Avoid suspicion, and spy not on each other, nor speak ill of each other behind their backs.'
>
> (surah 49:11–12)

The right to justice

Muslims believe that no human being should ever be imprisoned unless they are proved guilty of some crime, in an open and unbiased court. Nor should anyone be deprived of their liberty on the basis of suspicion only, or not given a reasonable opportunity to provide a defence. No individual should *ever* be arrested or imprisoned for the offences of others.

> 'No bearer of burdens shall be made to bear the burden of another.'
>
> (surah 6:164)

The right to protest

Muslims believe that the power of any human being is only given as a trust from Allah. It is therefore their duty to speak out against tyranny, and protect the weak from tyrants. To Muslims, a tyrant is a ruler who attempts to assert his own will upon the people in his charge, rather than seek for them the will of Allah – which will always be kind and just. If such a person takes power, it is the Muslim's right to point out their errors, and turn the tyrant back to the right way – even by force if this becomes necessary. This is because it is Muslims' duty to protect the weak and oppressed, and not hang back out of cowardice or thought for themselves.

> 'If anyone walks with an oppressor to strengthen him, knowing that he is an oppressor, he has gone forth from Islam.'
>
> (Hadith)

The right to freedom of expression

This is granted to every Muslim, provided it is used in accordance with the will of Allah. Muslims are *not* free to spread evil, wickedness, abuse or offence as those may lead to tyranny, and are therefore hurtful to others.

As with freedom of speech, Muslims are free to join any organizations or parties, so long as they are not evil or offensive to Allah and to others.

The freedom of conscience

Muslims believe that no attempt should ever be made to force people to act against their own consciences, so long as they are not acting against the welfare of humanity, and what they are doing is right by their own standards.

Muslims demonstrating

The right to religious freedom

Muslims believe it is impossible to force people to believe what they do not want to believe. Allah has allowed human beings free minds and the ability to reason. In Islam *all* religious sentiments are given due respect, and missionary work should not cause offence to others who are following different faiths. There is no need to hurry faith, according to Islamic scriptures. It will come, whenever it is to come.

'There should be no coercion in the matter of faith.'
(surah 2:256)

The right to equality

Muslims insist that all citizens must have completely equal rights. No individual should ever be above the law, no matter how powerful they are, or beneath the law, no matter how humble.

The right to participate in affairs of state

Islam teaches that all heads of government and members of ruling assemblies should be elected by free and independent votes of the people. They should never be elected by a clique, or granted power simply by means of family power. Dynastic rulers can be given allegiance, so long as their rulings do not break Islamic law.

KEY IDEA – THE IDEAL SOCIETY

To a Muslim, the ideal society is one in which there is justice, peace, love and cooperation, and everyone is free to worship God according to their own level of awareness.

FOR YOUR FOLDERS

► Explain, in your own words, what is meant by these terms
tyranny   honour   chastity   privacy   abuse   bias
► Why do you think that Muslims consider films, plays or books about Jesus or the Prophet Muhammad (peace be upon him), which they think are abusive or blasphemous, are a misuse of the right of freedom of expression?
► Why is it more important for a Muslim to protect the rights of others than always to act with 'civil obedience'?
► How do the Muslim examples of human rights lead towards the establishment of the Muslim ideal society?

FOR DISCUSSION

► *'Cooperate with me when I am right, but correct me when I commit error; obey me so long as I follow the commands of Allah and His Prophet, but turn away from me when I deviate.'*

This is an extract from Abu Bakr's first address to the Muslims after his election as caliph or successor to the Prophet Muhammad. How does this passage indicate Abu Bakr's acceptance of Islam as regards human rights?

Muslims believe that all human life is a gift of Allah, and is therefore sacred. Once a life has been given, no human has any right to try to end it.

'Do not take life – which Allah has made sacred – except for just cause.'

(surah 17:33)

Death

'Allah fixes the time span for all things. It is He who causes both laughter and grief; it is He who causes people to die and to be born; it is He who causes male and female; it is He who will recreate us anew.'

(surah 53:42–7)

Muslims believe that every life has an allotted length. No human being knows when their life will be required by Allah and taken back. Therefore it is the duty of all Muslims to live every day as if it was their last – in readiness for the moment when they will face Allah and answer to him for what they have done with their lives.

'The knowledge of the Final Hour is with Allah; none but He can reveal when it will occur. . . All of a sudden it will come to you.'

(surah 7:187)

Islam teaches that death itself should never be feared. It is human nature to dread pain and suffering, but Muslims are supposed to do their best to bear everything with patience and fortitude. Death is the natural end of human life. It cannot be avoided, and no one escapes it. It is rather pointless to resent the inevitable.

'When your time expires, you will not be able to delay the reckoning for a single hour, just as you cannot bring it forward by a single hour.'

(surah 16:61)

No true Muslim should fear death, or consider it to be the end of everything, as they believe in the afterlife. This should be a time of great joy and reward for all their efforts on Earth.

'Do you think that We shall not reassemble your bones? Yes, surely, yes – We are able to restore even your individual fingerprints!'

(surah 75:3–4)

The after-life

Many passages in the Qur'an describe in graphic terms the pleasant rewards or terrible torments in store for humans.

'For those nearest to God will come rest and satisfaction and a garden of delights, and . . . peace; but if you are of those who have . . . gone wrong, then your entertainment will be boiling water and hellfire. Truly, this is the absolute truth and certain.'

(surah 56:88–95)

Muslim mystics usually suggest that these passages are to be taken symbolically and not literally.

'In the Book are verses of fundamental meaning, and others which are allegorical.'

(surah 3:7)

'Eye has not seen, and it has not entered into the human heart what things God has prepared for those who love Him.'

(Hadith)

Beyond human control

Death is beyond human control. No person can choose the time of their passing unless God sanctions it.

'A soul cannot die except by Allah's permission, the life span being fixed as if by written contract.'

(surah 3:145)

Many people desperately try to put off their deaths and pray for Allah to grant them some miracle that will keep them alive – but Nature runs its course and miracles are not often granted. On the other hand, many people long to die, because they are very unhappy or in great pain, but Allah wants them to go on living.

Suicide

Muslims believe that every soul has been created by Allah, and is owned by him. In other words, no person owns their own soul, or is allowed to damage or attempt to kill the body in which it lives. For Muslims to kill themselves is just as much against Allah's laws as killing other people unlawfully.

'If you think you control your own destiny, try to stop your own soul from leaving its body at your hour of death.'
(surah 56:81–87)

'How can you reject faith in Allah, seeing you were without life and He gave you life; and He will cause you to die, and will bring you again to life?'
(surah 2:28)

Life may be full of hardships and terrible sufferings, but Muslims are taught to accept these as times of testing, and to face them with patience and humility. Real life, for a Muslim, begins in the Kingdom of God. Their life on Earth is a time of preparation. Therefore, not even the very worst things that could happen in life should make a person commit suicide out of despair.

Euthanasia

Sometimes life seems such a burden for someone that people think it would be better to end it, in as kind a way as possible. **Euthanasia** means a gentle and easy death, and is sometimes called mercy killing. It is usually thought of as being 'put to sleep' painlessly.

Muslims reject the idea of euthanasia, because the reason for any suffering will be known to Allah. 'Mercy killing' does not always give the affected person any choice.

Muslims regard every soul as being perfect, even though the body it is in may be damaged for some reason. They also believe that Allah has decided how long anyone is to live so it is not the personal choice of the individual. It is Allah alone who knows the reasons for our sufferings and our tests. This may seem very unfair when nobody knows the reasons – but Muslims believe that all will be revealed in due course, and that Allah is *never* unfair.

Capital punishment

'Do not take life except for just cause. If anyone is wrongfully killed, We give his heir the right to demand retribution or to forgive; but let him not exceed bounds in the matter of taking life, for he is bound by the law.'
(surah 17:33)

In Islam, there are two crimes which are considered **just cause** for giving the death penalty:

● murder
● openly attacking Islam in such a manner as to threaten it, having previously been a believing Muslim.

In the case of murder, the Prophet accepted the justice of taking a life for a life, although nobody is allowed to take the law into their own hands and seek revenge. The execution of a murderer can only be carried out after a proper legal trial.

One of Muhammad's sayings also suggests that the death penalty could be given for an ex-Muslim actively turning and attacking Islam, but it is not true that Muslims are condemned to death if they simply forsake the faith.

FOR YOUR FOLDERS

▶ Good Muslims live with a constant awareness of death. Why would Muslims say this is not a morbid preoccupation? Why should good Muslims live every day as if it was their last?

▶ If human life spans are fixed by Allah, how could this influence a person's attitude to battle, illness, famine and disaster?

▶ Why are suicide and euthanasia regarded as crimes in Islam?

'A man came to the Prophet and asked, "Who, among all people, is most worthy of my good company?" The Prophet replied, "Your mother." The man asked, "Who next?" The Prophet said, "Your mother." The man again asked, "Who next?" Again, the Prophet said, "Your mother." Only next did he say, "Your father."'

(Hadith)

KEY IDEA

A wise man loves and cherishes the mother of his family above all else.

Motherhood is the most valued of occupations

Birth control

Muslims believe it is only Allah who controls when births and deaths take place. If a child is born to a couple in spite of attempts to prevent conception, it is due to Allah's will. Conception, therefore, should be welcomed, and the parents should not seek an abortion. Muslims do not accept the argument that population growth must be controlled to avoid overcrowding the Earth, or because of poverty.

'Do not slay your children because of poverty – We will provide for you and for them.'

(surah 6:151)

Islam does permit some birth control, however, provided that special circumstances justify it. However, a man may not practise birth control without discussing it with his wife, and vice versa. Some Muslim scholars believe that the breath of life or **spirit** does not enter the body until the end of the fourth month of pregnancy, and therefore abortion in the early days is not forbidden and can be seen as a form of birth control.

'The creation of each one of you is brought together in your mother's belly for 40 days in the form of seed, then you are a clot of blood for a like period, then a morsel of flesh for a like period, then there is sent to you an angel who blows the breath of life into you.'

(Hadith)

So, if the soul enters the foetus after 120 days, an abortion, if it is absolutely necessary, should clearly be done before that time. After the fourth month abortion is unlawful.

Other Muslim scholars maintain that no one really knows what the soul or spirit is, and that when the Prophet was asked to define it he was told by Allah to reply that knowledge of the soul belongs to Allah alone. Therefore the foetus represents a potential life from the moment of conception, and should be protected and given all the rights of human life.

Reasons for birth control

The special circumstances accepted by some Muslims for birth control are:
● protection of the life of the mother
● strong indications that the child would be born deformed or handicapped
● to prevent a woman from becoming pregnant again while she is already breastfeeding a child (this is not recommended in Islam; the recommended period of breastfeeding is two years)

- personal reasons according to conscience (for example, the mother may be completing a course of study).

Abortion

'Slay not your children... the killing of them is a great sin.'

(surah 17:31)

Abortion is only lawful in Islam where the life of the mother is at stake. The principle is that the actual life of the mother is more important than the possible life of the baby. The mother is alive and has duties and responsibilities, whereas the foetus has not yet formed any personality. Abortion is *only* performed as the lesser of two evils.

Some women argue that it is a woman's right to decide what she does with her own body. They insist that she has the right to choose whether or not to give birth to a child. Muslims maintain that this means conveniently forgetting that what the mother does will affect another person's body – her child's. The Qur'an reminds these mothers that on Judgement Day the infants will want to know why they were killed.

'When the souls are sorted out; when the female infant buried alive is asked for what crime she was killed; . . . . . when the World on High is unveiled . . . then shall each soul know what it has put forward.'

(surah 81:7–9,11,14)

Test-tube babies and surrogate motherhood

Thanks to spectacular advances in medical science some women can now become pregnant when this would once have been impossible. There are three types of 'medical motherhood':

- **Artificial insemination by husband (AIH)** The husband and wife can produce their own sperm and egg, but the egg is unable to enter the uterus and be fertilized. Doctors can take the sperm and egg from the parents and bring them together so the egg is fertilized in a test-tube. They then return the fertilized egg to the womb of the mother. This is acceptable in Islam.
- **Artificial insemination by donor (AID)** The husband is sterile, so the sperm of another man is taken from a sperm bank, and used to fertilize the egg of the wife. The majority of scholars of Islam consider this to be unlawful because it is the closest possible thing to adultery. It also leads to confusion about who the father of the child is.
- **Surrogate motherhood** The wife is sterile, so sperm from the husband is used to fertilize the egg of another woman, the surrogate mother. She is paid to carry and deliver the baby, then the baby is given to the father and his wife. Sometimes, if the wife can produce eggs but not become pregnant, the 'test-tube' method may be used, but the fertilized egg may be implanted in another woman.

Opinions are divided as to whether surrogate motherhood should be allowed in Islam or not because:

- it destroys the special relationship between mother and baby
- in Islam, the mother of a child is the woman who gives birth to it and feeds it
- it commercializes childbirth if done for money
- difficulties arise if the surrogate mother cannot bear to be separated from the baby.

If the reason for surrogacy was simply because the husband of a sterile woman wanted to father a child then, by Islamic law, he is entitled to marry a second (or third or fourth) wife – with the previous wife's permission — or he could bring up a nephew.

Genetic experiments

Genetic experiments and engineering are **never** permissible in Islam. To attempt to alter genetic material is to take upon oneself the role of Allah. Human embryos are living beings, with human rights, and should not be manipulated, frozen or left to die.

FOR YOUR FOLDERS

- ▶ Why might Muslims justify birth control? Why do they see an important difference between those types of birth control that prevent the sperm from meeting the egg, and those that kill the foetus?
- ▶ Why does a mother's life take precedence over an unborn child's?
- ▶ Why is Islam basically against surrogate motherhood?

Islam teaches that males and females are equal. All living animals were created in pairs or **zawaj**. In fact, the principles of equality before Allah in Islam gave great freedoms and rights to women at a time when they definitely *were* considered to be inferior beings.

'Glory to Allah, who created in pairs all things that the earth produces.'

(surah 36:36)

O humanity, be careful of your duty to your Lord. Who created you from a single soul and from it created its mate, and from the two of them spread abroad a multitude of men and women.'

(surah 4:1)

Women in the forefront of Islam

Men and women have equal spiritual worth. Every instruction given to Muslims in the Qur'an refers to both male and female believers. They have been given the same religious duties and will be judged according to exactly the same criteria. Women should therefore live and work actively alongside men, and should try to gain all the knowledge and skills which they will need, to succeed.

'For Muslim men and women, for believing men and women. . .for men and women who are patient and constant, who humble themselves, who give in charity, who fast, who guard their chastity, who engage in the praise of Allah — for them Allah has prepared forgiveness and a great reward.'

(surah 33:35)

The right to be protected

'Men are the protectors and maintainers of women, because Allah has given them more strength. . .therefore righteous women are devoutly obedient, and guard in the husband's absence what Allah would have them guard.'

(surah 4:34)

Although Islam accepts that women are equal to men, it does take account of the physical differences between the sexes, and it makes allowances, to protect women and make them comfortable.

A Muslim woman has the right to remain a virgin, unmolested by strangers or by any male member of her own family. She has the right to go to her marriage untouched by any man, and to give herself to her chosen partner for life. She has the right to be cared for in times of physical pain and discomfort, for example, during her monthly periods, throughout pregnancy and while rearing her children. She may be excused from fasting during Ramadan, if necessary.

Muslim women have the right to be provided for, and should not be forced to work to earn money. However, there is no text which prohibits a woman from seeking work. The Prophet's wife Khadijah was herself a successful businesswoman.

She has the right to be looked after by her husband if she does not wish to go out to work. She also has the right to work without sexual harassment in her place of employment, and often safeguards this right by dressing modestly.

The right to modest dress

'Say to believing men that they should lower their gaze and guard their modesty. . .and that believing women should lower their gaze and guard their modesty; that they should not display their ornaments except as is normal, that they should draw their veils over their bosoms and not display their beauty except to their close male relatives.'

(surah 24:30–31)

(the surah gives the precise list of these relatives.)

Muslim women out on the street or at business will not try to draw attention to themselves, but will always behave modestly. If they catch a man's eye, they do not stare at him, but look away.

'Believing women should cast their outer garments over themselves when out: that is most convenient, that they should be recognized as such and not molested.'

(surah 33:59)

Muslim women usually cover their heads with some kind of scarf or veil; they cover their arms to the wrists and their legs to the ankles. This is called wearing **hijab**. Hijab (more properly called **satr**) indicates modesty in dress and behaviour. Hijab does not prevent women from going out on business, or taking an active part in society.

A Muslim woman's standards of behaviour and dress should never come from pressure by relatives, or the social norms of society, but because she herself has a desire to please Allah. In fact, many

Muslim women wear hijab *in spite of* opposition from husbands, or secular governments, and can actually become victims of harassment, violence and abuse.

Muslim women are not regarded by their men as sex-objects, who dare not show an ankle, or a lock of hair on their forehead, without attracting sexual attention. The purpose of Muslim dress for women is *modesty*. Muslim women think that wearing the kind of clothing that reveals naked limbs, is transparent, or clings very suggestively to the female figure turns a woman into a sex-object, and is worn simply to attract the attention of men.

Muslim women expect to be appreciated for their characters and minds. Their clothes can be smart or colourful, and vary according to the traditions of different countries – but they should never be indecent or vulgar. In fact, Muslim women regard their dress as the very opposite of female repression – it is real liberation.

A Muslim woman teaching

Suppression of women

There are many customs, in supposedly Islamic societies, which deny the rights given to women by Islamic law. Four are particularly significant, and have caused many Muslim women suffering, deprivation, lack of fulfilment, and boredom:
- the practice of **purdah** or the seclusion of women
- the restriction or prevention of women from going out, even to the mosque
- the voice of a woman being made **awrah** (forbidden to a stranger)
- daughters being given in marriage without their consent.

The first three of these restrictions were probably based on the following verses:

'O wives of the Prophet! You are not like ordinary women. If you fear Allah, don't be too casual in your speech, in case someone with an unsteadfast heart should be moved with desire. . .And stay quietly in your houses, and do not make a worldly display as in the times of ignorance; establish regular prayer and give regular charity, and obey Allah and His Apostles.'

(surah 33:32–33)

In fact, the seclusion of purdah has nothing to do with Islam, but was a practice extensively used by Hindus, Persians, Byzantines and even some Christians. The word 'purdah' is not found in the Qur'an. Purdah usually involves making women live separate lives from men, and keeping them out of public view. A woman in purdah may only walk in the streets if she is wearing a full-length black veil which also covers her face, except for her eyes.

Hijab is not like purdah, which is intended to segregate women from society. Hijab allows women to play a full and active part in society without fear of sexual harrassment or unfair treatment.

There are no instructions in the Qur'an or any of the universally accepted sayings of the Prophet which stop women going out. They are certainly not prevented from going to the mosque if they wish – it is common practice for them to go. Women take part in every aspect of life.

If it had been forbidden for a stranger to hear a woman's voice, then the warning to the Prophet's wives in surah 33:32 would not have been necessary. Many male scholars of Islam were taught by prominent women scholars!

In Islam a marriage is null and void if the free consent of both parties is not given. A father has no right to force his daughter into an arrangement she does not want. It is obvious from various reports that forced marriages do sometimes take place, but this is not Islamic in principle, and parents claiming to be good Muslims should bear this in mind.

FOR YOUR FOLDERS

▶ What evidence is there in Islam that men and women are equal, and of equal value?

▶ List the special rights granted to Muslim women, and explain why you think they see them as being so important.

▶ Why should Muslim women speak out against suppression of women?

Sex is a very important aspect of human behaviour. All humans have three parts to their personality – spiritual, intellectual and physical – and have urges to satisfy the needs of all three. Islam teaches that they should be satisfied according to the commands laid down by Allah, in a wholesome and pure manner, without excess, and without causing suffering.

'When a husband and wife share intimacy it is rewarded, and a blessing from Allah; just as they would be punished if they engaged in illicit sex.'
(Hadith)

Muslims do *not* believe that sex:
● is unclean
● is contrary to goodness, spirituality and faith in Allah
● should be resisted and suppressed.
Neither do they believe that sexual pleasures can be pursued regardless of moral considerations, since this only leads to preoccupation with sex and the development of sex as a business. Muslims maintain that both these extremes go against human nature, which requires that sexual desires are satisfied, but that the individual and the family are protected from dangerous consequences.

Permissiveness

Muslims believe that permissiveness leads to the breakdown of society, to selfishness, rape, lying and deception, lack of responsibility, drug addiction, theft and even murder. If Muslims are listening to Allah they should be able to resist temptation, and know right from wrong.

Sex before marriage

'Let no man be in privacy with a woman who is not lawful unto him, or Shaitan will be the third.'
(Hadith)

Islam prohibits any type of privacy between couples who are not married to each other. Muslims do not believe that sexual freedom before a commitment to marriage contributes anything to the future stability of that marriage. The assumption that the couple will have 'tried each other out' and so will 'know' each other is nonsense to Muslims. In societies where sexual freedom is tolerated, many marriages go wrong, and divorce is at a very high level. Muslims would not welcome marriage to a partner

who had experienced many previous 'trial encounters', because they might quite easily seek other 'trials' even after the marriage.

However, it is not true that Muslim couples are prevented from seeing each other before marriage. The Prophet actually commanded that bridegrooms *should* go and see the prospective brides, so that feelings of love, companionship and closeness would develop. He also said that they should not be left on their own, but be **chaperoned**.

Courtship

Courtship is only the first step towards marriage, and it *may not* always end in marriage – therefore the woman's reputation and chastity have to be protected. It is quite possible for an unscrupulous man to take advantage of a girl for his own satisfaction, and then abandon her without marrying her – perhaps even leaving her pregnant.

BASIC ISLAMIC RULES FOR SEEKING MARRIAGE

● A woman should be approached through representatives and may not be approached by anyone else until she has consented or refused.
● If she agrees the marriage can be contracted, but may not necessarily be consummated straight away.
● Agreements should not take place within the waiting period after a woman's divorce, in case the couple can be reconciled.
● Widows should not be courted within their period of mourning.
● It is important to check whether or not the couple are compatible.

Sex outside marriage

Adultery is regarded by Muslims as a form of theft, of the worst possible sort.

'Have nothing to do with adultery, for it is a shameful thing, and an evil opening the way to other evils.'
(surah 17:32)

Stealing another person's marriage partner is considered to be the most serious crime, because it would cause the break-up of at least one family unit, and possibly two.

'The man or woman guilty of adultery or fornication, flog them with a hundred stripes; do not be moved by pity. . .and do not let any person guilty of these sins marry any but others similarly guilty. . .unless they repent and change their ways.'

(surah 24:3–5)

If a couple no longer love each other, and do not wish to continue in marriage together, honourable divorce can be arranged. It must be done in such a way as to cause the least amount of damage to the respective families. Giving in to the urge to have casual sex outside marriage is despised in Islam, and seen as a major weakness and dishonour.

Homosexuality

Islam prohibits all illicit relationships and sexual deviations. Homosexuality is not regarded as a normal variation on the way things are, but is considered to be against the laws of nature. Human beings seem to be the only animals that have been tempted into homosexual activity.

There is nothing new about homosexuality. Lot, the nephew of Ibrahim, lived among a community of people addicted to it.

'Of all the creatures in the world, will you approach males and abandon those whom Allah created for you as mates?'

(surah 26:165–166)

Homosexuality is regarded by Muslims as a depraved practice which makes people slaves to their desires. It robs them of decency, morality and dignity.

'If two men are guilty of lewdness, punish them both. If they repent and change their ways, leave them alone. . .Allah accepts the repentance of those who do evil in ignorance and repent soon afterwards. . .of no effect is the repentance of those who continue to do evil.'

(surah 4:16–18)

In Islam, the only permissible form of sexual activity is that which takes place within a marriage.

Therefore, it can be argued *on these grounds* alone that homosexuality is unacceptable.

Islamic lawyers have different opinions about the punishment for homosexuality. Some even favour the death penalty in order to maintain the purity of society.

The Prophet declared that neither sex should ever imitate the other in their way of speaking, walking, dressing or moving. Such behaviour constitutes a rebellion against the natural order of things.

'Three persons shall not enter Paradise – the one who is disobedient to parents, the pimp, and the woman who imitates men.'

(Hadith)

Masturbation

At times, people have a fierce need to be relieved of sexual tension. Islam regards relieving oneself as a weakness, but it is tolerated under two conditions:
● the fear of committing sex before marriage, or adultery
● not having the means to marry.

The Prophet was well aware of the temptations of those unable to marry for some reason. His advice was to practise frequent fasting, in order to improve will-power and self-control.

'Young men, those of you who can support a wife should marry, for it keeps you from looking at women and preserves your chastity; but those who cannot should fast, for it is a means of cooling sexual passion.'

(Hadith)

FOR YOUR FOLDERS
▶ Why do Muslims think it is best if sexual activity only takes place in a marriage?
▶ Why do you think Muslims are against sexual permissiveness?
▶ Why is the Muslim attitude to homosexuality so severe?

Islam regards marriage as the normal human status for adults, and rejects **celibacy** (living without sex). The only proper way for a Muslim to take part in sexual activity is within marriage. Finding a good life partner, and building up a relationship together is regarded as 'half the faith'.

> 'Whoever gets married has completed half of his faith; therefore let him be conscious of Allah in the other half of his faith.'
>
> (Hadith)

Marriage is a social contract which brings rights and obligations to both husband and wife. Islam supports the basic equality of the sexes, but it does not prevent husband and wife from adopting different roles, which should be complementary.

Arranged marriages

In the Muslim world, because chastity and modesty are emphasized so strongly, there is little contact between young men and women. The selection of a marriage partner is often organized by the parents. Sometimes they will look for a known member of the family, preferably a cousin. For many couples, love comes *after* the marriage and not before.

Partnership in marriage

In Islam, marriage is a partnership. Muslim women accept only Allah as their master, and do not therefore consider themselves to be inferior to a husband.

Male dominance in marriage

For a marriage to work successfully, one person usually takes on the role of 'head of the family'. Muslims believe that most women, when they fall in love with a man, are happy to look after him and see to his needs and the needs of his children – on the understanding that the man keeps his obligation to provide for them. (See also page 122.)

> 'The best of treasures is a good wife. She is pleasing in her husband's eyes, looks for ways to please him, and takes care of his possessions while he is away; the best of you are those who treat their wives best.'
>
> (Hadith)

A Muslim couple, 'just married'

The right to compatibility in marriage

> The Prophet said, 'A woman should only be married to a person who is good enough for her or compatible to her.'
>
> (Hadith)

In Islam, the only compatibility that really matters is **piety**. The Prophet permitted marriages between people of vastly different social status and financial backgrounds, knowing it was not these factors which made for compatibility, but what they were like in their hearts.

The most important ingredients in a Muslim marriage are shared values and beliefs, so that even if the couple come from different cultures and backgrounds, they possess the same basic world view, attitudes and habits which will bind them together.

> 'Do not marry only for a person's looks; their beauty might become the cause of moral decline. Do not marry for wealth, since this may become the cause of disobedience. Marry rather on the grounds of religious devotion.'
>
> (Hadith)

The aim in marriage is that the partner should also be one's 'best friend', the one who shares the concerns and responsibilities of life, who offers peace, comfort and rest, and who helps to bear difficulties which are too much to be faced alone.

Polygamy

'Marry women of your choice, two, three or four; but if you fear that you shall not be able to deal justly with them, then marry only one.'

(surah 4:3)

The ideal Muslim family is, in fact, **monogamous**, but for a man to have more than one wife is neither prohibited nor unlawful. Islam did not introduce it. On the contrary, polygamy had been the normal practice in many ancient civilizations for centuries. Even in societies which encouraged monogamy, concubines were sometimes allowed, and very often men had numerous mistresses.

Although the practice of men having more than one wife is referred to as polygamy, in fact it should properly be called **polygyny**. True polygamy (either sex having more than one spouse) is not allowed.

Social reasons for polygamy

In any society where there is a greater number of women than men, strict monogamy means that many women would have no chance of marriage and could therefore be tempted into immoral relationships. A widow or divorcee whose prospects of marriage were small might prefer to be a second wife rather than face lifelong loneliness and struggle on her own.

Wives could suddenly become mentally or physically ill. Muslims think it is not reasonable to expect a husband to control his instincts for the rest of his life, or be forced to keep mistresses, or to divorce the unfortunate woman. A second wife, if he chose well, would be a second mother to his children, look after the household and, if necessary, help her husband to look after the first wife.

If a man's wife is sterile, taking a second wife may be preferable to never having children, or divorce, or taking mistresses, or adoption. (In Islam, a child can only be fostered, and not adopted in the Western sense – see page 129).

Disadvantages of polygamy

There are four considerable disadvantages to polygamy. These are jealousy, inequality, disharmony and conflicts between the children of different wives. Each of these must be taken very seriously when considering a polygamous marriage.

Equality in polygamy

If a man taking a second wife commits any injustice, that marriage can be declared illegal and against the principles of Islam. He should try to give all his wives the same quality and amount of food, clothing, medication, leisure, living space, time, compassion and mercy. The only area where complete justice is impossible is in the way that the man loves his wives.

'The Prophet prayed: " Oh Allah! This is my justice in what I could control; do not blame me for what You control and I do not control."'

(Hadith)

Polyandry

Islam is against a woman having more than one husband because a child has the right to know who its father is, and this would be impossible if the woman was married to more than one man.

Monogamy Having only one spouse or partner.
Polygamy Having more than one spouse.
Polygyny Having more than one wife (man only).
Polyandry Having more than one husband (woman only).

A Muslim family studying the Qur'an together

Islam teaches that the family is the basis of the whole social system. Society's structure and condition can be traced directly to the strength or weakness of the family. It is not a casual or spontaneous institution, but is divinely ordained. It is therefore regarded as noble and sacred.

> 'It is He who created you from a single cell with a mate of like nature, in order that they might live together.'
>
> (surah 7:189)

Who is included in the family?

The family is not just mother and father plus a couple of children. The Muslim family takes care of its old people, who include the actual parents *and* uncles and aunts. If tragedy hit any relative, or even a member of a neighbour's household, the family would be expected to rally round and give support during the time of need. The family also takes care of children who have lost their parents, for whatever reason – a common occurrence in some societies.

Old people

Today's old people were yesterday's providers and heroes, and are therefore always to be respected. In Muslim families age comes first, and the grandparents take priority over the children, who are taught to be respectful and considerate.

As people become old they often become confused, or bad tempered, or suffer from diseases, aches and pains. It is human nature for them to think that they are *always* in the right, and *always* superior to their children, even if the children are themselves in their sixties! Muslims behave towards their parents with tolerance and understanding. They know that there may come a time when the parents' judgement will be clouded, or they may not be able to cope.

> 'Your Lord orders that you . . . be kind to parents. If one or both of them attain old age with you, do not say one word of contempt to them, or repel them, but speak to them in terms of honour . . . and say, My Lord, bestow your mercy on them, as they cherished me when I was a child.'
>
> (surah 17:23–24)

It is considered unthinkable for a Muslim to pass over the care of their parents to a stranger. Just as the mother expects to bring her own child into the world and nurse it until it reaches independence, so the Muslim 'child' expects to care for parents who are approaching the end of life, and to nurse them safely into the next life.

'May his nose be rubbed in dust, who found his parents approaching old age and lost his right to enter Paradise because he did not look after them.'
(Hadith)

INSTRUCTIONS TO CHILDREN
- When dealing with your parents, be patient, grateful, compassionate, respectful and kind.
- It is impolite to call your parents by their first names.
- If your parents ask for something you can't afford or fulfil, apologize politely.
- Never interrupt your parents or argue with them (you can think your own thoughts!).
- Never draw attention to the care or support you are giving your parents, or what you spend on them, to make them feel a burden.

Adoption

'I, and the one who raises an orphan, will be like these two in the Garden.'
(Hadith – an occasion when Muhammad pointed to his middle and index fingers)

The Qur'an teaches that any orphaned or abandoned children should be looked after as an act of compassion, and given shelter, food, clothing and anything else they need – but there is *no* legal adoption in Islam. It is forbidden for Muslims to adopt a child of whom they are not the natural parents, or to make a child from another person's family an equal son or daughter to family members.

No 'adopted' children should ever be misled about their true parentage, or allowed the rights of the children born into a family. Human words or contracts cannot make an adoptive parent's blood run in the veins of an adopted child, or produce family affection and loyalty, or bestow genetic characteristics.

'He has not made your adopted sons your real sons: that is simply what you call them . . . Call them by the names of their fathers; that is more just in the sight of Allah. But if you do not know their fathers, they are your brothers-in-faith and your wards.'
(surah 33:4–5)

Milk brothers and sisters

If a baby's mother dies, and the baby is given to another woman to breastfeed, that child would be regarded as brother or sister to the mother's own children, and future marriage between them would not be allowed.

Spoilt children

No one child in a family should be made the favourite, but all should be treated equally, and with fair discipline.

'Do not ask me to be a witness to injustice. Your children have the right to receive equal treatment, as you have the right that they should honour you.'
(Hadith)

'Fear Allah, and treat your children with equal justice.'
(Hadith)

Parents always want to be proud of their children, but sometimes they can overestimate their talents and qualities, and this can cause stress. Muslims are expected to treat all people as individuals, and not to try to force their children to be something they are not.

Parents should avoid being over-protective, over-indulgent or too proud of their children. They should not push their children beyond their abilities, or be disappointed with them.

The most important thing a parent can do for a child is to set a good example, so that the child grows up devout, kind, mature, independent and able to help others.

FOR YOUR FOLDERS

▶ *'He who has no compassion for our little ones and does not acknowledge the honour due to our elders, is not one of us.'*
(Hadith)

How did the Prophet think compassion should be shown to (a) one's own children (b) orphans?

▶ In what ways can a Muslim honour the old people in the family?

'Either keep your wife honestly, or put her away from you with kindness. Do not force a woman to stay with you who wishes to leave. The man who does that only injures himself.'

(surah 2:231)

In some societies divorce is forbidden completely, which causes much distress. In others, it is freely available, and there are no checks on its abuse. Neither of these extremes is helpful in solving the problems that go along with divorce. Human beings sometimes choose to ignore, abuse or defy the laws of their societies.

Although Islam upholds the sanctity of marriage and the need for its continuance and permanence, it also recognizes that, human nature being what it is, not every marriage will be successful. Rather than condemn people to a life of misery, Islam makes provision for legal divorce, as a last resort – although it is highly discouraged.

'The most detestable act that God has permitted is divorce.'

(Hadith)

'If a wife fears cruelty or desertion on her husband's part, there is no blame on them if they arrange an amicable settlement between themselves; and such a settlement is the best way.'

(surah 4:128)

Muslims believe that divorce should always be the last resort, after all attempts to put things right have failed. A long series of procedures should have occurred before the pronouncement of a divorce. The fact that Islamic divorce does not involve long formal procedures does not mean that it is taken lightly (although obviously, some people abuse the system).

Divorce by mutual consent

The husband and wife can agree between themselves to terminate the marriage, and work out the financial arrangements to be made.

If the wife has a genuine grievance against her husband, she can obtain a divorce from him by returning his marriage gift to her in return for the dissolution of the marriage. The husband seeking divorce may not *demand* his gifts back, unless he finds his wife guilty of clear immorality. In fact, the necessity for the husband to return the wife's

dowry, and the influence of the extended family in trying to help or sort out difficulties, often discourages any husband who is inclined to divorce his wife casually.

CONDITIONS NECESSARY FOR THE DIVORCE TO BE VALID

- The partners must be sane, conscious and not under pressure from some outside party.
- The divorce must be clear to all.
- The partners must not be under the influence of alcohol or drugs, or so angry they do not appreciate what they are doing.

GROUNDS FOR A WIFE TO DIVORCE HER HUSBAND

- Inability or refusal of her husband to maintain her.
- Abuse or mistreatment.
- Impotence of her husband.
- Incurable, repulsive disease, or insanity of her husband.
- Extended absence, or desertion if the husband has not communicated.
- The husband's imprisonment.
- Deception at the completion of the contract, or concealment of important information concerning the marriage.

The waiting period, or iddah

The laws of Islam require a waiting period or **iddah**, before a divorce becomes final. This is usually three months, although it can be as long as nine months if the woman is pregnant, or as little as 31 days if the husband divorces the wife when he is certain she is not pregnant. During this period, the wife is entitled to continue living at the family home. She is also entitled to full maintenance and to be treated well.

If a reconciliation occurs, there is no need of remarriage if it is during the iddah. If the couple seek remarriage after the expiry of the waiting period, they may remarry, but with a new contract. Such remarriage is allowed a second and third time.

However, when the waiting period is over, the woman has no further claim on her ex-husband. Whatever she has received or been paid in that time is in consideration of the fact that she cannot marry anyone else in that period. It is a time in which both parties are given the chance to think again. In some societies, when the divorce is the fault of the husband, he is required to pay the woman's living expenses for one year.

If a wife has been divorced and remarried to the same husband twice, they are not allowed to remarry a third time until after the woman has been properly married to some other person. Islam does not allow couples to 'cheat' by arranging such a marriage – and a quick divorce – falsely in order to remarry. It is considered good practice for there to be at least one month between divorces.

After the waiting time, no one is allowed to prevent the woman from marrying whoever she chooses – not her ex-husband, nor her father or guardian. In some societies, the woman's family might try to prevent her from remarrying a disappointing husband whom they felt she was well rid of, but this is not allowed in Islamic society.

'Do not prevent them from marrying their former husbands if they agree among themselves in an honourable manner.'

(surah 2:232)

Divorce settlements

It is not the normal practice for Muslim men to pay maintenance to ex-wives for very long periods. A woman is entitled to be provided for by her husband if she is married, or by her father if she is not. After divorce, she can return to her parents' home and revert to her pre-marital status. If she has no parents, her closest male relatives must support her until she remarries, or she can be supported by her adult children. If she has no male relatives, an Islamic government is obliged to give her an allowance. Therefore there is no case for imposing on the ex-husband an obligation for life, which could lead to men trying to evade the law, or women seeking vengeance through heavy financial settlements.

'Some of you may be more eloquent in putting your arguments than others. Let a person reflect that if I award him something to which he has no right, I am only awarding him a piece of fire. He may take it or leave it.'

(Hadith)

Anxieties of Muslim fathers

From Mrs Zarina Choudry

Sir: Angela Lambert's informative article about the abduction of children by the parent denied custody ("Fighting the child-snatchers", 3 January) highlights the enormous differences and problems between Eastern and Western family life.

The reason a Muslim father is generally apprehensive about his child's future in a one-parent family in Great Britain is complex: first, to raise a Muslim child outside the folds of Islam is considered a grave sin. Obviously, a child brought up in Great Britain takes on board British characteristics and behaviour, therefore the father would have the additional burden of knowing that his Anglicised child would lose all contact with its Islamic heritage.

Second, as a child learns from its mother while father is out earning a living all day, how would it learn good manners and etiquette and "togetherness" which is still the norm in Muslim society? As Angela Lambert points out there would be no extended family network to nurture and protect this Muslim/British child during its formative years. It would feel at odds and not know its identity, pulled between two opposing cultures, one leading to excess, the other constraining.

Unfortunately women go into these romantic marriages without thinking through the consequences which so often lead to bitter trials and tribulations. Unless both parties have sound knowledge of Islam as set out in the Holy Koran (which stresses that divorce, although abhorrent, should be amicable for the sake of the children), then these tragic events will continue.

Yours sincerely,
ZARINA CHOUDRY
Islamic Education and
Cultural Society
Hayes, Middlesex
3 January

Custody of children

This is usually the hardest thing about divorce. In Islam, care of the children is the responsibility of the father, who either pays for their upkeep or takes them himself. It is believed that it is easier for a man to find another woman to mother his children than for a woman to find another man who will care for her children adequately. It also frees the woman from the burden of being a single parent.

FOR DISCUSSION

▶ Many Muslims think it is better for couples to stick together 'for better or worse', no matter what is going on. Why do you think so many Muslims are set against divorce?

FOR YOUR FOLDERS

▶ Why do Muslims disapprove of lifelong financial settlements for divorced wives?
▶ Why do Muslims regard children of broken marriages as the responsibility of the father?

'Riches are sweet, and a source of blessing to those who acquire them by the way; but those who seek them out of greed are like people who eat but are never full.'

(Hadith)

'No one eats better food than that which they have earned by their own labours.'

(Hadith)

'Accepting charity is forbidden for the rich and the able-bodied.'

(Hadith)

The importance of work

It is considered very important that a person *does* work, and does not stay idle. Anyone who tries to avoid work for *whatever* reason (unless they are incapable through illness) is disapproved of – even if the purpose is devotion to religion. It is the duty of a Muslim man to earn sufficient money for his own and his family's needs, so that he is not a burden to anyone. Muslims consider it dishonourable to live off other people.

Some mosques support full-time **imams**, but whereas this is accepted, it is not really preferred. In a thriving Muslim community there should be many people able to function as imams, and thus avoid dependance on one person. Any scholar of Islam should be able to contribute their knowledge without being paid.

Muslims have a duty to work

Similarly, it is thought dishonourable for a Muslim to beg, except in cases of extreme necessity. Muslims are expected to safeguard their dignity, develop self-reliance and not have to depend on others unless it is absolutely necessary.

'He who begs without need is like a person holding a burning coal in his hand.'

(Hadith)

'It is better that a person should take a rope and bring a bundle of wood on his back to sell so that Allah may preserve his honour, than that he should beg from people.'

(Hadith)

Times of need

'For a person who suffers calamity and loses his property, it is permissible for him to ask until he is able to stand on his own feet.'

.(Hadith)

Sometimes, inevitably, there do come situations and times of great need. Disasters, national and private, occur. People need help with housing or the business. They cannot be blamed if they are forced to ask for help from the government or from an individual.

Earning any interest on loaned money is totally forbidden by the Qur'an. (See surah 2:278–9; 30:39; 3:130 etc). **Riba**, the Arabic term for usury, means any unjustified advantage in trade dealings, and has therefore a wider meaning than the English term 'interest'. To be honourable, money has to be used as a facility not a commodity in Islam, or the owners of money gain an unfair advantage over the producers or traders. They can wait until the merchandise loses value (for example, fruit will only stay fresh for a limited time) and thereby force the merchant to agree to a lower price. To regulate this, Islam imposes a tax on all money which is not spent or in circulation. Charging interest forces others into debt and dependency. In Islam speculation and exploitation are removed, as providers of funds can only share the profits provided they are also willing to share the losses.

'If a debtor is in difficulty, give time in which to repay. If you could only accept it – it would be far better if you cancelled the debt altogether.'

(surah 2:280)

The dignity of work

The Prophet taught that there is no room in Islam for snobbery. The man who acts as a simple porter has as much dignity as the manager of a great business concern. What counts is his dignity, his honesty, and his attitude to the work he is doing.

Since communities need rubbish collectors just as much as brain surgeons, nobody need regard any useful employment as being beneath them – David was a metalworker, Noah and Jesus were carpenters, Moses was a shepherd and Muhammad was a market trader. Islam gave dignity to many professions which people had previously considered lowly and degrading.

Trading is regarded as acceptable employment, providing it is done honestly, and does not exploit anyone. Muslims are not allowed to hoard substances at times of glut in order to make a big profit in times of shortage.

'He who brings goods for sale is blessed with good fortune, but he who keeps them until the price rises is accursed.'

(Hadith)

Any form of cheating or unfair trading is dishonourable. This includes lying about merchandise or tampering with weights and measures in order to cheat people. An honest broker is to be treasured and commended. The Prophet himself spent much time as an honest merchant, and recommended them highly.

'On the Day of Resurrection Allah will not look at . . . the person who swears to the truth while lying about his merchandise.'

(Hadith)

Collective obligations

Muslims have a duty to develop crafts and industries which are essential and beneficial to the community. Such professions are known as **fard kifiyah**, or collective obligations. Every Muslim community should try to include enough people engaged in essential sciences and industries to meet its needs. These areas include medicine, education, science and technology, politics, community welfare and leadership, and the clothing, utensil and agricultural industries.

If there is a shortage of personnel, the whole community is held at fault, for it has a duty to see to it that the needs of the people are met, and that nobody suffers.

Individual freedom may have to be sacrificed if it interferes with the good of the community – the people as a whole must come before any private interest or individual's profits!

Forbidden work

Muslims are not permitted just to earn money in any way they can. Basically, the Islamic rule is that if someone's means of earning a living hurts another, or results in another's loss, it is **haram**. If it is fair and beneficial, then it is **halal**. Obviously, any form of making wealth that involves dishonesty, bribery, gambling, cheating, fraud, sexual degradation or any other means of making a profit by exploiting others, is forbidden to the Muslim.

Forbidden professions include:
- any form of activity deriving money from prostitution, pornography, indecency
- any form of drama or dance entertainment that is deliberately erotic or suggestive
- drawing, painting or photography that is sexually provocative
- manufacturing intoxicants and drugs, or trading in them
- working in any organization supporting injustice
- working in a bar, liquor shop, nightclub, dance hall, etc.
- being involved in armed forces fighting against Muslims.

'It is not poverty which I fear for you, but that you might begin to desire the world as others before you desired it, and it might destroy you as it destroyed them.'

(Hadith)

FOR YOUR FOLDERS

▶ Explain in your own words the meaning of these terms.
   speculation   commodity
   exploitation   riba
▶ Why are certain trades or professions forbidden to a Muslim? Give examples of forbidden work, and the specific reason why they are forbidden.
▶ How is a Muslim's honour affected by
   (a) unemployment (b) begging
   (c) dishonest marketing?

'You are niggardly at the expense of your own soul.'

(surah 47:38)

'He who eats and drinks while his brother goes hungry, is not one of us.'

(Hadith)

'Taqabbal Allah minna wa minkum.'
'May God accept the work we have done for his sake.'

(Muslim prayer)

Sadaqah and zakah

Muslims are expected to be charitable *all* of the time. Acts of charity that are a matter of personal choice and not of duty are known as **sadaqah**. These acts can be small, individual examples of giving – usually prompted by compassion on hearing of the plight of someone unfortunate. A baker's shop could give away what it had left on a Thursday night, for example, so that no one nearby need say their **Jumah** prayers in a state of hunger. Money could be sent away to a disaster fund.

Muslims are expected to tax their income and wealth as a matter of duty, and to hand over a certain proportion on an annual basis to those who are less fortunate. This is not regarded as a matter of choice, but as a religious duty, and is called **zakah**.

The zakah tax is the equivalent of one fortieth of a Muslim's surplus income, after the people being supported by them have been taken care of. There are different rates for goods, crops, and commodities. The zakah is usually collected and sent off during the fast of Ramadan.

Muslim parents often recite to their children some words of the Prophet to encourage giving:

'Every day two angels come down from Heaven; one of them says "O Allah! Compensate every person who gives in Your name." The other says "O Allah! Destroy every miser!"'

(Hadith)

The feasts

There are only two feasts of Islam – the **Eid-ul-Fitr**, which breaks the month-long fast of **Ramadan**, and the **Eid-ul-Adha** which falls during the time of **Hajj**. Both are seen as occasions on which to thank God for all his blessings by actual physical deeds.

Both feasts involve worship, purity, and thought for others. The whole family of Islam is brought together, to enjoy a time with loved ones and to share this good feeling by remembering all those who are poor or suffering in any way.

The requirements for feast days are simple:
- Cleanliness: baths are taken and clean or new clothes worn.
- Prayer: the whole family of Islam gathers together in huge gatherings, to be as one.
- Thought for one's own family: presents are given, especially to chidren, special meals are served.
- Thought for others: the zakah-collection is sent off for people who are less-fortunate, strangers are welcomed to share hospitality.

It is recommended that on feast days Muslims should go home after the prayers by a different route from the one they took coming, in order to create the largest possible opportunity for meeting other Muslims, and spreading the joy!

Eid-ul-Fitr

Zakah for Eid-ul-Fitr is a special payment of a set amount, the equivalent of two meals. This should be given to the poor on behalf of each member of the family by every Muslim who is financially able to do this. It is traditionally given before the Feast Prayer, so that the poor who receive it may be able to join in the festival. (If given afterwards, it does not count as obligation, but becomes a normal charity.)

Eid-ul-Adha

Eid-ul-Adha involves the sacrifice of an animal for the pilgrims on Hajj, and is a voluntary act for other Muslims round the world. The animal must be healthy and over a year old. Alms equal to the cost of the animal can be given by non-pilgrims.

The animal is dedicated to Allah, then slaughtered by the person best able to do this, as painlessly as possible; then it is divided up and shared. Parts of it may be kept or eaten by the person who paid for the sacrifice, but the larger part of it must be given to the poor. Selling any part of it, or giving any part of it to the butcher who slaughtered it as a form of payment, is forbidden.

Fasting

Fasting, especially during Ramadan, the ninth month of the lunar calendar, is an act of self-discipline and self-sacrifice. It requires a great deal of effort. During this month Muslims must not give in to the urges of the body for food, drink or sex during the hours of daylight, from the moment at early dawn when a black thread can just be distinguished from a white one, to the same moment at nightfall.

Muslim aid

'Those who spend their wealth day and night in secret and in public have their reward with their Lord; on them shall be no fear, nor shall they grieve.'

(surah 2:274)

There are many Islamic enterprises that organize charity on a large scale. The best known are:
Islamic Relief 517 Moseley Rd, Birmingham, B 12 (021 4403114)
This is an international relief organization, which helps needy Muslims in the UK and abroad.
Muslim Aid PO Box 3, London, N7 8LR (071 6004425)
This does similar work to Islamic Relief.
The Red Crescent (the Muslim equivalent of the Red Cross) carries out acts of mercy ranging from medical care on the battlefield to famine relief.
Muslim Relief Fund at the Islamic Cultural Centre, 146, Park Rd, London, NW8 7RG (081 7243363)
Smaller care organizations include:
Muslim Women's Helpline (071 7002509)
An organization which gives an emotional support service to Muslim women who have various problems. (Service available on Tuesday, Thursday and Sunday between 12 noon and 4 pm – Admin No 071 7000320).
Helpline – (081 4271751) offering advice on problems ranging from housing difficulties to racism; an offshoot of the paper *Muslim Voice*.

Appeals recently supported by these organizations have included the Bangladesh cyclone appeal, the Lebanese war victim appeal, the Mozambique famine appeal, the Afghanistan war appeal, the Somalia famine appeal, the Bangladesh flood disaster, the Ethiopia famine appeal, the Kashmir war damage appeal, the Sudanese locust famine appeal and the Iranian earthquake appeal.

The kind of detailed work done is supporting orphans and widows, sponsoring education and health visitors; building medical emergency units; digging wells and erecting water-pumps, and sending food, clothes, multivitamin tablets and medical equipment wherever it is needed.

An appeal for help

FOR YOUR FOLDERS

▶ *'How can you call yourself a believer while your brother goes hungry?'* (Hadith) Explain what you think Muhammad meant by this.
▶ If you were a Muslim, in what ways could you show that you were a believer?
▶ How do the Muslim feasts illustrate the principle of caring for others?
▶ What is the difference between sadaqah and zakah payments?

Jumah Friday midday prayers, usually with a sermon.
Hajj (Annual) pilgrimage to Makkah.
Ramadan Month of ritual daytime fasting.

'It is not permissible for a believer to keep away from another believer for more than three days! After the lapse of this period, he should go and meet him and salute him.'

(Hadith)

It is important in Islam that believers should not be detached from the world, or isolated. Individual salvation should not be sought away from society. Islam discourages its followers to withdraw from the world and live a life of religious seclusion. Rather, it encourages people to mix together, and calls for collective actions and cooperation. Therefore, to a Muslim, friends are extremely important.

Friendship plays a vital role in moulding the individual's personality. So much depends on the wisdom with which one chooses one's friends.

Good friends

'A person is apt to follow the faith of his friend, so be careful with whom you make friends.'

(Hadith)

'Good character melts away mistakes just as water melts away ice. Bad character spoils deeds just as vinegar spoils honey.'

(Hadith)

If friendship is based on love of Allah and commitment to the faith, then it will be blessed. Muslims are warned against friendships with people who may take them from the straight path.

'On that day, the wrong-doer will bite at his hands and say – "O would that I had taken the straight path! Woe is me! Would that I had never taken such a one for a friend! He led me astray!"'

(surah 25:27–30)

Muslims are not expected to mix freely with people who take faith as a joke, or belittle it. When Muslims see evil in a group, and are able to do something about putting it right, then it is their duty to act as best they can. If they cannot help the situation, then it is better for them to withdraw, and keep apart.

'Leave alone those who take their religion to be mere play and amusement, and are deceived by the life of this world; proclaim to them this truth – that every soul delivers itself to ruin by its own acts.'

(surah 6:70)

THE MEASURES WHICH MUSLIMS COMMEND AND PRACTISE TO NOURISH FRIENDSHIP

- Unselfishness, thought for others before self
- Spreading love and goodwill
- Social courtesies and politeness
- Visiting, out of love and concern
- Exchanging gifts
- Repaying kindness with kindness
- Accepting invitations with glad heart
- Avoiding corruption, hypocrisy and egotism

THINGS MUSLIMS ARE TAUGHT TO AVOID

- Belittling or mockery
- Hurting feelings or taunting
- Using disliked nicknames
- Backbiting and spying on friends
- Snobbishness and feelings of superiority
- Attributing evil motives to your friends' actions
- Acts that threaten community, such as drinking, gambling, cheating, etc
- Secret conversations

'Beware of suspicion, for suspicion is a great falsehood. Do not search for faults in each other, nor yearn after that which others possess, nor envy, nor entertain malice or indifference; be servants of Allah!'

(Hadith)

Positive action

Muslims should cooperate to do what is pleasing to Allah and to fulfil their individual roles as trustees on Earth. They *must* take positive steps – just to ignore a situation is no good, and words alone are not enough.

'The messenger of Allah said: If you see an evil action, change it with your hand [i.e. positive action]; or if you are not able to do this, then with your tongue; or if you are not able to do this, then with your heart.'

(Hadith)

REASONS WHY PEOPLE AVOID ACTION

- Fear of losing friends
- Individual fear of being the only one among millions who is taking action against this particular evil, and therefore what possible good can be done?
- Apathy, couldn't care less, someone else's business

If friends do not like their weaknesses and wrongdoings being pointed out to them – then the believer should think about the quality of those friends. Muslims should do whatever lies within their power, simply to please Allah – and leave the results to Allah.

Some criminals gain courage because they see people doing nothing to stop them, and so they think they are going along with their evil actions. Islam does not seek heroes, but it does want the general attitude in society to be that evil must be prevented from taking place.

Unity – the family of Islam

All Muslims belong to the **ummah** – the single 'family' of Islam. Muslims believe that Islam is so natural to human reason that *all* children are in fact born with **fitra** – the yearning to submit to Allah. They are born Muslims, and made into followers of

other faiths by their upbringing in their parents' homes. It is a common experience that when a non-Muslim turns to Islam, there is a very strong feeling that they are *coming home*. Such converts are often called **reverts**.

There is no distinction in Islam between a person who is born into Islam and one who comes to it in later life. Belief belongs to Allah alone – no one can be forced into it, and no one can be prevented from embracing it.

'Allah looks into your heart, and whoever has a pious heart, Allah will have compassion on him – you are all the children of Adam. Most beloved of you in the eyes of Allah is the one who is the most pious.'

(Hadith)

Ummah extends across all places and ethnic groups, and also links people in different historical periods. Each believer feels they are part of a given community, not only in their own time but also of the community extending from the past – all the followers of all the prophets, from Adam onwards!

The unity of believers takes precedence over all other relationships, including those of family. It is a unity of **faith**.

'Believers are like the parts of a building; each part supports the others.'

(Hadith)

'If any single part of the body aches, the whole body feels the effects and rushes to its relief.'

(Hadith)

FOR YOUR FOLDERS

▶ Explain, in your own words, the meaning of these terms.
ummah   fitra
▶ What do Muslims consider to be the most important aspects of a friendship? Do you agree?
▶ 'May Allah have mercy on anyone who gives me my faults as a gift.'
(Saying of Caliph Umar)
How does this saying illustrate the Muslim encouragement to see wrong put right?
▶ Why do Muslims sometimes call new converts to the faith 'reverts'?

'Do you not see that it is Allah whose praises all beings in the heavens and on earth celebrate, and the birds of the air with wings outspread? Each one has its own mode of prayer and praise. Allah knows well all that they do.'

(surah 24:41)

Muslims believe that Allah has handed the planet over to humankind, for them to look after and cherish and protect it. Human beings are to be guardians, responsible for every part of it. They are certainly not to damage, pollute or destroy it. On the Day of Judgement, Muslims expect to be asked questions about their responsibility towards Allah's Earth and the creatures on it, and the natural resources (animal, vegetable and mineral) which Allah has given for them to use and not abuse.

We are the guardians of our planet

'It is He who has made you custodians (khalifas), inheritors of the Earth.'

(surah 6:165)

'It is Allah who has subjected the sea to you . . . and He has subjected to you all that is in the Heavens and the Earth.'

(surah 45:12–13)

The balance

'Allah has lifted the heavens up high, and has set up the Balance.'

(surah 55:7)

That balance is very important. Muslims believe it is the very key to our survival. It used to be quite common for mathematically-minded astronomers to point out that there must be literally millions of planets in space with life on them, perhaps similar to our own. However, despite all the advances in science, there is still no evidence whatsoever of any other rock in space with a living ecology like our own. It is quite possible that we are, in fact, all alone in space – and the little spaceship Earth is a vitally important place.

The Muslim keeps an open mind as to whether or not there are other planets with life on them. What is vital is that our planet *does*, and that we must cherish it.

Responsibility

Muslims believe that Allah has given people free will, and that it is their duty to stop the present suicidal trend of selfish destruction of the Earth's resources. They should also be keenly involved in the battle against those selfish individuals who pollute our world for economic gain.

Muslim scientists have observed that human activity now affects the atmosphere and climate. Notable examples are the increase of the greenhouse effect caused by CFC gases which warm up the planet and destroy the protective ozone-layer, and 'seeding' clouds by dropping chemicals into them to produce rain. They consider that uncontrolled industrialization has been very wasteful with the Earth's resources. They also think that people who do not understand that they are Allah's guardians of the planet do not care about what is taken out of the Earth, how thoughtlessly it is used, and how waste products are disposed of or dumped. Moneymaking companies have disregarded the effect of their actions – as can be seen in the massive applications of herbicides and pesticides, or the polluting of the seas with poisons and chemical wastes.

Harmony in nature

Muslims – especially in such places as Bangladesh or the Sudan – are aware that there is violence in nature, but it is part of a deep balance which maintains all life. Many so-called natural disasters have been created by human beings. For example, famine in the Sudan (formerly a food-exporting country) has been caused by neglecting the ecology and growing too much cotton as a cash-crop to pay back interest on loans; flooding in Bangladesh is made worse by uprooting the forests.

If deliberate disruption is caused to the Earth's natural systems, the consequences are all too clear. Species of living things become extinct, deserts spread, the atmosphere is reduced, and millions are impoverished and suffer starvation.

Muslims regard this planet as a place created out of love, and therefore it should be sustained through love. The Muslim desires to live at peace with nature, and to bring about its wholeness.

How Muslims can be green

Muslims believe they cannot make the excuse that their own little contributions will make no difference to the big companies. They have to take the lead. Manufacturers will not go on producing things that people refuse to buy. There are many ways in which every household can help:
- re-use plastic bags, cartons, containers, etc
- whenever possible, buy recycled products, especially paper
- use bottle banks for returning glass products
- cut down the use of energy, by turning lights off, or washing up by hand instead of by machine
- ride a bike instead of going by car
- buy pine furniture in preference to rarer woods
- when buying furniture, try to make sure that it is made by a responsible company that plants replacement saplings.

'My heart is tuned
to the quietness
that the stillness of Nature inspires.'
(Hazrat Inayat Khan)

Some green hadiths of Prophet Muhammad

'The Earth is green and beautiful, and Allah has appointed you his stewards over it'.

'The whole Earth has been created a place of worship, pure and clean.'

'Whoever plants a tree and diligently looks after it until it matures and bears fruit is rewarded.'

'If a Muslim plants a tree or sows a field and humans and beasts and birds eat from it, all of it is love on his part.'

'O Lord!
I beseech thee for guidance, righteousness, chastity, and self-sufficiency.'
(Prayer of Muhammad)

FOR YOUR FOLDERS

▶ In what ways are Muslims expected to take responsibility for the use, and not misuse, of the planet in everyday life?
▶ What would be the Muslim attitude to a company that was only interested in making profit, and not in safeguarding the planet?
▶ Give reasons why you think Muslims would disapprove of:
  - using aerosols containing CFC gases
  - buying products obtained from the killing of rare or endangered species of animals (e.g. fur, ivory)
  - the unnecessary waste of paper and packaging
  - using products which will not break down and rot naturally
  - using detergents that pollute water supplies
  - not using unleaded petrol

THINGS TO DO

▶ Choose one of the sayings of Muhammad and copy it out carefully, giving it a decorative border. Give three reasons for your choice.

68 ANIMALS

'Once, during a severe famine, a student of religion saw a dog lying on the ground, so weak it could not even move. The student was moved to pity, and immediately sold his books and bought food to give to the dog. That very night, he had a striking dream. "You need not work so hard to acquire religious knowledge, my son. We have bestowed knowledge upon you."'

(Muslim story, *The Muslim Voice*, January 1990)

Islam teaches that mercy and compassion are to be shown to every living creature, for Allah loves everything that he has made. Therefore cruelty to animals is totally forbidden in Islam.

Beasts of burden should never carry or pull loads that are too heavy. They should be allowed to travel slowly in places where there is grass and water, but urged swiftly through barren deserts. Castration of male animals is regarded as cruel and unnatural and is therefore forbidden.

Blood sports

The Prophet forbade any 'sport' which involved making animals fight each other – a common enough practice in his time. By the same principle, modern blood sports such as fox-hunting, badger, bear or dog-baiting, or fights to the death between cockerels, are condemned.

Hunting

Islam teaches that no one should ever hunt just for sport. People may only take the life of animals for food or another useful purpose.

'If someone kills a sparrow for sport, the sparrow will cry out on the Day of Judgement, "O Lord! That person killed me for nothing! He did not kill me for any useful purpose!"'

(Hadith)

'Whoever kills anything bigger than a sparrow without a just cause, Allah will hold him accountable for it. The listeners asked, "O Messenger of Allah, what is a just cause?" He replied, "That he kill it to eat, not simply to chop off its head and then throw it away."'

(Hadith)

Where an animal or bird, such as a hawk, is a natural predator, it cannot be blamed for doing what comes naturally to it, since Allah has created the instinct in it – but deliberate cruelty is never to be encouraged. All hunting should be for food, and any animal used for hunting should be well trained, always kept under control, and not clumsy or savage.

If a weapon is used when hunting an animal it should be of a type that would pierce the animal, such as a spear, sword or bullet. Weapons which are used to club or throttle animals are forbidden. Clubbing a wounded animal or throwing stones at it is totally forbidden. The idea of people clubbing baby seals in order to get their fur for luxury garments is disgusting to a Muslim.

'O you who believe! Do not kill game while you are in the state of ihram.'

(surah 5:2, 5:98)

Killing for luxury goods is forbidden

When Muslims are in a state of **ihram** or purity for religious reasons, for example when on hajj, they experience total peace and serenity, and all living things, including animals, birds and insects, are safe in their presence. If a chicken appeared right in front of Muslims at such a time, they would be forbidden to harm it.

Branding

When domestic animals are branded, to show ownership, it obviously causes pain. Muhammad forebade the branding of any part of their body except the hindquarters.

'Do not brand any animal except on the part of its body furthest from its face.'

(Hadith)

140

The prophet's kindness

There are many stories which tell of the Prophet's kindness to animals. A famous one involves a cat that had given birth to kittens, on his cloak. Rather than disturb them, Muhammad took a knife and cut round them, leaving them a generous part of his cloak as their blanket.

A famous hadith told of a prostitute who found a dog (both are usually regarded as despised creatures) gasping with thirst. She took off her shoe and filled it repeatedly with water from a well, and offered it to the dog, until it had recovered. The Prophet commented that for such an act, Allah would certainly forgive her sins.

Similarly, he said that a man who had shut up his cat without food would not escape punishment for it in the life after death.

Animal experiments and vivisection

It is common, in the world today, for all sorts of experiment to be tried out on animals, for a variety of reasons. Some of these are genuinely beneficial to humanity, and bring about progress in medicine and medical welfare. Others are for cosmetic purposes, or involve testing reactions to various substances, even to cigarettes.

According to the Islam principle of compassion and kindness towards all Allah's creations, any experiment simply for the development of luxury goods is totally forbidden. Muslims should always find out if the things they buy have been produced using **halal** methods, without inflicting cruelty on any other living thing.

In the field of medical progress, if there were no possible alternative to an experiment on an animal, then Muslims might accept it. However, they would far prefer to look for some other method of investigation. Experiments on animals should never be attempted lightly, or without very good reason.

Halal slaughter

Muslims may not eat any sort of meat unless it has been killed in the quickest and most painless manner, and with prayer in the name of Allah. There is a growing trend towards vegetarianism for Muslims. Muslims do not agree with the methods of slaughter common in the West, in which animals are stunned electrically. They maintain that to cut the animal's throat, with a very sharp knife, is the

least painful method. If no knife is available, a sharp rock, piece of wood or reed can be used instead. The actual slaughtering is done by either cutting the animal's throat or by piercing the hollow of its throat. The best way is to cut through the windpipe, the gullet and the two jugular veins.

Every Muslim male has to know how to kill an animal. He should be prepared to take this responsibility upon himself if he is prepared to eat meat. Muslims regard people who simply buy meat from unknown sources, and who do not know how or where it was killed, as being irresponsible.

When Muslims kill an animal, they have to observe certain rules. The knife that will kill the beast is never to be sharpened in front of it. The animal is to go to its death in a calm atmosphere, well fed and watered, not suspecting what is about to happen – and certainly not in an atmosphere of torture and terror. It is forbidden to deny food or drink to an animal on the grounds that it is just about to be killed. Islam prohibits the slaughter of one animal in front of another, for the same reason. Animals should be killed quickly, while a prayer is being said.

'Ibn Abbas once reported that the Prophet saw a man who was sharpening his knife after laying down a sheep to be slaughtered. He rebuked him saying, "Do you intend to make it die two deaths?"'
(Hadith)

Animals in confinement

Some animals are kept in appalling conditions – for example, in factory-farms or in zoos. It is against the spirit of Islam to keep any animal tied up, in dirty conditions, or confined in a small space, just for convenience. Muslims believe that people who treat animals and birds like this will be answerable for their actions on the Day of Judgement.

FOR YOUR FOLDERS

▶ What are the rules governing halal slaughter?
▶ Why do you think Muslims are so against (a) factory farming (b) the practice in UK and other western slaughterhouses?
▶ Why are Muslims sometimes in conflict with the fashion industry?

'Intoxicants are the key to all evils. A man was brought and asked either to tear the Holy Qur'an, or kill a child, or bow in worship to an idol, or drink a cup, or sleep with a woman. He thought the less sinful thing was to drink the cup, so he drank it. Then he slept with the woman, killed the child, tore the Holy Qur'an and bowed in worship of the idol.'

(A story of Othman ben Affan)

Alcohol is strictly forbidden to the Muslim. This applies not only to wine – which existed at the time of Muhammad – but to any form of alcoholic liquor. There is one major reason for this. Alcohol causes people to lose control over their own minds and bodies.

The word **khamr** means *intoxicant* or *poison*, and is used for any alcohol. It was defined by the Caliph Umar as 'that which befogs the mind.'

The problem

'O believers! Intoxicants, gambling, and trying to foretell the future are the lures of Shaytan; if you wish to prosper, you must keep away from these things. It is Shaytan's plan to stir up enmity and hatred in your midst with them, and lure you away from remembering Allah, and from prayer.'

(surah 5:93–94)

Muslims believe that **Shaytan**, or the **Devil** uses all sorts of devious tricks to combat belief in Allah, and alcohol is one of his greatest successes. It is a powerfully addictive drug. Even when people know perfectly well what the harmful results can be, most of them still carry on drinking until disaster strikes. It is even sometimes used as a 'medicine' given to someone who is upset, shocked, bereaved, hurt or in distress. The media often present taking alcohol as a pleasant social habit – the expression of hospitality.

Disastrous effects of alcohol

Muslims are against alcohol for many reasons. Firstly, it is forbidden in the Qur'an. Also, it damages people by harming their minds, it harms their general health, affects their ability to work, and can lead to mental breakdown, despair, suicide, and bankruptcy. It can damage family life by causing harmful behaviour such as neglect and cruelty, and this can bring shame and dishonour on partners or parents. It can damage other people by causing accidents. Innocent people may be hurt, immoral behaviour may be encouraged and hospital beds may be filled unnecessarily.

Islamic prohibition

At the time of the Prophet, many people drank a great deal of alcohol. It was perhaps even more widespread than it is today! The teaching of Allah in the Qur'an took human weakness into account, and the prohibition of alcohol was given gently, in stages.

Allah points out that both nourishing and harmful products could come from the same plants – the date and the vine. People should start by thinking about this.

'And from the fruit of the date-palm and the vine you can derive wholesome drink and food. Behold, there is a sign in this for the wise.'

(surah 16:67)

Another verse points out that the harm caused by alcohol by far outweighs its pleasant effects, but people were still left to form their own judgement.

'When they ask you concerning wine and gambling, say, "In them is great sin and some profit; but the sin is greater than the profit."'

(surah 2:219)

There is also the request that Muslims should not have their minds intoxicated when they come to prayer.

'O you who believe! Do not come to prayer with a befogged mind, but come when you can fully understand all that you are saying.'

(surah 4:43)

Since prayers were said five times during the day, this would mean that those praying were already virtually willing to give it up! Finally came the complete prohibition (surah 5:93–94) given above.

As the news of this latest revelation spread through Madinah, the effect was dramatic. People poured away the drinks in their hands, and smashed their wine containers, pouring the liquid out on to the sand. No truly believing Muslim has ever touched alcohol since, a period of some 1400 years.

Alcohol used in medicine

'Alcohol is not a medicine but a disease.'   (Hadith)

The only time a Muslim would be allowed to take medicine which contained alcohol would be if there was no alternative medication available. Since the principle of Shariah is always to promote welfare, in the conditions described, it would be allowed.

Keeping a barrier

True Muslims will keep a barrier between themselves and any contact with alcohol. They regard even being in the presence of alcohol to be a danger. Some Muslims are now beginning to compromise when they live in communities that accept alcohol. They will sit in pubs, or mix socially in houses where people are drinking, even though they themselves will have a fruit juice.

People who offer a drink to a Muslim may not realize that it is forbidden for them even to:
- trade in alcohol
- own or work in a place which sells it
- sell grapes to someone who they know will make wine with them
- give alcohol as a gift, even to a non-Muslim, on the principle that they should not give or receive anything that is not pure.

Respect

Sometimes, when Muslims mix with people who do drink alcohol, a conversation might start up about religion, or about the Qur'an. This may be out of interest, or simply to be polite. No Muslim should discuss the things of Allah in the presence of alcohol. Muslims should be aware of evil, and try deliberately to eradicate it. If this is not possible, then they should leave the place and stay away.

HADITHS CONCERNING ALCOHOL

'Allah has cursed khamr, those who produce it, those for whom it is produced, those who drink it, those who serve it, those who carry it, those it is carried to, those who sell it and those who buy it.'
(Hadith)

'If someone stockpiles grapes during harvest time in order to sell them to a Jew or Christian or anyone else who produces khamr, he will be leaping into the Fire with his eyes open.'
(Hadith)

A CAUTIONARY TALE

There is one story about a Caliph ordering the flogging of people who were not themselves drinking alcohol, but just sitting with people who were. These included a religious person who was fasting – actually going without food and drink. The Caliph ordered this man to be flogged first – because he was the one who should have known better!

'If you sit with them, you will be like them.'
(surah 4:140)

The penalty for drinking

There is no penalty for drinking alcohol laid down in the Qur'an, but in Islamic countries where alcohol is totally forbidden it could be punished by flogging – an immediate physical and psychological pain that makes the wrongdoer think twice. This is not regarded as excessive cruelty, but as an example and warning to others, and is intended to deter the damage caused by drunkards. Wrongdoers are not imprisoned, but may return immediately to their work, their household and their living.

FOR YOUR FOLDERS

- *'Every intoxicant is khamr, and every khamr is haram.'* (Hadith) What is meant by 'khamr' and 'haram'?
- Why do Muslims consider that TV programmes which present alcohol as a harmless social convention are dangerous and immoral?
- Muslims know that it is hard to give up harmful habits. Why do they think people should be made to realize the serious consequences of their habits?
- Why do Muslims think it is wrong for people to 'drink themselves to death'? What other people, besides the drinkers, are affected by their habit? Why do Muslims feel they have the right to try to stop them drinking?
- What is meant by the barrier against alcohol, in Islam? How might this barrier affect a Muslim in the UK?

Drugs

Drugs such as marijuana (hashish), cocaine, opium and nicotine are powerful intoxicants which affect the human mind, and are therefore also khamr.

'Sinful people smoke hashish because they find it produces rapture and delight, an effect similar to drunkenness . . . it produces dullness and lethargy . . . it disturbs the mind and temperament, excites sexual desire, and leads to shameless promiscuity.'

(Sheikh Ibn Taymiyyah)

Drugs are often used by people as a means of avoiding the pains and distresses of their lives. They can escape to an exciting world of fantasy and bring on a 'high', a feeling of well-being and euphoria. The problem is that 'fantasy' experiences may be dangerous, and the good feelings are artificial, not real. All these things are against the spirit of Islam.

It is well known that using drugs has bad physical, mental and moral consequences. Muslims point out that they:

● impair the user's reasoning and decision-making abilities, and lead to irresponsible behaviour
● cause physical decline and lethargy
● affect the nerves
● cause a lowering of the user's general health, as the state of the body becomes less important
● cause moral insensitivity, less concern for others and increasing concern for personal satisfaction
● weaken will-power
● cause the user to neglect the family, and have gradually less desire to please them or look after them
● cause the user to neglect responsibilities
● lead the user into crime to pay for the drugs.

The general principle against drug use is based on the acceptance that Muslims are not the owners of their own bodies, but Allah is. Any substances which are harmful or injurious to the body, or might even cause death, are haram.

The penalty for taking drugs in an Islamic country where they are forbidden is the same as for taking alcohol, a flogging.

KEY IDEA

Becoming dependent on drugs is a downward spiral, often leading to the gutter, and death.

Making drugs legal

'Do not be cast into ruin by your own hands.'

(surah 2:195)

'Do not harm yourselves or others.'

(Hadith)

Nowadays there are frequently attempts to make drug-taking legal, in the hope that this will reduce the black market value of the drug. This would force big drug dealers out of business because they would no longer make an enormous profit. However, Muslims believe that more and more people would become addicted, thus giving the dealers an ever growing market. It would certainly put a bigger burden on society, because of the greater need for rehabilitation centres, increase in crime and family break-ups, and so on.

FOR YOUR FOLDERS

▶ Some drug-takers argue that they are not harming anyone else. What they do is their own business. Do you agree? How far do you think a Muslim would agree with this opinion?
▶ A Muslim might argue that the effects of drug-taking are against the spirit of Islam. How would they justify this?

An unpleasant habit

Smoking

Although there is no mention of smoking in the Qur'an (which was given before the discovery of tobacco), if Islamic principles are applied, the use of tobacco should also be haram.

Until quite recently, tobacco advertisements implied that smoking helped concentration and creativity. The image they set was that an 'elegant' cigarette was a mark of sophistication, or that smoking was a 'manly' social activity. The truth is that if people are hooked on tobacco, they begin to lose concentration and suffer as their need for the drug builds up. *Then* a smoke calms them down. It should be obvious that this dependence is harmful. Muslims believe that people should give up smoking if at all possible, and allow their bodies to be restored to health.

Rules of behaviour

If Muslims do smoke, they should observe certain rules of behaviour in order not to give offence to others.

- It is not acceptable for Muslims to force people who do not wish to smoke to share their tobacco fumes. It is dangerous to their health, and Muslims have no right to harm others.
- It is not polite for Muslims to smoke in the company of non-smokers, who do not wish to suffer the unpleasant smell of stale smoke on their clothes, etc.
- It is not polite for Muslims to smoke in the houses or rooms of non-smokers. Smoking makes rooms and furniture smell, and discolours the environment. It is most impolite to cause this damage and discomfort to those who do not smoke themselves.
- Smoking in any public place where there are young people is not encouraged. It might induce someone to think it was 'grown up', and copy the habit.
- It is wrong for a Muslim to encourage any person to start smoking.
- It is wrong for a Muslim to tempt back to smoking any person who has given it up. Especial care should be taken not to smoke in the presence of a friend who is struggling with withdrawal symptoms.

KEY IDEA – A FACT TO REMEMBER

The tobacco industry needs to hook around 300 new smokers every day in each country – to make up for the 300 or so customers who die every day from its harmful effects!

THINGS TO DO

▶ Cut out a few pictures illustrating people smoking. If possible get pictures used for advertisements, and also photographs of smokers in genuine situations. How does the reality of the second group of pictures compare with the glossy view presented by the advertisements?

FOR YOUR FOLDERS

▶ How would Muslims find advertisements for smoking completely deceptive and immoral? Why does the tobacco industry need to create more smokers?

▶ Is there any reason why non-smokers should have to 'pay' for the smokers? What is the attitude of Muslim smokers to non-smokers?

▶ In some countries where tobacco is grown, the local people go hungry while the landlords grow rich on this export crop. What do you think Muslim opinion would be on this practice?

▶ Muslims think it is vital that human beings are trained in discipline and self-control from an early age. What is a Muslim's duty towards the care of (a) their own body (b) the bodies of other people?

▶ Muslims believe in human freedom. How might a Muslim try to help someone who had become a slave to drugs? (Think of the possible causes of addiction in these people.)

145

In the service of Allah

'O Lord! I seek Thy protection against creeping sloth and cowardice and miserliness, and I seek Thy protection from oppressive debt and the tyranny of people.'

(Prayer of Muhammad)

Jihad, or 'striving', applies to any sort of activity made by a person because of love of Allah. The word comes from **juhd** which means *effort*, and the verb **jahida** means to be tired as a result of making an effort.

For most Muslims, the concept is purely a personal one, and refers to the deliberate effort made by each of them to serve Allah to the best of their ability, by a life of devotion, self-sacrifice, and love and compassion for others.

The great jihad

The Prophet pointed out that the **great jihad** was against one's own personal desires, which so often were selfish and conflicted with the wishes of Allah. It is jihad:

- Whenever a Muslim is called upon to make an extra effort – for example, to get up before dawn in order to pray.
- When a Muslim tries to love and forgive someone who has hurt them or insulted them.

- When a Muslim does not cling to personal possessions, but gives them up in the service of others.

Military jihad

'The Prophet was asked about people fighting because they are brave, or in honour of a certain loyalty, or to show off: which of them fights for the cause of Allah? He replied, "The person who struggles so that Allah's word is supreme is the one serving Allah's cause."'

(Hadith)

The word jihad is often used in speaking about a military situation, when Muslims are called upon to fight for the honour or preservation of their faith. **Harb al-Muqadis**, or Holy War, is the logical extension of fighting for their rights. Jihad does not mean forcing other people to accept Islamic beliefs, but striving to bring about a society in which Muslims are free to obey Allah's laws, leaving others free to worship or not as they wish.

Usually, when people feel oppressed, or are aware that tyranny is spoiling the life of a community, they hope that if they point out the injustices, then the consciences of the rulers will cause them to put things right.

Sometimes, however, this is not the case, and it becomes necessary to make a decision about what to do next. If a conquering force is poised to overrun a community, what should that community do? Sit back and accept it? Or resist in every way possible?

Democracy is government or rule acceptable to the majority. This is a basic principle of Islam, and when a country is ruled fairly by democratic principles, everything usually goes peacefully and well. Once an individual – or group of individuals – begins to have unacceptable authority over the rest, or once the government tries to impose rules that are unacceptable to the will of Allah, they should be resisted – at first by reason, and in the end by force if necessary. A Muslim who strives in such a way is called a **mujahid** (plural **mujahideen**).

Justifiable war

Can war ever be justified? Muslims believe that it can, in certain circumstances:

- in self-defence
- in defence of family, tribe, or country
- to fight oppression
- to put right injustice.

'If anyone walks with an oppressor to strengthen him, knowing that he is an oppressor – he has gone forth from Islam.' (Hadith)

'The most excellent jihad is to speak the truth in the face of a tyrannical ruler.' (Hadith)

Peace

One of the basic aims of Islam is to bring about peace. However, in order for peace to be genuine, there *must* be absence of oppression and injustice. The kind of peace where the weak are simply putting up with things because they are afraid or unable to tackle the strong is not recognized as peace in Islam.

The Muslim warrior is honoured as the protector of the faith and the community's rights, who has to suffer pain and discomfort and self-sacrifice in order to protect what he loves.

Humane treatment of enemies

Fighting in a jihad is to be prolonged only so long as the tyrant continues to oppose. Once the enemy is defeated, the principle of mercy is to be applied instantly, and all hostilities should cease. The enemy should never be executed vindictively after their capitulation.

Wounded enemy soldiers are to be given exactly the same treatment as wounded members of one's own forces. The women and children of the enemy should never be molested or harmed. It would be a gross sin for a Muslim soldier to rape the women of the defeated enemy.

'Hate your enemy mildly; he may become your friend one day.' (Hadith)

Martyrs

Any person who is literally martyred in the cause of serving Allah is called **shahid**. Martyrdom for Allah is not the same thing as nationalism. Someone can lay down their life for their country without being religious at all – and this is *not* shahid. Sometimes it is very difficult to distinguish between the two forms of sacrifice – it depends on the principles involved.

For the true martyr for Allah, Muslims believe that the sacrifice of their life will earn them forgiveness for any wrongs they committed during their lifetimes, and they will go straight to Paradise.

RULES OF JIHAD

There are very strict rules for fighting a jihad.
- It must be started and organized by a religious leader, not just by any politician.
- It must be for a recognizably just cause, in the name of Allah, and according to the will of Allah.
- It must be to bring about good and not evil.
- It must always be as a last resort, after every other means for settling the problem has been tried and has failed.
- It should never be fought out of aggression, or desire to gain territory.
- Killing is not to be indiscriminate.
- Innocent people should not be made to suffer.
- Trees, crops and animals should be protected.

Obviously, under these conditions, mass destructions such as would take place in nuclear war would never be called jihad, and are totally forbidden in Islam.

FOR YOUR FOLDERS

▶ Explain in your own words the meaning of these terms.
jihad   Holy War   mujahid   shahid   martyr   nationalism
▶ What is the true meaning of jihad? Give some examples of things that are jihad in the everyday life of a Muslim.
▶ *'Whoever proclaims the cause of Nationalism is not one of us; and whoever fights the cause of partisanship is not one of us; and whoever dies in the cause of nationalism is not one of us. Nationalism means helping your people in unjust causes.'* (Hadith)
Why do you think Muhammad was so against nationalism?
▶ What are the rules that govern a military jihad?
▶ Why could the use of nuclear weapons never be justified as jihad?

Justice

'Goodness and evil cannot be equal. Repay evil with what is better, then the person who was your enemy will become your intimate friend.'

(surah 41:34)

Muslims believe in strict justice, carried out according to the principles of honour, tempered with mercy. If someone has been wronged, then it is the duty of all Muslims to unite to put the wrong right. If they ignore the wrong done, they are themselves in the wrong, and have submitted to a tyrant. It is not considered right just to let it go, and ignore it.

If someone does wrong to themselves in private, then it is between them and their Creator. He may punish or he may forgive. If they do wrong publicly, upkeeping public morals may have to take precedence, so if Muslims admit to some wrong (even if it is done only to themselves), or boast of it, punishment may follow.

If someone has wronged another person, *their* demands of justice have to be satisfied first, before the wrongdoer can be forgiven. The wronged person could ask for compensation, or insist on punishment for the wrongdoer. It is accepted that Allah *always* forgives the truly penitent person; gaining forgiveness from another human being is harder!

If some wrong has been done against a Muslim, then it is always considered better in Islam to forgive and be charitable, as long as refusal to take revenge is consistent with honour. The first move should be to reason with the wrongdoer, in the hope that they will stop their offensive action and become a friend.

'The reward for an injury is an equal injury back; but if a person forgives instead, and is reconciled, that will earn reward from Allah.'

(surah 42:40)

'If the enemy starts leaning towards peace, then you also start leaning towards peace.'

(surah 8:61)

No one is above the law, or unprotected by it

No citizen should ever be above the law, no matter how powerful, or beneath the protection of the law, no matter how humble. No one should ever be forced to act against the dictates of their own consciences. (See also page 117.)

No human being should ever be imprisoned unless they have been properly convicted of a crime by an unbiased court of law. No person should ever be threatened or punished or imprisoned because of the fault of others, or in order to intimidate others.

Public justice

Muslim justice should always be carried out publicly. This is not done for the sake of barbarity, or to please a blood-thirsty audience, but because it is important:
- that justice is seen to be done,
- that judges should not have the opportunity for corruption and brutality behind the scenes.

Muslims cannot approve of trials and punishments being carried out in secret, with the possibility of inhumane treatment and torture.

Final judgement before Allah

'No bearer of burdens shall be made to bear the burden of another.'

(surah 6:164)

'Let them bear, on the Day of Judgement, their own burden in full – and also something of the burdens of those without knowledge whom they misled!'

(surah 16:25)

Every Muslim believes that human judgements can be wrong, or influenced by bias or ignorance of circumstances – but Allah sees and hears everything, and no person can escape his true judgement on their life. On that Day, no one will be able to make excuses for another – all will stand alone, as individuals.

Crime and punishment

Three things are regarded as being particularly dishonourable in Islam – **theft**, **sexual permissiveness** and crimes associated with **drunkenness or drug-addiction**.

There are strict limits for penalties laid down in Islamic law. In some countries which are supposed to be Muslim some savage punishments are carried out – but these are *not* Islamic and are the culture of the particular country.

Theft

'As to the thief, male or female, cut off their hands: a punishment by way of an example.'

(surah 5:41)

'A woman of a high and noble family was brought to the Prophet accused of theft, and they begged that she be spared the punishment. He said, "I swear by Him who holds my life in His hands, that even if my daughter Fatima had committed this crime, I would have amputated her hand myself."'

(Hadith)

The Qur'an lays down a severe punishment for theft, but it is not true that Muslim countries are full of people who have lost hands! On the contrary, a true Muslim would not even consider committing theft, because of the belief that Allah sees everything. Only a fool would sacrifice nearness to Allah in the afterlife for the sake of a temporary temptation.

Where theft has been committed, the circumstances leading up to it are examined very carefully. If it can be proved that the thief stole out of dire need, because the family or individual was starving, and the state had not been able to fulfil its obligation as regards providing for them, then there would be no question of losing a hand. Hands are only amputated when it can be proved that the person is a persistent thief, and there is no chance of reforming their character. Then and only then is it done in Islam, to act as a deterrent.

"As to the thief, male or female, cut off his or her hand – a punishment from Allah by way of example for their crime. And Allah is exalted in Power, Wise."

An example of Islamic law

Adultery

The theft of someone's wife or husband is regarded as the most serious crime, and a complete betrayal of honour. The punishment laid down in the Qur'an for adultery is 100 lashes – no more and no less – but this is only when the adultery is flagrant and has been witnessed by four people. A person may admit the crime four times, which would count as four witnesses. This practice has been condemned as

being open to possible abuse, in case the person was coerced into confession in private – but this is not in keeping with the spirit of Islam. (See also pages 124 and 125.)

Consumption of alcohol and drugs

As regards alcohol or drugs, there is no fixed penalty laid down in the Qur'an other than the warning about consequences at the Day of Judgement. Many Islamic countries tolerate the private behaviour of non-Muslims, but object strongly when consumption of alcohol becomes public. They do not wish their own society to be corrupted.

Nowadays, anyone caught flagrantly drinking alcohol would probably lose their job and be sent home if they were from a different country. (See also pages 142 and 143.)

Capital punishment

(See page 119.)

FOR YOUR FOLDERS

▶ Muslims are usually peace-loving people. Under what sort of conditions can they be provoked into action?
▶ What is the Qur'anic penalty for theft? Why would a true Muslim never be a thief in any circumstances? What are the only conditions for which a Muslim court should consider cutting off a hand?
▶ Why do Muslims believe in public execution of justice?

FOR DISCUSSION

▶ *'If Allah were to punish people according to what they deserve, He would not leave on the earth a single living being; but He gives them a chance for a certain length of time.'*

(surah 35:45; 16:61)

What does this passage teach us about Allah's attitude to justice and mercy?

*It has been told to you, O man, what is good and
what the Lord requires of you; only to do justice
and love kindness and walk humbly with your God.*

(Micah 6:8)

Imagine you and your class were cast away on a
desert island. As well as needing food and shelter,
you would have to agree on some rules of conduct
so that you could all survive.

You might perhaps start by making it unlawful for
anyone to kill. That much is easy. But deciding what
to do in specific cases might not be so easy. Would
you execute a murderer? Would you regard abortion
as murder? What about euthanasia? How would
you decide these things?

Stop reading for a few moments to think or
discuss how you would set about it.

You might have found it difficult to make
decisions in this activity – and even more difficult to
explain why. Jews would understand this. These
are *moral* questions, and Judaism teaches that
human beings are unable to create their own
morality. People can apply moral guidelines, but
they have to be given them in the first place by God.
For Jews, these guidelines are set down in their holy
book, the **Torah**. They are expressed in the form of
mitzvot, commandments that Jews are expected to
live by.

The role of humankind

'In the beginning, God created the heaven and the earth.'
These are the first words of the Torah. It goes on to
describe how God set the world in order, and
created the first human pair: a man and a woman.
He gave them

*'control over the fish of the sea and the birds of the
sky, over the animals and over the whole earth.'*

(Genesis 1:26)

He also gave them some rules to live by.

With this story, the Torah sets down one of the
most basic beliefs of Judaism – that human beings
are unique in creation because of their ability to
make moral choices; to distinguish between good
and evil, right and wrong. Jews believe that when
people choose to do good, they refine themselves
and come closer to God.

Other Jewish writings explain that 'God desired a
dwelling place among low creatures' (i.e. in this
world). This does not mean that Jews expect God to
appear on Earth in human form, but that they look
forward to a time when everyone will feel God's
presence and know him (see Jeremiah 31:33–34).
Judaism teaches that this will happen after the
coming of the **messiah**, a great leader who will
usher in a new age (see page 184). They believe that
doing good helps to bring the messianic age nearer.

The Seven Commandments

As the Torah's story unfolds, it describes how
people became increasingly wicked, and how God
destroyed them with a great flood.

A certain righteous man called Noah, together
with his family, was chosen by God to survive the
flood and start the human race anew. Noah and his
descendants were to live by the seven rules that
God now wanted people to keep. He commanded
them not to worship anything but himself, not to
blaspheme, murder, steal, commit sexual
misdemeanours, nor be cruel to animals, and to
establish a system of law and order so that people
could live in harmony.

These seven laws became known as the **Noahide
Code** (called after Noah). They are not the sum total
of morality, but rather the minimum requirements
for building a moral and spiritual life. They form the
basic Jewish statement of morality for all
humankind. Jews call them the **sheva mitzvot**, the
Seven Commandments.

The Jewish ideal: all humankind living under God's rule

The 613 commandments

As the generations came and went, people slid back into wickedness. God spoke to another righteous man, Abraham, and told him that if he would live by God's rules, his descendants would be raised to become a great nation. Abraham was the first Jew.

Abraham's descendants became slaves in Egypt. After several generations, God sent a great prophet, Moses, to set them free. Moses led them into the desert and there, around Mount Sinai, the people heard God proclaim his will to them. Moses went up the mountain to speak to God, and brought back two blocks of stone. Cut into them were the **Ten Commandments**:

- *I am the Lord your God, who brought you out of slavery in Egypt.*
- *You must have no other god besides me.*
- *You must not use the name of the Lord your God without reason.*
- *Remember to keep the Sabbath day holy; on it you must not do any work.*
- *Respect your father and your mother.*
- *You must not murder.*
- *You must not commit adultery.*
- *You must not steal.*
- *You must not give false evidence against your neighbour.*
- *You must not desire your neighbour's house, wife nor anything that belongs to him.* (Exodus 20:1–14)

The Torah tells of many other commandments that God told Moses to teach the people. There are 613 altogether, embracing every area of life.

THINGS TO DO

▶ Look at the Ten Commandments carefully. Pick out the ones that deal with behaviour towards people. Jews refer to them as 'mitzvot between one person and another'.

How would you describe the others? Jews regard both types of **mitzvah**, which means *commandment* (singular of mitzvot) as equally important.

There are many other 'mitzvot between one person and another', for example, taking care of the poor and the stranger, telling the truth or paying a worker a fair wage. These, the moral teachings of Judaism, are the ones studied in this book.

What is Jewish morality?

Morality can never be a matter of simply keeping rules. People have to develop inwardly. 'The mitzvot were given to refine people,' says an ancient Jewish teaching. For Jews, living by the commandments is the way to develop a moral sensitivity. Jewish morality can be summed up in five points:

- God created people to serve him.
- Moral behaviour is an essential part of serving God.
- By serving God, people refine themselves and bring holiness into the world.
- People could not have known how to do this, so God gave them commandments.
- Keeping the mitzvot, and making them one's normal standard of behaviour, allows people to develop as moral beings.

Judaism expects all people to serve God and behave morally, but it demands very much more from Jews.

Rabbi   Jewish spiritual teacher or leader.

FOR YOUR FOLDERS

▶ Judaism teaches that people are answerable to God for the way they lead their lives. Is such a belief necessary to ensure that people behave morally? Explain your answer.

▶ What are the similarities between the Seven Commandments (Noahide Code) and the Ten Commandments? What are the differences? To whom do they apply? How might a Jew respond to the view that they are not all relevant to today's world?

▶ Think of three crimes you have read about recently or seen on the news. How far would it have made a difference if people had kept the Noahide Code?

▶ Imagine that you are a rabbi, and that you have just given a talk on Jewish morality. Someone in the audience comments, 'Jews aren't really moral people, they just keep rules.' What would you say?

'You must do according to the instruction which they give you and the judgment which they tell you. Do not turn aside from it.'

(Deuteronomy 17:11)

The ideal and the practical

The Torah sets down the basic ideals Jews are expected to live by. However, the way these ideals are meant to work in practice might not always be clear. For example, the Torah teaches that people should help those in need (Leviticus 25:35–37); never be untruthful (Exodus 23:7); and respect their parents (Exodus 20:12).

But just how are people to balance the time and effort they devote to the poor and needy against the needs of their own families? What does someone say when a terminally ill friend asks, 'Am I going to live?'? How can a child respect a father who gets drunk and holds the family in terror?

These are **moral** questions, and as soon as they are raised people are asking how ideals work *in practice*. This is the central concern of *all* moral thinking. For Jews, trying to live by the Torah's ideals is trying to do God's will in day to day situations. It has always been the task of rabbis and other religious thinkers to provide guidance as to how this might be done.

Priests, prophets and rabbis

The basis of Jewish morality is the Torah. This is sometimes called the **Written Torah**. Jews believe that while Moses was on Mount Sinai (see page 151), God showed him how the Torah was to be interpreted. The guidelines, which were then passed on from teacher to pupil over the centuries, became known as the **Oral Torah**. The Written Torah provided ultimate knowledge of God's will; the Oral Torah provided the means of determining when and how it should apply. Together they made it possible to know God's changeless will, yet continually to apply it to changing conditions.

Originally, it was the **priests**, descendants of Moses' brother Aaron, as well as the **judges**, to whom people turned for moral guidance. The task of teaching morality was also taken up by the **prophets** – outstanding people who were very close to God. The moral guidance they taught was written down, and their books, together with the Torah, became part of the **Tanach**, the Jewish Bible.

By about the 5th century BCE, there were no more prophets, and the priests had ceased to be the main interpreters of the Torah. The teachers who followed were known as **rabbis**. They were wise and pious men who taught people to live in God's way. Unlike the prophets, they never claimed to have heard God speaking to them. Instead, they used their knowledge of the Tanach and Oral Torah, as well as their experience and understanding of human nature, to teach people how the Torah's ideals should be applied to everyday life.

Their teachings were collected into a large work called the **Talmud**. This was written down in about the year 500 CE, though it contains the sayings of rabbis and other wise people over many centuries. The Talmud deals not only with moral issues but with many topics. It was set down as a kind of loose commentary on an earlier work, the **Mishnah**. One part of the Mishnah, the **Ethics of the Fathers**, deals solely with moral guidance. Another important Jewish work, the **Midrash**, is a rich store of stories and parables with moral meanings. Many of these teachings were put in order by an important Jewish philosopher, **Rabbi Moses ben Maimon** (1135–1204), often called **Maimonides**.

Over the centuries, rabbis have continued to teach morality. Some of them wrote their ideas down, others had their teachings preserved by their disciples. These writings have helped successive generations of Jews to live by the Torah's ideals. In the pages that follow we will meet the teachings of some of the more influential of them.

Jewish life

The holy days and other events of Jewish life have immense value in shaping the feelings and attitudes of the people who observe them. For example, during the busy week, it is often not possible for families to spend much time together. For this reason, Jews value the weekly **Sabbath** (Saturday), when they are not permitted to do any work, as an opportunity to devote time to their families (see page 154). The **Passover**, when Jews celebrate their ancestors' release from slavery, is a time for reflecting on freedom; the **Day of Atonement** is an occasion for thinking about forgiveness.

The destruction of the Jerusalem Temple, in the year 70 CE, is still remembered in many Jewish prayers and marked by several fasts throughout the year. The rabbis of the time saw it as a punishment for the unfriendliness that then existed between one

Jew and another. They taught that the time of the messiah (see page 150), when the Temple would be rebuilt, could be brought nearer by acts of love and compassion towards other people.

The destruction also resulted in the **dispersal** of the Jews throughout the world. The rabbis taught that this had come about in order to enable Jews to play their part in the general moral advancement of humanity.

The cycle of festivals and special days provides repeated opportunities to reflect on these and other moral themes.

Jews and morality today

Nowadays, life is changing much more rapidly than in the past. There are new moral issues to face, and it is the task of modern rabbis to guide Jews in applying the teachings of the Torah to the challenges of today. It would be wrong, though, to think that all Jews follow the guidance of the rabbis, or even think the same way or believe the same things. There are various reasons for this. Many Jews live secular lives, upholding some Jewish values while ignoring others.

Different movements

A small proportion of Jews identify with the **Reform** and **Liberal** movements that have grown up since the early years of the last century. Most of their religious leaders teach that God did not give the Torah on Mount Sinai, that Judaism evolved from an early form of tribal religion, and that many of the commandments are not to be regarded as eternally binding.

These movements differ from one another mainly in their readiness to make changes in Judaism. Some of the changes they have introduced are discussed later in this book. The majority of Jews, sometimes called **Orthodox**, do not regard these movements as authentic, as they preach a different understanding of what Judaism is.

Some Jews base their moral standpoints on non-Jewish moral philosophies. A number of Jews today, in particular young people, are returning to traditional values. Others are not interested.

All this means that anyone who questions different Jews about their religion and morality, is likely to find widely differing attitudes. Nonetheless, for Jews who are serious about their Judaism, other sources of moral inspiration are always secondary to the Torah's moral teachings.

THINGS TO DO

▶ Isaiah, Jeremiah, Hosea and Micah are some of the prophets who preached morality. Use an encyclopedia to find out about their teachings.

FOR YOUR FOLDERS

▶ What is (a) the Written Torah (b) the Oral Torah?
How are they related? What might have happened to Judaism had it not had an Oral Torah?

▶ *'Love your neighbour like yourself.'* (Leviticus 19:18) is one of the best known moral statements of the Torah. What do you think it means? Suggest realistic ways in which it might be put into practice.

▶ Why does life change more rapidly today than in the past? Can you think of three contemporary moral issues that could not have been raised 50 years ago?

▶ The following lines come from one of Shakespeare's plays:
'This above all, to thine own self be true; and it must follow as the night the day, thou canst not then be false to any man.'
(*Hamlet*, Act 1, Scene 3)
What does this mean? Explain how Jews might regard it as a source of moral inspiration.

'Honour your father and your mother.'

(Exodus 20:12)

Parents and children

A distraught father once came to Rabbi Israel Baal Shem Tov (1698–1760). 'Rabbi, what shall I do?' the man asked. 'My son is drifting into evil ways.' 'You must love him,' replied the rabbi. 'But Rabbi,' the distressed man continued, 'you don't understand. He lies and cheats. He works on the Sabbath. He even steals.' 'Oh, that's different,' said Rabbi Israel, 'in that case you must love him even more.'

What does this story say about the parent–child relationship? In the past, Jewish families were close-knit. This is largely true today too. Sadly, it is also true that the breakdown of family life in society at large has affected many Jewish homes. There are families where parents and children do not get on with each other.

A Yemenite family celebrate the Passover

However, where Jewish values are central to the life of a family, they often protect them from many of the problems that are experienced elsewhere. The weekly Sabbath, for example, is a special time for families to be together (see page 152). With no one rushing to get to work, the Sabbath meal is eaten in a relaxed atmosphere with traditional songs round the table, and stories about the great men and women of the Jewish past. Other holy days are the same, and Jews often spend them with their families.

TALKING POINT

● Why do relationships between parents and children sometimes break down? Why might this be less common where Jewish values are upheld?

Judaism teaches that parents and children have certain responsibilities towards one another. Parents are expected to feed, clothe and educate their children, and see that they can support themselves. 'Teach your son a trade,' says the Talmud, 'or you teach him to become a robber.'

The Talmud also recommends that parents teach children to swim, i.e. basic survival skills. In today's terms this would include such things as road safety and wariness of accepting lifts from strangers. While much of this is plain common sense, for Jews these things are religious obligations.

For their part, children are expected to take care of their parents, 'See that they eat and drink, and take them where they need to go.' (Talmud). They must treat their parents with respect, and avoid hurting their feelings or causing them even minor irritations.

FOR DISCUSSION

▶ 'How far does respect for parents go?' asked one rabbi in the Talmud. 'Go and learn from a certain heathen called Dama (who was a dealer in precious stones),' replied another. 'On one occasion, some people came to buy a very expensive gem. However, the key to the safe lay under the pillow where his elderly father was sleeping. Dama refused to wake him up, even though it meant losing the sale.' What does this tell you about the importance of respect for parents in Jewish thinking?

Naturally, parents are only human and they sometimes do wrong. Judaism insists that children be as tactful as possible when pointing out their parents' shortcomings. It would be wrong for them to shout at their parents or be sarcastic.

Moral development

Jewish parents are expected to raise their children to be moral people. They are to give moral guidance, and (more important) show a personal example.

THINKING POINT

● A certain rabbi once said, '"Honour your father and your mother" is not only a command to the child, but also to parents. It says to parents, "make yourselves the kind of people your child will want to respect".'
What do you think he meant?

Sometimes it is necessary to punish a child but, says the Talmud, 'Do not threaten a child. Either punish him straight away or let the matter drop.' It reinforces the point by an appalling story of a child who committed suicide because his father threatened to punish him.

COMMENT

'Children understand their parents very well. When they see their parents consistently leading moral lives, and not out simply to satisfy their personal pleasure, they respect them and try to be like them.'
(Rabbi Moses Chaim Luzzato, 1707–1747)

The extended family

In her book about the time she spent with a **Hasidic** (religious) family, Lis Harris, a former editor of *New Yorker* magazine writes:

'. . . Bassy, the youngest, who was nineteen, was with her grandmother. Bassy, a slim, spirited girl who in the secular world would probably be taken for the captain of her field hockey team, had explained to me several hours earlier, as she hastily gathered a few belongings together and headed for the door, that she spent Shabbat (Sabbath) with her widowed grandmother who lived around the corner. "Sometimes she comes
here for Shabbat but sometimes she likes to stay at home, so I help her prepare everything and I stay overnight to keep her company." When I said that most of the girls her age that I knew would not be eager to do that, she looked genuinely surprised.

"But I don't mind at all. It's no problem. You'll see when you meet Bubbe (Grandma). She's great. Actually I've spent every night with her since she had to have one of her fingers removed because of cancer last year. It's really no big deal."

'All the Bubbies' and Zeydes' (grandfathers') places in their families were secure, of course, because though personality conflicts were as common in the Hasidic world as anywhere else, the values of the older and the younger members of the family were the same. There was no generation gap.'

FOR DISCUSSION

▶ Look at the quote from Rabbi Luzzato. Discuss ways in which parents might try to help children grow up to be moral adults.

FOR YOUR FOLDERS

▶ What do the extracts by Lis Harris tell you about the place of the elderly in religious Jewish families?
▶ How do you think the point about the values of the old and young affects family relationships?
▶ Why do you think Jews regard family relationships as important?
▶ A Jewish teenager wants to go out with friends on a Friday night (Sabbath). The parents are very unhappy about this. Write out the conversation that might take place.
▶ If a parent tells a son or daughter to do something which is against the teachings of Judaism, what do you think the child ought to do? Try to give an example and explain the child's dilemma.

'A man shall leave his father and his mother and cleave to his wife, and they shall become one flesh.'

(Genesis 2:24)

The Torah, Talmud and later Jewish writings all stress the importance of marriage. Jews call marriage **kidushin**, which means *sanctification*.

'A man without a wife lives without joy, without blessing and without good,' says the Talmud. Marriage creates a stable environment for raising children. It also provides companionship, and enables people to develop as personalities. Although some Jews do remain single, deliberate celibacy is seen as inconsistent with God's will (see Genesis 2:18, Isaiah 45:18).

Partner selection

The Midrash tells the story of a Roman noblewoman who asked a rabbi what God had been doing since he created the world. 'Arranging marriages,' came the reply. 'What?' exclaimed the woman. 'Even I can do that.'

She lined up a thousand of her male slaves with a thousand of her female slaves, and decided who should marry whom. The next day, they all came to her with complaints. Some were injured. 'I don't want her,' said one. 'I don't want him,' said another.

The lady sent for the rabbi and told him, 'What you said is true. There is no god like your God.'

FOR DISCUSSION

▶ What do you think the story illustrates? What does it tell you about the way Jews think of partner selection?

It is very important for Jews to marry Jewish partners, since only the child of a Jewish mother is recognized as Jewish. A Jewish man does not determine the Jewishness of his child.

Some years ago, leaders of the **Liberal Movement** (see page 153) decided that the child of a Jewish father should be regarded as Jewish, as well as anyone who had been brought up a Jew, regardless of parentage. This has led to some people thinking of themselves as Jewish, even though they cannot be accepted as such by the majority of congregations.

Marriage and personality

'God created the first human being half male, half female. He then separated the two parts to form a man and a woman.'

(Midrash)

Until marriage, people lead their lives as individuals. However, in Jewish thought they are lacking something – single men lack female qualities and single women lack those of the male. A married couple is considered as a complete organism, where the qualities of each contribute to the fulfilment of the whole. In Jewish thought marriage makes it possible for men and women to develop their personalities as complete individuals.

Marriage and sexuality

Judaism considers it wrong for anyone, Jew and non-Jew alike, to have sexual relations outside marriage. However, it attaches no stigma to the children of unmarried parents.

'The mating of animals is a temporary and purely physical act. Through the sanctification of marriage, a husband and wife become the closest of relatives.'

(Maimonides)

Within Jewish marriage, sexual behaviour is regulated by the Torah's code of conduct, called **family purity**. Each month, during the wife's menstrual period, and for a complete week afterwards, all physical contact between husband and wife ceases. Sexual relations only resume after the wife has visited the **mikveh**, a special pool where she immerses her entire body in water.

Jewish couples who observe family purity find that this actually enhances their relationship. It is like stepping back into their engagement period, when they expressed their love for each other in non-physical ways. This can sometimes be a time of great closeness. Where family purity is observed, couples are less likely to become bored with one another.

Inside the mikveh. Building a Mikveh takes precedence over building a synagogue. Can you suggest a reason why?

'A wife returning from the mikveh is as fresh to her husband as on their wedding day.'

(Talmud)

It also ensures that a wife is seen as a person, not as a sexual object. Today, an increasing number of Jews are re-discovering this mitzvah.

Divorce

Where a relationship has completely broken down, Judaism puts no obstacles in the way of divorce. No grounds are required; a mutual decision to terminate the marriage is sufficient.

A civil divorce has no standing in Jewish law. A Jewish marriage can only be terminated by a Jewish divorce. This consists of a scribe writing out a divorce document, called a **get**, and the husband handing the get to his wife in a **rabbinical court**.

A Jewish couple who divorce in the civil court but do not have a get are still married in Jewish law. If they take new partners they will be committing adultery, creating serious problems for any children who might be born.

If husband and wife do not wish to face each other in the court, or if they live in different places,

each may send a representative – he to give the get, she to receive it.

The get must be given of the husband's own free will, and the wife must receive it in the same way. No one can be compelled to divorce against their will.

'The Torah lists the forbidden sexual relationships, and then says "You shall be Holy" (Leviticus 19:2). This tells you that even in a permitted relationship you must sanctify yourself.'

(Rabbi Moses ben Nachman, 1194–1270)

Judaism has always taken a very natural view of sexuality. The Talmud discusses sexual matters with amazing frankness. At the same time, however, it treats them in an atmosphere of **modesty**.

Modesty is not the same as a negative attitude to sexuality. Judaism teaches that sexuality plays an important role in human relationships. However, it also recognizes that the sexual urge can generate very powerful emotions, and that for this reason sexual behaviour must be carefully regulated.

Acceptable sexual behaviour

(*Read this section together with pages 156–7.*)

In Jewish thinking, sexual behaviour is only acceptable within marriage – a stable relationship between one man and one woman. Although sexual intercourse serves to bring children into the world, Judaism recognizes that this is not its only purpose. It is also a way in which two people who are committed to sharing their lives can express their love for one another. For this reason it is considered natural and purposeful even beyond the age of childbearing.

Forbidden sexual behaviour

The Torah strictly forbids **adultery** (a sexual relationship with someone else's husband or wife) and **incest**. Incestuous relationships are those between brother and sister, father and daughter, mother and son, and other people related by family or marriage (see Leviticus 18:6–23).

Among the sexual relationships the Torah forbids is that between one man and another.

'You shall not lie down with a man in the same way that you would lie down with a woman; it is an abomination.'

(Leviticus 18:22)

Lesbianism is not mentioned in the Torah, though the Talmud refers to it with disapproval.

In recent years, homosexual pressure groups have campaigned to make their sexual preferences acceptable to people. Whereas some spokespeople of the Reform and Liberal Movements (see page 153) have accepted their views, the Orthodox have remained unconvinced by their attempts to redefine sexual normality. Gay men and women often put forward the belief that homosexuals are by nature different, and cannot be other than what they are. No one has yet produced satisfactory *evidence* to support this. There is, however, strong medical opinion that people *develop* homosexual tendencies for a variety of reasons, and that nearly all of those who have can, if they wish, be helped by regular psychotherapy.

In Jewish thinking, a man feeling attracted towards another man is no different from him being attracted to someone else's wife. In both cases, allowing his attraction to lead to a sexual relationship is a **sin**. However, Judaism does not permit men or women with homosexual leanings to be persecuted or discriminated against.

Judaism also forbids prostitution – either becoming one or using the services of one. Prostitutes have always been regarded with disdain. Nonetheless, Jews can feel profound sympathy for a man or woman driven to prostitution through poverty, and would want to bring them back to what they see as a respectable way of living.

Contraception

The Jewish holy writings teach that when

'God formed the world . . . He created it not to remain empty; He made it to be populated'.

(Isaiah 45:18)

This is because of his desire that there should be people who will fulfil his will and bring holiness into the world (see page 150). Judaism sees contraception as impeding God's will.

On the other hand, Judaism regards preserving life as being of prime importance. Where it might be hazardous for a woman to become pregnant, the rabbis insist that contraceptives should be used. The same holds true where pregnancy might put a woman under such psychological strain that she becomes a danger to herself. Using contraception for the sake of convenience, for example, where a couple want to finish paying off their furniture before having children, is not acceptable in Jewish teaching.

Where contraceptives are used, it is normally only the woman who is permitted to use them. The rabbis felt it important that intercourse be as natural as possible.

Abortion

In Jewish thinking, abortion is more objectionable than contraception. It not only impedes God's will; it actually destroys potential life. The destruction of a viable foetus is sometimes regarded as murder, and is forbidden for Jews and non-Jews alike.

At the same time, Judaism does not give the foetus, which is only potential life, the same importance as the mother, who is actually alive. Abortion is therefore acceptable if a pregnancy becomes hazardous for the mother (or might become so), or if she is likely to be severely psychologically affected. Some rabbis permit abortion where a child is likely to be so retarded that it would never function as a human being.

Judaism could *never* agree with terminating a pregnancy because it got in the way of holiday arrangements or might disrupt a woman's career.

FOR YOUR FOLDERS

▶ *'A woman has the right to do what she wants with her own body.'*

How might Jews respond? Explain your answer.

Infertility

Due to the great importance Jews attach to raising a family (see pages 154–5), the rabbis have explored every means of helping infertile couples. They have permitted **artificial insemination by husband** (*never by donor*), though with strict safeguards, to ensure that only the husband's semen is being used. Some even permit masturbation (which is otherwise strongly disapproved of), where no other method is available for obtaining semen for sperm counts or insemination procedures.

In vitro fertilization (fertilizing an ovum in the laboratory and implanting it in a woman's womb) is still very new. Some rabbis have welcomed the procedure, though they insist that it should be governed by the same safeguards as for genetic engineering (see page 161). However, *none* agrees with implanting a woman's fertilized ovum in another woman's womb (**surrogate motherhood**).

Paying a woman a fee to 'lease' her womb could lead to all sorts of abuses. Women could have children without the 'inconvenience' of being pregnant. Others could turn pregnancy into a profitable business, and know that they will not be tied down with a child afterwards. The possible psychological stresses on *both* women are completely unpredictable. The rabbis see all this as destroying the sanctity of marriage and childbirth.

Many rabbis also regard it as morally wrong to freeze a husband's semen for use after his death, as this deliberately brings orphans into the world. This could only be sanctioned when a man is undergoing some treatment (e.g. for cancer) that might destroy his sperm, and he expects to be alive to raise his child.

Equally important is the spiritual help and moral boost that religious leaders have given in this area. Priests, prophets and rabbis have always given their blessings to childless couples (see 2 Kings 4:14–16). Today's rabbis often encourage couples to continue seeking medical help, even though they themselves have felt like giving up.

THINGS TO DO

▶ The advertising industry often uses sexual imagery as a means of selling products. Find some examples in newspapers and magazines. Do you think using sexuality in this way is consistent with Jewish teaching? Explain why.

▶ According to British law, doctors can make contraceptives available to girls under the legal age of consent without having to inform the girls' parents. Write a letter from a Jewish mother to her doctor, giving her views on the subject.

'Keeping the body fit and healthy is part of serving God, for it is impossible to know and understand anything of the Creator's will if one is ill. Therefore a person should avoid whatever undermines bodily health.'

(Maimonides)

In Jewish teaching, keeping the body clean and healthy is a religious duty. This does not mean that Jews are expected to buy only from health-food shops, and exercise every day. It *does* mean that they are to treat the body sensibly, keep it clean, and avoid anything that might harm it.

Cleanliness

The Talmud tells the story of Hillel, a 1st century rabbi, who once told his disciples that he was going to carry out an important mitzvah. When they asked him what he was going to do, he told them that he was going to the bath-house. 'Is that a mitzvah?' they asked. 'Yes,' he replied. 'See how the statues of kings which are set up in the theatres and arenas are scrubbed and kept clean by specially appointed officials. Should not we, who are created in the image of God [see Genesis 1:27], have even greater regard for the cleanliness of our bodies?'

'A person must wash his face, hands and feet each day in honour of his Creator.'

(Talmud)

The Talmud also teaches Jews not to pray without having rinsed their mouths in the morning (except on fast days), and to wash their hands before meals and after leaving the lavatory. These are all *religious* duties. However, there have been 'fringe benefits'. For example, during the Great Plague of London (1665), when people were dying by the hundreds, hardly any Jews became ill.

Health

Today, people are more health-conscious than in the past, but even in ancient times, people were aware that there were simple ways of taking care of their bodies. The Talmud contains a good deal of sound practical advice for healthy living. For example, it advises people to eat and sleep at regular times but never to excess; and not to sit, stand or walk for long periods. It also points out that the body is affected by mental and spiritual health. *'Three things drain a person's health: worry, travel and sin.'*

Jews are also commanded to avoid harming their bodies. Today there are three widespread habits that are known to be harmful:
● drinking alcohol
● smoking
● taking drugs.

Alcohol

Jews are not forbidden to drink alcohol. Indeed, they use wine in various religious ceremonies. However, Judaism strongly disapproves of consuming alcohol in large quantities.

'Do not be among the wine bibbers, or the gluttons who fill themselves with meat.'

(Proverbs 23:20)

The Midrash warns:

'Wine enters, sense goes out; wine enters, secrets come out.'

In some circumstances, drinking even a small amount of alcohol would be inadmissable. For example, in Jewish law a judge who had drunk one glass of wine would be considered unfit to pass judgment until a suitable time had elapsed.

Tobacco

Tobacco smoking is much more recent, and over the years large numbers of Jews have taken up the habit. However, as it gradually became known that tobacco smoking was a major cause of lung disease, many Jews came to regard it as inconsistent with their religious teachings.

Today, it is known that people can be harmed by breathing in other people's tobacco smoke – passive smoking – and in 1982, Rabbi Eliezer Waldenberg, a major authority on medical matters in Jewish law, wrote:

'There are sufficient grounds to forbid smoking according to the Torah. Similarly, when someone is smoking in a public place, those in the vicinity who are concerned about their health have a right to object.'

How far is this poster consistent with Jewish moral teachings?

Although the majority of rabbis have not wanted to issue an outright ban on smoking, many have tried to discourage it, urging parents not to let children take up the habit. Today, although there are very many Jews who do smoke, there are fewer than in the past.

Drugs

Some young Jews are becoming addicted to drugs, though the problem is virtually unknown in religious families. A number of Jewish care organizations now run drug counselling services (see page 172), and it has been suggested that drug education should be given in synagogue religion classes.

'God created the world because He wanted people to serve him. Putting oneself at risk amounts to rejecting the Creator's will.'
(Rabbi Moses Rivkes of Vilna, 1595–1671)

THINGS TO DO

▶ How far are Jewish people likely to agree with people who say that the use of drugs, alcohol and tobacco is up to individuals to decide?

Genetic engineering

Genetic engineering means altering the structure of human cells. It is proving increasingly useful as a means of eliminating hereditary disorders. Some rabbis welcome genetic engineering. They see correcting hereditary abnormalities as no different from correcting physical defects through surgery.

It could, however, be abused so some rabbis have called for safeguards.

Suicide

In Jewish thinking, God is the giver of life, and the only one who has the right to take life away (Deuteronomy 32:39). Judaism only gives people the right to take life in self-defence, war (see page 178) or where a court of law passes a death sentence (see page 175). Suicide is regarded as such a serious sin that a Jew who does commit suicide is not buried together with other Jews, but in a separate part of the cemetery.

THINGS TO DO

▶ Why do Jews regard cleanliness as a religious duty? According to a Talmudic expression, 'A rabbi with a stain on his clothes deserves to be put to death.' What do you think this saying means?
▶ Discussions about drinking and driving often revolve around the idea of a 'safe level' of alcohol consumption. What bearing might Jewish teachings have on these discussions?
▶ You are the secretary of a synagogue. The committee has voted to set aside a room for people who wish to smoke. Compose the letter you intend sending to all members, explaining the new ruling.

FOR YOUR FOLDERS

▶ What does the story of Hillel tell you about the importance of cleanliness in Judaism?
▶ Why do you think that very few Jews died in the Great Plague of London? Find out all you can about it. How was it spread?

79 WEALTH AND POVERTY

'Who is rich? He who is satisfied with what he has.'

(Ethics of the Fathers)

Judaism has always steered a middle path between striving after wealth and shunning it.

'Give me neither poverty nor riches. . . in case I become too full and deny, and say "Who is God?", or in case I become poor and steal. . .'

(Proverbs 30:8–9)

Materialism

'Do not weary yourself trying to become rich.'

(Proverbs 23:4)

The prophets and rabbis often warned against materialism. In Jewish thinking a person's wealth is decided each year by God, so any amount of effort is, in the end, pointless.

Materialism can make a person's life a misery.

'He who loves silver can not be satisfied with silver.'

(Ecclesiastes 5:9)

The Midrash adds:
'He who has a hundred, craves for two hundred.'

Worst of all, materialism can actually lead a person to sin.

'Take care not to forget the Lord your God. . . in case when you have eaten and are satisfied, and have built fine houses and live in them, and when your herds and flocks increase, and your silver and gold and all that you have has increased, then your heart be lifted up and you forget the Lord your God.'

(Deuteronomy 8:11–14)

FOR DISCUSSION

► How might people caught up in materialism respond to the needs of others?

Poverty

Although Judaism rejects materialism, it never went to the other extreme and turned poverty into an ideal. 'Poverty is worse than fifty plagues,' says the

Talmud. Throughout the Talmud and Midrash, the poor person is variously described as miserable, crushed or in a rut.

TALKING POINT

● In one place the Talmud says, '*A poor man is reckoned as dead.*' What do you think the Talmud means by this?

Deliberately impoverishing oneself is regarded as morally wrong since, in effect, it makes other people responsible for one's upkeep.

'It is better to make your Sabbath like a weekday [i.e. eat frugal meals] than to need other people's support.'

(Talmud)

The Talmud sees a decent standard of living as necessary for a person's psychological well being.

Using wealth

Jews are expected to budget their income to provide for themselves and their families, as well as for those in need. Indeed, setting aside money for charity comes first.

Judaism teaches that a tenth of anyone's income is not their own property at all. It belongs to the needy. A person only has the right to decide which charity to give it to.

Although very poor people are excused from giving a tenth, they are expected to contribute something. In Jewish thinking, everyone has a responsibility to help people in need – even those who are themselves in need.

Jews are also expected to set aside money for celebrating Sabbaths and other holy days. Poor Jews often cut down on their weekday expenses in order to make the Sabbath a special experience.

Tzedakah (charity)

Charity implies doing someone a favour. Jews prefer to speak of **tzedakah**, which means *correctness* – not doing someone a favour at all, but handing over what rightfully belongs to the poor person. Not to give tzedakah is, in effect, robbing the poor.

Jews regard some ways of giving tzedakah as preferable to others. Handing a coin to a poor person is the least acceptable way, because it might humiliate the one who receives it. Judaism stresses the importance of preserving human dignity, and the Talmud and Midrash tell several stories of people who put money through a poor person's door and then run away, not to cause embarrassment.

Better still is not to 'give' at all, but to 'lend' to the poor person indefinitely and without interest. Of course, the giver knows that it is not really a loan, but this avoids embarrassment by offering the poor person the possibility of repaying 'some day'.

The disadvantage with most methods of giving tzedakah is that the poor person remains poor, and will soon need more help. The best possible thing one can do is to help the poor person to become self-supporting.

Pushkes in a Jewish home

FOR YOUR FOLDERS

▶ How many different ways are there of giving to charity? Do you think some ways are better than others? Explain your answer.

FOR DISCUSSION

▶ *'The greatest tzedakah is to enable the poor to earn a living.'*
                                            (Maimonides)

Can you suggest ways of doing this?

Many Jewish homes keep **pushkes**, collection boxes for various worthy causes. People put in small change left over after shopping, and the pushkes fill up surprisingly quickly. Pushkes are regarded as part of the home furnishings.

An important part of the education of Jewish children is encouraging them to put part of their pocket money in the pushke. In Jewish kindergartens, children often make their own pushkes, and bring a few pennies each day to put in them. This trains them from the earliest age to share what they have with others.

FOR YOUR FOLDERS

▶ A shabby young man is sitting on a street corner, holding a piece of cardboard with *HOMELESS AND HUNGRY* written on it. What dilemmas might this create for a Jew who is serious about living by Jewish values? What might he or she do?
▶ The following lines are from Shakespeare's play, *The Merchant of Venice*:

   If you repay me not on such a day,
   In such a place, such sum or sums as are
   Express'd in the condition, let the forfeit
   Be nominated for an equal pound
   Of your fair flesh, to be cut off and taken
   In what part of your body pleaseth me.
                                            (Act 1, scene 3)

   The speaker is Shylock, a Jew who has agreed to lend money to a Venetian merchant on these inhuman terms. Literature like this has done much to sustain the belief that Jews will do anything for money. How does such a stereotype relate with what you have learnt in this section?

Why does God let people suffer?

'Not to have known suffering is not to be truly human.'

(Midrash)

How can anyone explain the suffering of innocent people? Why does a child have an incurable illness? These are questions as old as humanity itself.

For Jews today there is a further question. Why were six million men, women and children murdered by the Nazis between 1933 and 1945 in the **Holocaust** (see page 170)? Many have asked, 'Where was God in the concentration camps?'

These questions have led some people to lose their faith. Others have come to believe that God is limited, and that he, too, struggles to overcome evil. Judaism, however, has always taught that God is all powerful, all knowing, always present and completely good. If he is anything else at all, he is not God. But if he is all of these things, how is it that he lets people suffer?

Suffering in the Tanach

The Tanach tells the stories of such people as Joseph, who was sold as a slave by his brothers (Genesis 37:28), Ruth, who endured young widowhood and poverty (Ruth 1:2–5), King David, whose infant son died (2 Samuel 12:15–18) and how they coped with their suffering. The book of Job deals entirely with suffering. It is about a man who lost his home and family, and suffered appalling pain, yet never once turned against God.

Stories such as these offer ways of understanding suffering. It might be a punishment sent by God (Judges 3:7–8), a test (Genesis 22:1–2) or a way of prompting people to return to God (Leviticus 26:41).

Whatever the reason, the Tanach teaches that suffering is intended for a person's ultimate benefit.

'As a man chastises his son, so the Lord your God chastises you.'

(Deuteronomy 8:5)

'When God brings suffering upon people, he is educating us – making us realize our mistakes, just like a loving father sometimes has to smack his child.'

(Rabbi Meir Simcha Hacohen of Dvinsk, 1843–1926)

Suffering in the Talmud and Midrash

The rabbis of the Talmud offered some very important insights into suffering. Here are some extracts:

1 *'If a man should suffer, let him examine his deeds. If he finds he has sinned, let him repent. If he finds nothing, let him attribute his suffering to neglect of Torah study. If this, too, is not so, then for sure his afflictions are sufferings of love.'*

2 *'The righteous suffer for the sins of their generation.'*

3 *'The potter does not test cracked vessels, because if he taps them even once they break. He only tests good vessels, because no matter how many times he taps them they do not break. So God does not test the wicked, but only the righteous.'*

4 *'Which way leads a person to the World to Come? (see pages 184–5). The way of suffering.'*

5 *'God says, "If I grant you happiness, give thanks; if I bring you suffering, give thanks."'*

FOR YOUR FOLDERS

▶ How is suffering presented in extract 1? What is the meaning of 'let him repent'? What might this achieve? What do you think is meant by 'sufferings of love'?

▶ What does extract 2 suggest to you about group responsibility?

▶ Read extract 4 and pages 184 and 185. What do you understand by the term World to Come? Why do you think suffering is seen as the way that leads there?

▶ Read extract 5. It is obviously easy to thank God for happiness. But what might it do for people if they can bring themselves to thank God sincerely for suffering? How might it change their outlook on life?

SUFFERING IS MANY-SIDED

In all of these extracts, the rabbis of the Talmud never try to *justify* suffering. They accepted it as a fact of life. However, they understood that suffering comes from God and therefore has to have a positive side.

Although different rabbis highlighted different aspects of suffering, it would be wrong to imagine that Judaism views it solely as a punishment or a test or a way of changing a person's outlook on life. Suffering is many-sided.

The important thing is that, whatever the reason, if people are to come through suffering they have to draw upon inner reserves of strength they might otherwise never have known they had. They sometimes emerge as better people.

Jewish philosophy

Many Jewish philosophers have discussed the problem of suffering. They saw suffering as necessary so that people should have freedom of choice.

Judaism teaches that people are totally free to choose between good and evil. If God only showered us with blessings, we would have no choice but to love him. As a result we would have to do good.

Suffering makes it possible for us to reject God, and do evil. Suffering, therefore, maintains the balance of our free choice.

Relief of suffering

Although Judaism has always shown that suffering has a positive side, it also teaches that every effort should be made to relieve it.

The Talmud contains a good deal of sound advice for avoiding illness (see page 160). Jews have always regarded it as a religious duty to visit the sick, provide for the poor or comfort the bereaved. Jewish communities have always had organizations that provided these services. Some of these are listed on pages 172 and 173.

Jews also appreciate the role of entertainment in relieving suffering.

The Talmud tells the story of a rabbi who wanted to see someone who had earned a place in heaven. He was shown two men in the market place. He ran up to them and asked, 'What is your occupation?' They replied, 'We are clowns; we try to lift people out of their sadness.'

Euthanasia

In Jewish thinking, killing people to put them out of their misery is murder. It is forbidden even if a sick person requests it.

Where a person is on a life support machine, Judaism regards it as murder to switch it off if the patient has any heart, brain or lung functions of their own. Once these are gone, it may be turned off, for then the machine is not *supporting* life – it is *providing* it.

Although Jews may not actively terminate someone's life, the rabbis do permit withholding treatment from patients who are really beyond help, especially where the treatment is likely to cause pain or distress (e.g. chemotherapy). At the same time, however, Jews insist that it is essential to keep the paitent as comfortable and pain-free as possible.

'O my God, guard my tongue from evil and my lips from speaking deceitfully.'

(Prayer Book)

FOR YOUR FOLDERS

The Midrash tells the story of a man who had a wise servant. One day he told his servant to go and buy the best meat in the market. The servant brought back a tongue. The next day he sent him to buy the worst thing in the market. Again, the servant returned with a tongue. When he asked the servant to explain what he had bought, he replied, 'Nothing is better than a good tongue, and nothing is worse than a bad one.'
▶ What do you think the story illustrates? Write your answer down and put it to one side – you will need to refer to it later.

Judaism has always stressed the importance of the spoken word. Jews are expected to be truthful, neither to humiliate nor mislead another person, nor spread rumours:

'Death and life are in the power of the tongue.'
(Proverbs 18:21)

Naturally, all of this also applies to words in writing or in print.

Truth and falsehood

Being truthful is an important Jewish ideal. The Torah tells Jews to *'Keep far away from a false word'* (Exodus 23:7), and again, *'That which goes out of your lips you shall keep and do'* (Deuteronomy 23:24). The Talmud calls truth **God's seal**.

At the same time, the difference between truth and falsehood is not always clear and simple.

FOR YOUR FOLDERS

What would you do if telling the truth might lead to another person being upset or harmed? Try to give two or three examples and then explain how you would react.

Elisha, one of the great Jewish prophets, was asked by a sick Aramean king whether he would recover. Although Elisha saw that he would die, he told the king's messenger, 'Go, say to him "You shall certainly live".' (2 Kings 8:7–15). There are various reasons for this. Some see it as a situation where telling the truth would have been unnecessarily cruel.

THINGS TO DO

▶ Jewish teaching disapproves of boasting. The Talmud permits people to withhold the truth when questioned about their achievements. It also recommends, when praising people, not recounting all of their achievements in front of them. Can you suggest a reason for this? How might it affect
● the one who is boasting
● those who are listening,
● the person being praised?

Truth can very easily be misused to gain some advantage. This happens fairly often in advertising. For example, a manufacturer of washing-up liquid might claim to have a product that contains no nitrates. This would be perfectly true, since washing-up liquids never contain nitrates! However, such a statement is clearly calculated to make the product appear more environmentally friendly than its competitors so that people will want to buy it. The Talmud calls this **genevat daat**, or 'deception'. It is a practice Judaism strictly forbids.

'God made humans superior to the animals by giving them the power of speech. Those who misuse it make themselves inferior, for animals cannot do any harm with words.'
(Rabbi Israel Meir Kahan of Radin, 1839–1933)

Oaths

An oath is a statement made with reference to God or some holy object as a means of declaring it to be true.

The Talmud teaches that oaths are very serious things indeed. When statements are made under these conditions, the slightest deviation from the truth, even unwittingly, becomes a sin. For this reason the Talmud advises people to avoid making oaths. Many Jews, called to give evidence in a court of law would often choose to 'affirm' that they will tell the whole truth rather than swear to it.

Spreading rumours

'Do not go about as a tale-bearer.'

(Leviticus 19:16)

One of the most serious offences for a Jew is **lashon hara**, literally, 'a tongue of evil'. Jews use this term to describe passing on unpleasant information about another person. The Torah strictly forbids this, even though the information might be true.

It is all too easy to slip into this kind of talk. People do it even without thinking. For this reason the Talmud calls lashon hara one of the sins that a person treads underfoot.

FOR YOUR FOLDERS

▶ There are always circumstances when passing on unpleasant information is necessary, and permitted. For example, would you consider it right to warn a shopkeeper to be careful about accepting cheques from a dishonest customer? Explain why. Can you think of any other examples?

Causing embarrassment

'Someone who humiliates another person in public has no share in the World to Come.'

(Ethics of the Fathers)

Unkind words can make people feel very uncomfortable. People who have been humiliated will sometimes continue to feel the discomfort whenever they think about it.

'You can kill a person only once, but when you humiliate him, you kill him many times over.'

(Talmud)

FOR DISCUSSION

▶ Can you think of a situation in which keeping the Jewish teaching about not humiliating someone could lead to speaking untruths? How might a Jewish person deal with this?

THINGS TO DO

▶ In English law, a person can be sued in court for libel, slander, perjury or violating the Trades Descriptions Act. Find out what these are. How might Jews feel about these things?

▶ Read through the answer you gave to the first question in this chapter (just after the story about the wise servant). How far would Jewish teaching agree with your answer?

▶ How might (a) a shopkeeper (b) a journalist (c) a detective (d) a film critic (e) an estate agent have to take care in order to live by the teachings discussed in this section?

▶ Can you think of any other examples of *genevat daat*? Why do you think Jews regard it as wrong?

▶ The Midrash tells the following story: *'One day Truth came into the world. She went to a big city expecting to be greeted with joy, but instead everyone turned their backs on her. The same thing happened in city after city; Truth was shunned everywhere. Saddened, Truth left the towns, and sat down by the roadside. Along came Parable, and asked her, "Why are you crying?" Truth told him what had happened. "I just don't understand why people turn away from me," sobbed Truth. "But just look at you," said Parable. "You are naked. That's why no-one wants to acknowledge you. Come, I will clothe you." So Parable clothed Truth, and wherever she went people accepted her.'*
Explain what you think the story means.

▶ A company offering package holidays abroad has asked you to help design their travel brochure. Write two drafts of the same paragraph, one which includes genevat daat and the other not. Which do you think the company will prefer? Explain why.

'Great is work. God's presence only rested upon the Jewish people when they began occupying themselves with useful work.'

(Midrash)

THINGS TO DO

▶ List some reasons why you think people should work. Try to think not only about earning money and being able to buy things, but also about how work affects the individual *as a person*.

The importance of work

In Jewish teaching it is necessary for people to have an occupation. The Midrash sees idleness as harmful to the individual, pointing out that it can lead to immoral behaviour and depression. It is also bad for society. 'Teach your son a trade,' says the Talmud, 'or you teach him to become a robber.'

It is also important for people to feel that they are productive. The Talmud tells the story of an old man who was planting a tree. A Roman officer who was passing by pointed out that he would not live to eat the fruit. 'Just as my father planted for me,' replied the old man, 'so I am planting for my children.'

The Torah describes the sin of Adam, the first man, and tells how God expelled him from the Garden of Eden, where all his needs had been provided (Genesis 2:16). From now on, he was to find his own food. The Talmud retells the story, and shows Adam stunned at the thought of having to search for food together with the animals. Then God tells him, 'By the sweat of your face you shall eat bread.' (Genesis 3:19). On hearing this Adam revives. He then knows that he will be able to work, and that this will set him apart from the rest of creation.

For Jews, work is also necessary for fulfilling God's will. Judaism has no place for **hermits** – people who withdraw from the world of work and human contact to spend their time in spiritual pursuits. It teaches that people have to serve God by being active in the world, bringing God's will into every sphere of activity (see pages 150–1).

All the rabbis of the Talmud and Midrash had an occupation. Among the most influential was a blacksmith, a cobbler, a stone-mason, a weaver and a carpenter; some were merchants, others were farmers.

'The study of the Torah together with an occupation is an excellent thing.'

(Ethics of the Fathers)

Jews are permitted to take up any occupation they wish, except those which are likely to bring harm to people physically (such as drug trafficking) or morally (like selling pornographic literature). Indeed, in Jewish thinking, such things are forbidden to non-Jews too.

Business ethics

Very often, business ethics depend on doing what is profitable. For example, a trader with a reputation for fair dealing is likely to attract more customers than one with a bad name.

FOR YOUR FOLDERS

▶ Do you think that doing what is profitable is a good basis for business ethics? Explain your answer.

Judaism rejects such a view because it takes no account of a person's *intentions*. It is all too easy for a business person to give unsound advice or withhold information from a customer, and still keep a good reputation. Jewish business ethics depends on fulfilling God's will. For this reason almost every time the Torah lays down a rule about business conduct it adds, *'and you shall fear your God'*. God knows what a person's intentions really are.

The Midrash tells the story of a man who came up to a rabbi while he was praying, wanting to buy some goods. The rabbi did not answer. The man thought that the rabbi wanted a higher price for the goods, and offered more. Again the rabbi did not answer. Again the man raised his offer. At that point, the rabbi finished his prayer and said, 'My son, at the moment you approached me I made a quick mental agreement that I would sell, and then put the matter out of my mind because I wanted to concentrate on my prayers. Since I agreed to accept your first offer I shall sell you the goods at that price.'

How would you feel if you had been sold what you understood to be good tomatoes, and found a few bad ones in the bag? Would you be entitled to a refund? In Jewish law you would. The Torah demands that people conduct their business with total honesty.

'You shall do no unrighteousness in measurement, neither in land measure, in weight nor in liquid measure.'

(Leviticus 19:35)

If a salesperson measures something wrongly, the sale is invalid and the buyer can demand a refund. The same applies to a sale where inferior goods have been substituted for or mixed in with better ones. Judaism rejects the principle (which sometimes applies in British law) of *caveat emptor*, 'let the buyer beware'. It makes the seller largely responsible for the fairness of the sale.

In Jewish law, a sale is also invalid if a trader has charged too high a price. This is reckoned as a maximum of one sixth over the estimated market value of any goods.

The Talmud mentions the ancient practice of shopkeepers giving out nuts to children to get them to shop in their establishments. Today's equivalent would be the various free gifts and special offers that businesses use to compete with their rivals. In Jewish thought this is acceptable business practice.

It is also acceptable business practice for people to promote the goods they sell or the services they offer by honest advertising. However, Judaism considers it morally wrong to try to sell a product by running down someone else's.

THINGS TO DO

► Can you think of any examples of this? It happens fairly often in advertising.

Total honesty is also expected from employers and employees in their dealings with one another. Judaism sees their relationship as a contract. Employees fulfil their side of the contract by working during their hours of employment, and not doing other things. To do so would be to rob their employers of the time they are paying for.

Employers, for their part, are expected to pay wages on time, and not demand longer hours than are written into the contract or determined by local custom. Where other amenities are expected of employers, e.g. providing a midday meal, they must provide them.

Leisure

'When God stopped work on the Sabbath he created contentment, peace of mind and rest.'
(Midrash)

Although Judaism places great value on work, it also recognizes the need for taking a break. Traditionally, the Sabbath was the main form of rest for Jews. However, this was not so much a relaxation as an opportunity to set aside time for spiritual matters.

Today, when most people live high-pressure lives, leisure is perhaps more important than at any time in the past. Jews have many different forms of leisure. Some have hobbies, others take activity holidays, play sport or simply relax with a book.

Some forms of leisure are not acceptable in Jewish thinking. Jews are forbidden to watch or take part in anything immodest or obscene. They are also forbidden to take part in cruel sports such as fox-hunting.

FOR YOUR FOLDERS

► What does the story of Adam tell you about the importance of work in Jewish thinking?
► In Jewish law, a sale is invalid if a trader has charged more than 15% above the market value. How do you think this profit limit of one sixth might affect markets?
► Can you describe some of the ways in which traders or manufacturers try to persuade people to buy their products? Which might Jews regard as legitimate, and why?
► How might a religious Jewish cabinet minister try to influence the government's employment policies?
► What might Jewish teaching regard as a legitimate role for trade unions? How might they view strikes?
► Why do you think Jewish teaching considers it wrong to trade in harmful things? Might this raise dilemmas for shopkeepers who sell (a) kitchen knives (b) fireworks?
► To what extent do you think Jewish business ethics depend on mutual trust between buyer and seller, or employer and employee?

'And if a stranger should live in your country, you must do him no wrong. The stranger who lives with you shall be as the home-born among you, and you shall love him like yourself.'

(Leviticus 19:33–34)

THINGS TO DO

▶ Give a definition of (a) prejudice (b) discrimination. Check your definition by looking up the words in a dictionary.

▶ Write down two or three examples of prejudice. Why do you think some people are prejudiced against others? Explain your answer, before reading further.

In its very first chapter, the Torah tells us that 'God made man in his image'. The word **man** used in this way is a general term for humankind.

God did this because he wanted people to serve him. In Jewish thought all human beings are partners in fulfilling God's desire for 'a dwelling place among low creatures' (see page 150). For Jews to think of another person as inferior, or having less of a share in God's plan, would be to deny some of their most basic beliefs.

FOR YOUR FOLDERS

▶ Actually discriminating against another person is more serious. What do you think it does
(a) to the victims
(b) to those who practise it
(c) to relationships in society?
In Jewish thinking, discrimination hampers God's plan. Can you explain why?

Racism

Racism is the belief or feeling that people of a certain race are inferior. There is racism in many parts of the world today, some of it in Britain.

The worst form racism can take is when it becomes official government policy, for then people can no longer expect the law to protect them. This is what happened to Jews in Germany during the 1930s.

Racism can start from seemingly small things. Where can it lead?

Germany was suffering from an economic slump, large-scale unemployment and widespread discontent. In 1933, the National Socialist (Nazi) Party came to power. They blamed the Jews for all Germany's problems. They claimed that the Jews controlled the banks, the press and the universities, and that they were plotting with Communists to take control of the country.

The Nazis began passing racist laws to remove the Jews' citizen rights. Eventually, they built concentration camps and herded the Jews into them. By 1945, 6 million Jewish men, women and children had been systematically murdered. Jews refer to this as the **Holocaust**.

One of the sickest aspects of racism is that it can even be given a 'religious' basis. For example, in the southern states of America, the Ku Klux Klan persecutes blacks and Jews, claiming that the Bible teaches white Aryan supremacy.

For Jews, racial differences do not affect a

person's value before God. The Torah teaches that *all* people have the same responsibilites towards God, expressed in the Noahide Code (see page 150).

Jews are sometimes called 'the chosen people'. Jews do not think of themselves as chosen to be God's favourites, but chosen for additional responsibilities. They have 613 commandments to keep (see page 151). Judaism teaches that for God's plan to be fulfilled, it needs Jews and non-Jews to serve him in partnership – each in their respective ways (see page 185).

Sexism

FOR DISCUSSION

▶ Do Jews believe that women can only be given respect if they have total equality and do the same things as men?

Judaism recognizes men and women as completely equal before God. At the same time, Judaism places fewer religious duties on women than on men. This, together with the fact that synagogue prayer is primarily an obligation for males, with the women sitting in a separate section, has led to a good deal of confusion over the place of women in Judaism.

Although in the West feminism has a history of some 200 years, it was only in the 1960s that the movement really began to make people aware that women have often been treated unfairly. Some feminists tried to achieve equality by persuading women that they should become as much like men as possible. Women had to get to the top in their careers, and being a wife and mother was seen as a hindrance.

This is not a view Judaism could ever agree with. Judaism sees marriage and motherhood as important parts of a woman's full development as a human being.

The importance Judaism attaches to raising children and creating a family structure is discussed on pages 154 and 155. Women, as the carriers and bearers of children, are well suited to nurturing children, particularly in their earliest (and in many ways most formative) years. This is considered so important that the Torah makes women exempt from fulfilling many of the commandments which have to be performed at specific times. A woman cannot be tied down with such obligations. The exemption applies both to women who have families and those who do not.

Many Jewish women, like others, do go for higher education and careers. However, Jewish teaching would encourage them also to put time and effort into marriage and children, both for their own personal fulfilment as well as to create a firm basis for the next generation.

Other faiths

Jews do not believe in a single religion for everyone. They do believe that Judaism is the only correct path *for Jews*. Of humankind in general however, the Jewish holy writings say, *'The righteous of all nations have a share in the world to come'* (see pages 184–5).

What do Jews expect people to do to be righteous? (If you are not sure, turn back to page 150 and re-read the paragraph about the Seven Commandments of the Noahide Code.) In Jewish terms, people are righteous if, at the very least, they live by these commandments.

This means that although Jews do not agree with everything that other religions teach, they do accept they can lead people to God, provided they encourage their believers to live by the Noahide Code. However, Jews also look forward to an age when all humanity will worship the same one God (see page 184).

THINGS TO DO

▶ Anti-semitism is a form of racism. Find out what it is. What do you think the causes are? How do you think Jewish people feel about it? Suggest ways in which racism might be overcome.

FOR YOUR FOLDERS

▶ You might sometimes hear Jews referred to as the 'Chosen People'. What does this phrase seem to mean?

▶ Several schools in your area are planning a programme of activities to promote racial harmony. What suggestions might a Jewish teacher make?

▶ List some of the ways in which women have been treated as inferior. How have women tried to overcome sexism? Why do you think Jewish teachings see wifehood and motherhood as important?

'*Regard the needy as members of your household.*'

(Ethics of the Fathers)

In Jewish literature, God himself is described as caring for the disadvantaged.

'*The Lord gives food to the hungry, the Lord frees those imprisoned, the Lord opens the eyes of the blind, the Lord raises up those that are bowed down, the Lord loves the righteous, the Lord takes care of strangers, He supports orphans and widows.*' (Psalm 146:7–9)

The Talmud urges people to take God's example.

'*"Just as I am righteous," says the Lord, "so you, too, be righteous. Just as I visit the sick, feed the hungry and clothe the naked, so you do the same."*'

Responsibility

Judaism insists that it is not only up to the poor and disabled to find the help they need. Disadvantage is everyone's problem. The Talmud and Midrash tell many stories of people who went to great lengths to help others in need. These stories drive home the importance of helping other people.

'*If someone is looking after a sick person and goes away to join the community in prayer, his prayer is no mitzvah at all – it is bloodshed.*'
(Rabbi Nathan Zvi Finkel of Slobodka, 1849–1928)

Helping the disadvantaged is not only up to individuals, it is a responsibility for the whole community. Since ancient times, wherever Jews have settled they have set up organizations to care for those in need.

FOR YOUR FOLDERS

► Three ways in which organizations can be more effective than individuals.

The needs of the disadvantaged have always been a major concern of the rabbis. They frequently permitted the disadvantaged to do things that would have been forbidden to other Jews. For example, on the Sabbath (Saturdays), Jews are forbidden to carry any object from the house into the street or vice versa. However, the rabbis permitted people with walking difficulties to go out with crutches or a walking stick.

The use of machinery is also forbidden on the Sabbath. Today, rabbis, working closely with Jewish scientists, have helped design hearing-aids and hospital lifts which are acceptable. (Pace-makers and similar appliances are always permitted, since people's lives depend on them. Preserving life overrides the Sabbath.)

Care organizations

These are a few Jewish care agencies in Britain.

NORWOOD CHILD CARE

Norwood began in 1795 as a Jewish orphanage in South London. In those days it had fewer than 20 children. Today, it provides a complete range of social services to hundreds of Jewish children and their families each year, and works to an annual budget of over £1 000 000.

Norwood is called upon by people going through marital difficulties, unemployment and those trying to cope with drug and alcohol dependence or with a handicapped child. The organization always makes children its priority, and offers various kinds of help, including counselling, residential fostercare and financial assistance.

Some families just need some extra cash to buy clothes for their children. Others need a holiday they could not otherwise afford. At Norwood's residential homes, trained staff care for young people who have grown up with violence or neglect. Some are on drugs, others are anorexic.

THE JEWS' TEMPORARY SHELTER

The Shelter was set up in 1885 to help penniless Jewish refugees from Eastern Europe. More recently, it has provided emergency accommodation and funds for Jews who have been forced to leave Egypt and Iran. The Shelter runs a day centre for the elderly, and a kosher 'meals on wheels' service for those who are house-bound.

JEWISH CARE

This organization has been formed from a merger of the **Jewish Welfare Board**, the **Jewish Blind Society** (both nearly 300 years old) and the **Jewish Association for the Physically Disabled**.

Jewish Care runs six housing schemes, providing elderly, disabled or blind people with sheltered flats. This enables them to be independent but, at the same time, to know that help is near at hand. The organization also runs 17 residential homes for the elderly, two day care units for elderly, mentally frail people, and hostels, group homes and a health care centre for people with mental health problems.

They send trained care staff to visit housebound people who need help with dressing, washing and feeding. Jewish Care also runs eight day centres, providing elderly people with companionship, hot meals, activities and outings. In all, the organization provides help and support for over 10 000 people and their families each year.

There are many care organizations such as these. One very popular organization supported by British Jews is the Magen David Adom, the Israeli ambulance service. However, Jews do not only support the specifically Jewish care organizations; Judaism teaches them to contribute to any deserving cause that comes their way.

Caring for the care organizations

A few Jewish care projects receive local council grants. The majority do not. The bulk of the money these organizations need has to be raised from voluntary contributions.

There are many ways of doing this; there are fund-raising events, sponsored walks and appeals in the press. Many Jews have collection boxes in their homes (see page 163); some remember the care organizations in their wills.

The success of these ventures depends on the Jewish ideal of **tzedakah** (see page 163). Alongside tzedakah, where people help others with their money, Judaism also teaches the importance of **gemilat chassadim**, donating one's own time and effort. This ideal has enabled the care organizations to call upon the help of volunteers, who work alongside the trained staff.

Youth, caring for the aged

THINGS TO DO

► Name three charities you would like to support. Give your reasons for choosing them. Would a Jewish person necessarily support them for the same reasons as you do? Explain your answer.
► Why do you think rabbis and Jewish scientists work together to design aids that disabled people can use on the Sabbath?
► You are the secretary of a Jewish youth club. A local hospital is looking for people to play with the patients on the children's ward. Write a letter to club members asking for volunteers.

'Pray for the welfare of the government; if it were not for the fear of it, men would swallow each other alive.'

(Ethics of the Fathers)

THINKING POINT

● What does this parable tell you about good and bad government?

The role of government

The Talmud not only tells stories about Jews. To illustrate the difference between good and bad government, it tells of Alexander the Great's visit to King Katzia.

ALEXANDER AND KATZIA

Katzia offered his royal visitor silver and gold, but Alexander told him that he only wanted to see how justice was carried out in his country.

At that moment two men came before King Katzia. One of them said, 'Your majesty, this man sold me a field. When I began to dig in it I found a treasure. I want him to take the treasure back because I only bought the field from him.'

The other man responded, 'No, your majesty. I sold him the field, and therefore anything he finds in it belongs to him.'

King Katzia turned to the first man and said, 'Do you have a son?' 'Yes,' he replied. Katzia turned to the other man. 'Do you have a daughter?' 'Yes.' 'Then let your son marry your daughter and give them the treasure as a wedding present,' ruled the King.

King Alexander started to laugh. Katzia turned to him. 'What would you have done?' he asked.

'I would have killed them both,' replied Alexander, 'and taken the treasure for myself.'

Katzia was shocked. 'Does it rain in your country?' he asked.

'Yes,' replied Alexander.

'Are there cattle in your country?'

'Yes.'

'Well,' said King Katzia, 'if that is the way you carry out justice, then the rain surely falls only for the benefit of the cattle. The people do not deserve it!'

The law of the land

In biblical times, almost all Jews lived in the part of the world now known as Israel. The law of the land was the Torah, and Jews obeyed it because they understood it to be God's will (see page 150). By the 5th century BCE Jews had begun to migrate, and towards the end of the 1st century they were scattered throughout the known world.

This meant that Jews had to live by two systems of law at the same time: the laws of the Torah and the laws of the country in which they lived. This could sometimes present difficulties, for example where the laws of the country permitted something which the Torah disallowed or vice versa. To meet this difficulty, the rabbis ruled that *'the law of the land is the law'*.

Naturally, they never applied this principle when the law of the land actually compelled Jews to violate the commandments of the Torah. For example, in the 2nd century BCE, a Syrian king tried to force the Jews in his empire to change their religion. At first, the Jews just disobeyed him. Eventually, however, he began to persecute them. They rose in armed revolt and fought for their right to worship as they wished.

How much power should an organization like the United Nations wield?

Justice

'You shall appoint judges and officers in all your towns . . . and they shall judge the people righteously.'

(Deuteronomy 16:18)

From the earliest times, Jews were commanded to set up a system of justice. This consisted of law courts, where judges would try offenders, settle disputes and issue rulings on religious matters. The Jewish legal system comprised three levels of **Bet Din** or court. Ordinary trials were conducted by a Bet Din of three judges. They questioned the witnesses themselves and, after considering the evidence, gave a verdict.

When someone was standing trial for an offence that carried the death penalty, a Bet Din of 23 judges tried the case. Matters of national importance required a **Sanhedrin**, a court of 71 (see page 178).

THINGS TO DO

► What arguments might Jews put forward in a discussion on capital punishment?

In Jewish law, the death penalty was sometimes used for offences that were regarded as particularly serious, such as murder, the rape of a married woman or violating the Sabbath. This was not only a punishment and a deterrent to others, it was also an **atonement** for the offender.

Circumstantial evidence was never admissible. A person could only be executed if witnesses had given a warning, pointing out the possible punishment, and had then actually seen the crime carried out in front of them almost immediately.

If people had heard a scream, and then rushed into a building to find a man standing over a body holding a knife that was dripping blood, there was no way that the death penalty could be enforced. No one had actually witnessed the crime.

Although the death penalty was always there as a possibility, it was rarely carried out. It was, in effect, a way of indicating which crimes were the most serious. The Mishnah even states that a Bet Din that executed a person once in 70 years was a 'destructive Bet Din'. No Jewish court has carried out a death sentence since Roman times.

Nor is there any place for mutilation in Jewish law. The often misunderstood verse, 'an eye for an eye' (Exodus 21:24) is taken in the Talmud to refer to monetary compensation. It teaches that if someone's eye is injured, they may only claim the value of an eye as compensation, i.e. *no more than the value of an eye for an eye.*

Nowadays, there is only the Bet Din of three judges. They are very learned rabbis with many years of communal experience. There are several such rabbinic courts in England, four of them in London alone. They are concerned mainly with divorce cases, conversions and business disputes between Jews.

The workings of the Bet Din depend on the careful examination of witnesses by impartial judges. Very high standards of truth and reliability are expected of them both, and it is very easy to be disqualified. For example, people with criminal records may not appear as witnesses in a Bet Din; nor may dishonest traders or gamblers.

A judge, too, may be disqualified if there is the slightest risk that he might be partial. The Talmud tells the story of a rabbi who was getting into a boat. A man standing nearby put his hand out to help him. As the rabbi thanked him, the man mentioned that he was due to appear before him in court. 'In that case,' said the rabbi, 'I am disqualified from being your judge.'

FOR YOUR FOLDERS

► Look back to the story of King Katzia. Do you know of any good or bad governments today? How would you decide?
► How do you think the ruling 'the law of the land is the law' helped Jews?
► The following are some Jewish teachings about government and justice.
 (a) *A habitual borrower cannot be a judge.* (Talmud)
 (b) *A government can be brought down because of a single injustice.* (Rabbi Israel Meir Kahan, 1839–1933)
 (c) *The laws of governments are determined by everyday life; the laws of God determine everyday life.* (Rabbi Joseph Isaac Schneersohn, 1880–1950)
 What do you think these sayings mean? What do they teach you about justice and government in Jewish thought?
► What do you think 'atonement' means? Try to find out.

'May every mouth give thanks to You, every tongue swear to You, every knee bend to You, every human frame bow before You . . .'

(Prayer Book)

In Jewish thinking, people are created by God to serve him (see page 150). Although Jews and non-Jews have different obligations, and therefore different ways of serving God (see page 185), Jews think of all people as partners in refining the world and making it God's dwelling place.

People can carry out this task best if they are free to develop their full potential as individuals. However, in today's world there are two major factors that prevent people developing – poverty and denial of human rights.

World poverty

'For hunger is a curious thing . . . at first it is with you all the time, walking and sleeping and in your dreams, and your belly cries out insistently, and there is a gnawing and a pain as if your very vitals were being devoured, . . . the strength drains from your limbs, and you try to rise and find you cannot, or to swallow water and your throat is powerless, and both the swallow and the effort of retaining the liquid tax you to the uttermost.'

This is an extract from a book by an Indian writer. What he describes is an ongoing experience for millions of people in underdeveloped countries. They are too poor to afford basic human needs, like food and clean drinking water, that people in the West take for granted.

World poverty is not only due to natural causes like poor harvests. It is also caused by the high rate at which people in developed countries use the planet's resources for themselves. According to a recent report, *the amount of money West Europeans spend on pet food each year is enough to provide 12 million Asian children with decent meals*.

In Jewish terms, this makes world poverty a *moral* issue on two counts:

- people have a responsibility to see that other people are able to fulfil God's will

- it is our own high consumption of resources that is partly to blame for them not being able to do so.

THINGS TO DO

▶ How could people in developed countries help relieve world poverty? Do you think that relief is only up to governments, or can individuals help? Describe briefly any relief programmes that you know of.

Would the programmes you have described just provide for immediate needs, or would they help people to become self-sufficient? Read the section on Jewish teachings about tzedakah (charity) on page 163. How might the ideas in that section be applied to relieving world poverty?

Human rights

FOR YOUR FOLDERS

▶ Write down three or four examples of human rights. Why should people have these rights?

You might find it easy to list some human rights. However, while we take it for granted that people should have them, it is not always so easy to explain why. Why do you think this is so? What reasons might Jews give for considering human rights important?

After World War 2, the nations of the free world drew up a **Universal Declaration of Human Rights** (see pp 221–2). For several years, the General Assembly of the United Nations worked to turn this into international law. In 1976, its terms became legally binding on the 45 countries (including Britain) that accepted them. Among the terms are:

- No one shall be subjected to arbitrary arrest, detention or exile.
- Everyone charged with a penal offence has the right to be presumed innocent until proven guilty.
- Everyone has the right to freedom of movement. Everyone has the right to leave any country.
- Everyone has the right to work, to free choice of employment, to just and favourable conditions of work and to protection against unemployment.

● Everyone has the right to a standard of living adequate for health and well being. Motherhood and childhood are entitled to special care.

Most of these appear to have their roots in the Tanach and Jewish moral teachings. However, in Jewish thinking, people should exercise their rights in a moral way. This means recognizing that having rights creates responsibilities.

Poverty in the middle of wealth. Why is this a moral problem?

According to Jewish thinking, in insisting on their son's right to be educated, the boy's parents should also have ensured that he carried out his responsibility to allow other people to have *their* education. If he was not able to be responsible in this way, it was clear that he needed special help. His parents should have tried to make some arrangements for him, rather than sue the authority for not taking him back to his old school.

THINGS TO DO

▶ What might Jews say about people playing loud music late at night, claiming that they have the 'right' to listen to what they like whenever they like? Can you think of other examples of where the claim to rights ought to depend on responsible behaviour?

▶ Find out what you can about the work of a relief organization that you do not already support or know about. How do its administrators decide where and how the work should be carried out? What *moral* issues are involved in the decision making? How far might a Jewish person agree with their decisions?

THINGS TO DO

▶ Some time ago, the papers carried a report about a 14 year old boy who was suspended from school. His behaviour had been so bad that he disrupted every class he was in. If he was sent out, he made so much noise in the corridor that several classes were disturbed. The head teacher suspended him. Each time the school took him back, the same thing happened, so he kept on being suspended. As a result, he was away from school for many weeks.

His parents took the local education authority to court. Under the terms of the Universal Declaration of Human Rights, 'every person has the right to an education'. They claimed that the school was denying their son this basic human right. Do you think the parents were right? Explain your answer. How would you have ruled if you had been the judge in this case?

FOR YOUR FOLDERS

▶ You are on a committee concerned with famine relief in Ethiopian villages. You only have limited funds. How would you use them?

Would you expect the Jewish committee members to want to use the available funds
(a) to provide grain and other foodstuffs
(b) to build a system of pipelines to bring clean water to the villages
(c) to provide tractors and fertilizers and train the villagers to use them?

Would they distinguish between short- and long-term objectives? Explain your answer.

▶ What are 'prisoners of conscience'? Do you know of any? From what you already know about Jewish teachings on the role of human beings, what would you expect Jews to say about these prisoners? Are Jews likely to regard them as all the same? Explain your answer.

'The world stands on three things, on justice, on truth and on peace.'

(Ethics of the Fathers)

Peace as an ideal

From biblical times to the present day, Jews have greeted each other with **Shalom**, which means *peace* (2 Kings 4:26). This is more than just a greeting. Jews have always hated war, and shalom expresses the hope that one day all humankind will live in peace.

This does not mean that Judaism teaches total pacifism. Although it regards war as evil, it recognizes that there are times when someone has to fight. Nonetheless, it teaches that they must go to great lengths to avoid war.

'If your enemy is hungry, give him bread to eat; if he is thirsty, give him water to drink.'

(Proverbs 25:21)

Kindness and understanding can sometimes defuse a tense situation (see 2 Kings 6:21–23).

Obligatory and optional wars

This extract is from the book of Joshua:

'. . . The Lord said to Joshua . . . rise up, cross over this River Jordan, you and all this nation . . . Every place where the sole of your foot treads I will give to you . . . be strong and courageous, for you will lead this people to take possession of the land which I have promised to their ancestors . . .'

These words were said to Joshua, Moses' successor, as the Israelites were about to enter the promised land. However, the land was not empty, and the Israelites were going to have to fight for it.

That war was a **milchemet mitzvah**, an obligatory war – one which the Israelites were commanded by God to fight. Jews distinguish between this and the **milchemet reshut**, the optional war. There are three other kinds of *milchemet mitzvah*.

First, if they are attacked by an enemy army, Jews regard it as a religious obligation to defend themselves (Exodus 17:8–13).

Second, an extension of this is the **pre-emptive war** – attacking an enemy who is about to strike, in order to avoid being attacked. In the summer of 1967, Israeli intelligence discovered that Egypt and Syria were about to launch an attack. The Israeli airforce struck at those countries' airfields and destroyed most of their aircraft while they were still on the ground. As a result, the war was over in six days and thousands of lives on both sides were spared.

Third is going to the aid of a country that is under attack, to stop war reaching one's own country. In 1939, when Germany invaded Poland, Britain had a pledge to help the Poles if they were attacked. The British government realized that if the German armies were not halted, they would eventually invade this country. Britain declared war on Germany.

A milchemet reshut is an optional war. It can only be undertaken if there are sound reasons for fighting, diplomacy has failed (Judges 11:12–33), and if the **Sanhedrin**, the Supreme Rabbinical Council, approves it (though, in practice, there has not been a Sanhedrin since Roman times). For example, by the time of King David, the most famous Jewish King, Israel had been fighting its neighbours on and off for three centuries. David decided to subdue them. The court gave its approval as this seemed the only way to secure a lasting peace.

Fighting any other kind of war, whether to build an empire, colonize or to take revenge, is forbidden to Jews.

COMMENT

'The generals are regarded as clever men. They commission powerful weapons and calculate how to kill thousands of people. Can there be any greater foolishness than this?'

(Rabbi Nachman of Breslov, 1772–1810)

The non-military heritage

Due to their longstanding hatred of war, Jews have never had a military heritage. Traditionally, they have only taken up arms to defend their lives, their homes or their beliefs. Even today, Jews do not bring up their children to glorify war.

FOR DISCUSSION

▶ Some Jewish parents do not allow their children to play with toy guns. Can you suggest why? Do you think they are right?

The army in Israel

Throughout the centuries, Jews in the Holy Land (Israel) lived mostly at peace with their neighbours. However, during the 19th century more Jews started to return to their ancestral homeland, and hostilities broke out.

In 1945, when World War 2 ended, Israel (then called **Palestine**) was under British control. Thousands of Jews who had survived the Nazi concentration camps (see page 170) wanted to come to Palestine. The British and Arab governments wanted to slow down immigration.

Various Jewish military groups emerged, and began fighting for the rights of these survivors to settle in Palestine, have homes of their own and build up their lives again. These groups became the basis of the present Israeli army.

In 1948, the Jews of Palestine declared their independence, and the State of Israel was born. From then on the army was to be known as the Israel Defence Force.

Since 1948, Israel has been involved in several conflicts with its Arab neighbours. Israelis are aware of their history as a persecuted people, and have no wish to oppress others. However, maintaining peace has not always been easy, and if individual soldiers have committed abuses it is because the teachings of the Torah have not yet become a central part of the Israeli consciousness.

Israeli soldier at the Temple site – ready for war but praying for peace

FOR YOUR FOLDERS

▶ Here are some Jewish teachings:
  (a) *Seek peace and run after it.*

  (Psalm 34:15)
  (b) *Peace is the vessel for receiving God's blessing.*

  (Mishnah)
  (c) *The Torah was given to establish peace.*

  (Midrash)
  (d) *Peace is to the world what yeast is to dough.*

  (Talmud)
  What do you think these sayings mean? What do they tell you about the Jewish attitude to peace?
▶ Think of three wars you have learnt about in history. Explain whether Jews would regard them as milchemet mitzvah, milchemet reshut or neither.
▶ What does the name 'Israel Defence Force' tell you about the role of the Israeli military?

'A righteous man pays attention to the needs of his animal.'

(Proverbs 12:10)

In its opening chapter, the Torah describes the creation of animals:

'Then God said, "Let the water team with swarms of living creatures, and let birds fly above the earth . . ." and God made the animals according to their kinds, the beasts according to their kinds and all the things that creep upon the earth'.

It then tells us that humans were created

'to have control over the fish of the sea and the birds of the sky, over the animals and over the whole earth.'

(Genesis 1:20–26)

FOR YOUR FOLDERS

▶ How do you think these verses have shaped the Jewish attitude towards animals? Write down your ideas before reading further.

Jews derive two important principles from these verses:
- animals must be treated with the respect due to something created by God
- animal life can never have the same value as human life (see page 150).

The Torah permits the use of animals for human benefit, but never their abuse. Jews are strictly forbidden to cause unnecessary pain to any animal. This is also one of the Seven Commandments of the Noahide Code (see page 150), binding on all humankind.

The Talmud tells the story of Rabbi Judah, who once saw a calf being led to the slaughter-house. The animal ran towards him and hid its head in his robe, as if seeking his protection. 'Go,' he said to it, 'this is what you were created for.' That day it was decreed in heaven that since he had shown no compassion, he should be afflicted with sufferings. Some weeks later, his servant was cleaning the house, and wanted to sweep out some young weasels that had made their nest there. Rabbi Judah called out, 'Leave them, God's mercy extends to all His creatures.' On that day it was decreed that his sufferings should end.

FOR DISCUSSION

▶ What does this story tell you about the relationship between people and animals in Jewish thought?

'Teachers must see that children respect the smallest and largest animals which, like people, have feelings. The child who gets enjoyment from the convulsions of an injured beetle will grow up to be insensitive to human suffering.'

(Rabbi Samson Raphael Hirsch, 1808–1888)

Animals for work

Jews are permitted to use animals for work, and both the Torah and Talmud lay down guidelines for their care. The rabbis ruled that a farmer should not buy more animals than he could afford to feed properly, and that he was to feed his animals before sitting down to his own meal. Even the very strict Sabbath laws were relaxed to help an animal that had fallen into a pool or pit.

Animals for food

Although Jews may be vegetarians if they choose, the Torah permits them to eat the meat of certain animals (Leviticus, chapter 11). However, Judaism insists that if meat is to be eaten, the animal has to be killed by a method that is totally pain-free. The Jewish method of slaughter is called **shechitah**.

Shechitah is a cut made across the animal's throat. Its painlessness depends on two things, the sharpness of the blade and the smoothness of the cut.

The shechitah knife (its blade can be as long as a metre) is kept razor sharp. The knife is drawn across the animal's throat with a smooth action, severing the carotid arteries, the two blood vessels that carry blood to the brain. When these arteries are cut, blood pressure in the brain drops to zero. The animal loses consciousness immediately – before it has been able to feel any pain.

If shechitah is performed without a smooth stroke, or with too much pressure or with a knife that has the slightest defect, Jews are forbidden to

Animal abuse – to what extent do these practices square with Jewish moral teachings?

eat that meat. The animal might have been caused pain.

Jews are not only forbidden to cause physical pain to animals, but mental anguish too. Keeping animals in cramped conditions, or feeding them with substances that cause pain or distress, are a violation of Jewish moral principles.

Experiments on animals

The Jewish approach to experiments on animals turns on the two principles already mentioned:
- animals may be used for the furtherance of human needs
- no unnecessary pain may be inflicted.

This rules out experiments for the production of cosmetics. There is no way that blinding rabbits to test eye-shadow can be thought of as 'furthering human needs'.

Jews regard medical experiments as different. Finding cures for diseases, or perfecting surgical techniques, are extremely important human needs. Killer diseases such as diphtheria and smallpox, which were widespread in Britain earlier this century, have been more or less wiped out due to experiments that involved animals. So has polio, which once left children paralyzed. Surgeons have learned to transplant hearts, kidneys and livers by operating on animals before trying out the techniques on people.

In all of these examples the consideration of not causing unnecessary pain would mean that Jews would like to ensure that the experiments were carefully monitored, and were only performed when no other method was available.

THINGS TO DO

▶ Write a short conversation between two people who are arguing over whether it is right to keep animals in zoos. Alternatively, make this the topic of a class discussion. What might Jews think about it?

▶ A scientist who experiments on animals is nearly killed by a car bomb planted by an animal liberation group. Imagine you are a Jew writing a letter to the editor of a newspaper, giving your comments.

▶ You are a Jewish head-teacher. Someone rings you up to tell you that two of your pupils have drowned a kitten in a nearby canal. What would you say or do to those pupils? What would you say at school assembly?

Is preserving rare flowers more important than growing crops?

'The earth, and everything that fills it, is the Lord's.'
(Psalm 24:1)

FOR YOUR FOLDERS

▶ Are you light green, dark green or not green at all? Pause for a few moments to think about it or discuss it. Now write down your answer, and explain it. (If you are not sure what these terms mean, find out before going further.) Now look back to what you have written. Did you simply consider strictly *environmental* issues, or did you include the *moral* side of things?

Very often, the terms 'light green' and 'dark green' refer only to how far people are willing to make changes in their lifestyle to take account of the environment. They say nothing about the **moral** issues involved. Judaism teaches that this is God's world, that we are entrusted with its care and that we must exercise that care in a moral way.

Conservation

In his memoirs, Rabbi Joseph Isaac Schneersohn of Lubavitch (1880–1950) writes of how, as a young child, he used to walk through the Russian countryside with his father. He once reached up and plucked a leaf off a tree. His father bent down and shook his head. 'No, my son,' he told him in a gentle voice, 'at the time of creation God decided that this leaf should grow on this particular tree at this very time. Everything in nature is put there to serve God's purpose. We can use them for our needs, but we must be careful not to destroy things unnecessarily.' He wrote that, for the rest of his life, he never wantonly destroyed anything again.

TALKING POINT

● How do you think seeing the planet as God's world affects a person's attitude to the environment?

The Torah speaks of human beings being put on this planet *'to work it and to look after it'* (Genesis 2:15). The Torah, Talmud and later Jewish writings all give guidelines for doing this. One of the most important is the principle of not destroying anything unnecessarily.

'When you lay siege to a city . . . you must not destroy its trees by taking up an axe against them; . . . for the tree of the field is man's life . . .'
(Deuteronomy 20:19)

In ancient times, an army attacking a city would lay siege to it – they would build a wall around it so that no one could get out. Jews were commanded not to cut down fruit trees for their siege walls.

In the Oral Torah (see page 152) this is taken as an example of not wasting things in general. Judaism forbids the purposeless destruction of anything. *'Fill the world and have control over it.'* (Genesis 1:28), is taken to mean that God wanted people to use the world's resources wisely. In Jewish thinking, wasting natural resources is a misuse of the position God has given us.

Another important Jewish conservation principle is the **migrash** – an area of open land surrounding towns (Numbers 35:2). In ancient times all the cities of Israel had them.

In some ways, the migrash resembles today's 'green belt'. However, unlike the green belt (which is often the site of golf courses, cemeteries or rubbish tips), the migrash was to be preserved as open land. No one was permitted to grow crops or set up a business there. It provided the town with a light, airy and pleasant setting, where people could sit, stroll or picnic.

The Talmud also describes the ancient practice of enhancing the beauty of a town by surrounding it with a ring of fruit trees.

Pollution

In Jewish thinking, people's health and well-being always come before commercial interests. The Talmud, applying this principle to town planning, insists that businesses that cause annoyance or that produce harmful substances must be kept at a suitable distance from towns, and always away from the prevailing winds.

Today, it is not simply a matter of keeping industrial plants away from towns. The problem is much more complicated.

Manufacturing processes always produce waste, much of it toxic. It might be given off as smoke, poured into the sea or buried in land fills. Whichever way, it is sooner or later absorbed by fish, or seeps into the soil and finds its way into plants and the animals that feed on them. Eventually, it enters our own food chain. There is no simple way of preventing these substances from reaching people. Applying the Talmud's principles to today's conditions, Judaism would consider it essential for *all* factories to have waste treatment facilities *before* they started operating.

The moral dimension

A few years ago, a zoologist in Africa allowed himself to be charged down by a white rhino rather than use his rifle to shoot a member of an endangered species. Some time later a British motorist was killed when another driver swerved to avoid hitting a swan that was crossing the road. At that time, the AA issued a warning telling drivers not to endanger human life for the sake of animals.

These incidents reflect a trend that is growing out of our present day concerns about the environment – *people are beginning to regard themselves as just another part of the ecosystem.* In Jewish thinking, such a view is misguided and dangerous. It leads to denying the supreme value of human beings.

When Rabbi Schneersohn's father protected a tree in a remote Russian forest, he did so not because he saw himself and the tree as two parts of the same ecosystem, but because he saw nature as created by God to be the place where we humans can carry out his will. For Jews, environmental concerns have to take into account the special place of humanity in creation. In other words they have to have a *moral* dimension

For example, should Brazilian rain forests be cut down to make room for farms? In Jewish terms it is not simply a matter of balancing the amount of carbon dioxide being given off into the atmosphere against the amount the trees can re-absorb. It is also a *human* question.

If the trees are cut down, the forest dwellers lose their home and their way of life; if they are not, there will be insufficient farmland for a poor country with a growing population.

There are no easy solutions. But, for Jews the human dimension is a central part of any discussion of these issues.

THINGS TO DO

▶ Make a survey of the environmentally friendly products used by members of your class. Some Jewish pupils are designing a poster to promote the use of such products. How might they word it?

▶ When coal is used to produce energy it gives off a number of environmental pollutants. However, closing down the mines and going over to cleaner sources of energy would result in massive unemployment, and hardship for thousands of people. How would you expect a Jew to respond to the problem?

▶ Imagine that a religious Jew has just been appointed Secretary of State for the Environment. What steps do you think they might take (a) immediately (b) as long-term projects?

'And so we wait for you O Lord our God, to see very soon the glory of your power . . . to establish the world under the kingship of the Almighty . . . when all human beings will call upon your name . . . when they will all accept your kingship . . .'

(Prayer Book)

With these words, Jews conclude each of their three daily prayers. They pray, as they have prayed for centuries, for the dawning of a new age when all humankind will be united under the rule of God. They expect this to happen through the coming of the messiah.

FOR YOUR FOLDERS

▶ Before going further, write down your own idea of a perfect world. Now put what you have written to one side; you will need to refer to it later.

The messiah

'King Messiah will, in the future, arise and restore the Kingdom of David to its former glory . . . anyone who does not believe in his coming or who does not await it denies the Torah and the prophets . . .'

(Maimonides)

In Jewish thinking, human history, as we know it, is not open-ended. It will be brought to an end when God finally comes to take up his dwelling place in this world, making his presence felt by all people (see page 150). That, as Jews understand it, is what the world was created for, and that is the destiny to which it is moving.

The new age is to be brought in by the messiah. The books of the prophets describe many of the things that are to happen when he comes. From the Tanach, the Talmud and Midrash we learn that the messiah is to be a descendant of King David, and a man of exceptional wisdom, piety and qualities of leadership. Jews do not think of him as a divine being, but a person sent by God to carry out certain tasks.

According to an ancient Jewish teaching, in each generation there is someone ready to assume the role of messiah as soon as God calls him. He will be called either if people are so righteous that they deserve the new age, or so wicked that they need a powerful spiritual leader to save them from themselves. Otherwise he will be revealed only in his pre-ordained time.

During the last century, leaders of the Reform Movement began placing a different emphasis on those biblical passages that referred to the time of the messiah. They took them to mean the dawning of a 'messianic age', rather than the appearance of an actual messiah. They think of this not as a new world order but a moral ideal, and so they do not look forward to the rebuilding of the Temple (see pages 152 and 153), or many of the things that Jews have prayed for for centuries.

The world to come

'This world is like an entrance hall in front of the World to Come; prepare yourself in the entrance so that you may enter the dining hall.'

(Ethics of the Fathers)

The time of the messiah is sometimes called 'the world to come'. It is expected to be a period of moral perfection. One of the messiah's first tasks will be to establish peace all over the world.

'They shall beat their swords into ploughshares and their spears into pruning hooks. Nation shall not lift up sword against nation, nor shall they train any more for war.'

(Micah 4:3)

There will be no violence of any sort, and people will be able to go about their daily tasks, or simply relax, without fear.

'Every man shall sit under his vine and fig tree; and no one shall make them afraid.'

(Micah 4:4)

There will also be a change in people's values. The Talmud tells the story of a rabbi who was ill and fell into a coma. When he revived his father asked him, 'What did you see?' He answered, 'I saw a world turned upside-down. Those who are powerful here were low there, those who are low here were raised up.' 'My son,' his father replied, 'you have seen the pure world.'

In this world people often reach the top through aggressiveness – trampling over other people to get what they want. Sometimes, success is achieved through dishonesty. In the messianic age, such undesirable qualities will bring a person down; only through virtue will a person be able to advance.

'In this world one man builds a house but another uses it; one man plants trees and another eats the fruit. But in the world to come "they shall not build and another inhabit, they shall not plant and another eat . . ." (Isaiah 65:22)'

(Midrash)

The whole period will be one of friendship and cooperation.

'In the world to come there will be neither jealousy, hatred nor rivalry.'

(Talmud)

One of the messiah's most important tasks will be to rebuild the Jerusalem temple. This was originally built by King Solomon in the 10th century BCE, and destroyed many centuries later by the Babylonians. Seventy years later, a second temple was built on the same site, but was destroyed by the Romans in 70 CE. The messiah is expected to build the third and final temple. It is to be a spiritual centre for the whole of humanity, and all nations will come to worship there.

Towards an ideal world

When Jews speak of an ideal world they usually mean the time of the messiah. Each day, for many centuries, Jews have prayed for this new age to dawn.

Although the Talmud teaches that long ago God decided when the time of the messiah will come about, it also teaches that people can bring the ideal age nearer by the way they live their lives now (see page 153).

In Jewish terms this means that Jews would have to live by their 613 **mitzvot**, and non-Jews by their seven (see pages 150 and 151).

Jews are expected to help other Jews to keep God's commandments. They are also expected to encourage all people to live by the Noahide Code (see page 150).

'Moses commanded us, by the word of God, to bring all the inhabitants of the earth to accept the commandments that were given to Noah and his descendants.'

(Maimonides)

This means that, to some degree, perfection can be attained here and now. It also means that bringing the glorious future about is in our hands, and that Jews and non-Jews, in their different ways, can be partners in working towards an ideal world.

The Sikh religion began in a part of India known as the Punjab almost 500 years ago. It is based on teachings revealed by God to ten **Gurus**. A guru is a special teacher who helps people to develop their spiritual lives and also becomes a guide generally, helping them in making family and career decisions. They might refer to him as **babaji** which means *grandad*. This is a term of respect as well as affection. Indian culture puts great stress upon honouring older people. A very special relationship exists between children and grandparents.

Learners and disciples

The word 'Sikh' means **learner** or **disciple**. The first Sikhs were men and women who were disciples of a man called **Guru Nanak** who lived from 1469 to 1539 and began his preaching mission round about 1499. He was a man who was very concerned for the ordinary people, the Indian villagers whose lives were often miserable and hopeless. He taught them in their own language, *not* Sanskrit which was the ancient language used by Indian holy men. Guru Nanak believed that God cared for everyone. To have used a language which only a few could understand would have been to deny this.

One god and one humanity

The key teaching about God which Guru Nanak preached is that God is one. God is the only eternal reality. Men and women, the universe, planets, trees and oceans, all kinds of life forms are created by God and will eventually disappear. God will remain. This one God is present in creation and also in each human being. People of vision and insight can be aware of this. Guru Nanak's task was to tell them that this was true and then help those who were interested and believed him to discover it for themselves.

Because God is one and is present in all human beings it follows that all should be respected equally. All humanity is one. This should be a guiding principle in matters of behaviour and attitude. Women should be given the same opportunities as men. In the Sikh place of worship, the **gurdwara**, they can conduct all services and ceremonies. There are no priests because this would suggest that some people are more important in the eyes of God than others are. Discrimination on grounds of gender, colour of skin, race, or religion should not be found among Sikhs and they should oppose it wherever they come across it, because all human beings are equal whether they be Muslim, African, a king or a beggar. In the gurdwara everyone sits on the floor. This is a practical way of showing that no one is superior or inferior to anyone else.

Pray, work, and give

Sikhs often quote a brief Punjabi saying, '*Nam japo, kirt karo, vand chako*' which means 'meditate on God's name, work honestly, give to those in need'. This tells Sikhs that a right relationship with God, based on the Gurus' teachings, is the foundation stone of life. Daily meditation and joining with other believers in worship develops this. However, honest hard work is not an option that is to be avoided if at all possible. God has put humankind in the world to work as well as to meditate. The saying also teaches that the money or goods people get from working must be used to care for others. Caring is not an option either. Religion must not be a selfish effort to save one's own soul. These ideals of Sikhism will recur many times in this book because teachings about such things as the family, justice, the use of alcohol and tobacco, as well as obvious matters like attitudes to wealth and racism, are based on them.

Sikhs have almost always been ruled by other cultures and have not been able to make their own laws. For a time, from 1799 to 1849, there was a Sikh state in the Punjab, but then it became part of British India. After Independence, in 1947, India introduced a new code of laws. Since 1956 Hindu laws on marriage, divorce, adoption, and inheritance have applied to Sikhs, Jains and Buddhists. Muslims, Christians and Parsees have their own family law.

Sikhs have migrated to other parts of India and to most countries, though most still live in the Punjab. There are about 16 million Sikhs world wide. Outside India the largest population is in Britain where about 400 000 live.

The Guru Granth Sahib

Guru Nanak taught through poetry which was set to music, as songs are easy to remember. He had nine successors who taught the same message and cared for the growing Sikh community, or **Panth** as Sikhs call it. Six of his nine successors also composed religious poetry but the tenth and last of them, **Guru Gobind Singh**, refused to include any of his hymns in the scripture which he finally

The Guru Granth Sahib is the focus of Sikh worship and life

compiled, the **Guru Granth Sahib**. This book occupies a central place in all gurdwaras. There are no human Gurus among the Sikhs today. They worship the one God, using the hymns of the Gurus to offer praise and to guide them in their everyday lives. Passages from the Guru Granth Sahib will be quoted in most sections of this book. All copies are of a standard form, 1430 printed pages long. It is sometimes also called the **Adi Granth** so it is customary to refer to a passage in the Sikh scripture by using AG and a page number only, for example AG 1429. This will be done in this book.

Dress

Sikhs are often recognizable by their appearance. Many of them keep their hair uncut, so Sikh boys may have their hair tied on their heads in a top knot and covered with a handkerchief. When they are older they will wear a **turban**. This is not to keep the hair tidy, it serves as a mark of identity. Women often wear Punjabi dress, **shalwar kameeze**, a kind of trouser suit. Many women who live in the western world dress like the people among whom they have settled. They do not need to wear the turban though some do. Almost all Sikhs, men, women and children, wear a steel wristlet, called a **kara**, on the right wrist. Although Sikhs lay great emphasis upon appearance, they should not forget that it is obedience to the spiritual and ethical teachings of the Gurus that matters most of all.

FOR YOUR FOLDERS

▶ Sikh means *learner* or *disciple*. What learning should Sikhs value most? How do they get this learning?
▶ How do Sikhs show their equality in the gurdwara?
▶ Sikh men may use the name 'Singh' instead of the family name and women may use 'Kaur'. For example 'Jaswant Singh', 'Rani Kaur'. How can this express the idea of equality?

FOR DISCUSSION

▶ Why do you think Sikhs in Britain still say that knowing Punjabi is important?

THINGS TO DO

▶ Try to find out more about the Punjab. Try to link up with people of your own age in the nearest Sikh community so that you may be able to talk about some of the issues in this book with them.
Discover why it is important for Sikh men to wear a turban.

People are divine

Sikhism teaches that human beings are created by God and that God lives in them. In other words, people are part of God. Guru Nanak said:

'O, my body, God infused divine light in you and you were born into the world.'

(AG 921)

'You are immanent in all beings.'

(AG 1291)

This means that for Sikhs all human beings are divine in essence, even if sometimes we have to dig deep to find the essence! Therefore everyone should be respected in the way God is honoured. If anyone curses a human being they are cursing God. In practice the rich and powerful are respected because they can choose to help other people or do them harm. The poor and weak are ill-treated because people like to feel that they have some power over others. The truth is forgotten or ignored.

The Sikh Gurus taught that two things were necessary if human beings were to respect one another. The first is **meditation**. As someone recites the Gurus' teachings and reflects upon them, the divine spark they are born with will be blown into a flame. God's completely undeserved love, known as grace, brings this about.

'The mind which is defiled by vices is purified by the love of God.'

(AG 4)

Secondly, the Gurus were wise enough to realize the value of mixing with like-minded men and women. Negatively, Guru Nanak taught:

'He who associates with evildoers is ruined.'
(AG 1343)

Positively, he said:

'In good company one becomes good, pursues virtues and cleans oneself of vices.'
(AG 414)

Haumai

Sikhs do not believe that people are evil by nature. The reasons why they exploit one another in so many ways, they say, are **ignorance** and **self-centredness**. Ignorance, because they are blind to reality. They fail to see God in others as well as in themselves. Self-centredness because they think that they are at the centre of the universe.

KEY IDEA

Self-centredness leads me to imagine I am the most important person in the universe. This means that everyone else is likely to become the victim of my selfishness – unless I am afraid of them.

Sikhs use the word **haumai** to describe this falsehood which prevents them from realizing the truth and doing it. Haumai turns love into lust, partnership into the wish to dominate, and a healthy appetite of any kind into greed.

Friendship

Sikhs teach that human friendships should be genuine and open, not based on a calculation that the friend can help in some way. In practice Sikh friendships are traditionally with people of the same sex. Indian society doesn't encourage young men and young women to mix freely outside the family after puberty. This is an important reason why marriages are usually arranged. Friendships are often formed most closely with cousins and other members of the extensive kinship group, who tend to have the same values and share the same interests. As Indians, Sikhs have shared these attitudes to friendships, but changes are taking place among Sikhs born in Britain, especially if their parents were also born in the United Kingdom.

Love

The love of God has already been mentioned. Love is a characteristic of God which has been implanted in human beings. Sikhs should love one another which, once again, means that they should treat them with respect. It will be obvious, for example, that an arranged marriage is different from the love marriages which are usual in western countries. People who have not met cannot be in love with one another. For Sikhs, emotional love is not the best foundation for a marriage relationship.

Relationship problems

Sikhs, like every other group, experience personal problems. When individuals cannot sort them out for themselves they will go to the family, which is a kind of vast counselling service. If the problem is debt, someone will try to find the money to pay off the debts. If a mother needs a break from a large family because her health is suffering, there will be sisters, parents and cousins available to bring relief for a few days, weeks or even months. In Britain this network does not always exist, but Sikhs would be very reluctant to share their problems with social workers. Pride requires them to keep things in the family or at least in the Sikh community. It is a bad family, not to be respected, which cannot solve its difficulties.

In the Punjab, life is more disciplined than in Britain. The different groups, Hindus, Muslims, Christians, Jains and Sikhs share a very similar culture of arranged marriages, and no sexual relationships before or outside marriage. The family even choose what careers their children will follow. Most children live in the family home until they marry, and often after the wedding. *Independence* and *individuality* for young Sikhs have different meanings than they do for many western young people. The wisdom of their parents is trusted and the rules they lay down are generally accepted and regarded as sensible.

A Sikh family is 'extended'. What does this mean? What do you see as the benefits and drawbacks of an extended family?

FOR YOUR FOLDERS

▶ Haumai is self-centredness. In Punjabi it means, 'I-I'. What would Sikhs say is the difference between
(a) love and lust
(b) ambition and exploitation
(c) trying to win fairly and unfairly?

▶ What do Sikhs mean when they say respect for others begins when you have discovered the divine within yourself?

FOR DISCUSSION

▶ The third Guru, Ram Das, wrote, *'Just as the castor oil plant imbibes the scent of the adjacent sandalwood, similarly even those who have fallen are freed by the company of the true ones.'*

(AG 861)

Explain this verse and discuss the wisdom of the advice. Think of some actual examples.

THINGS TO DO

▶ Think of one or two family problems. Imagine you live in a Sikh extended family. Through role play, work out possible solutions. Characters could include grandparents, a paternal uncle and his wife, as well as parents and children. Remember you should play a number of different roles to try to understand various points of view.

▶ Act out a situation where a newly married Sikh couple try to persuade their parents to let them set up their own home.

The family is the key to Sikh relationships and to their outlook on life. It is in the family that children should first become aware of God, learn how to live with other people and gain values. The Gurus often said:

'Why look for God in the forest when God is at home?'

(e.g. AG 684)

This was a reference to the accepted Hindu practice of leaving the family to embark upon the fourth stage of life, that of **sannyasin**, to concentrate completely on the search for spiritual liberation. Such men, for the possibility was not open to women, came from the three highest castes. They rejected not only their families but their wealth and their names. They denied themselves all luxuries and tried to live without as many necessities as possible. For example, they ate only simple food which they begged because they had nothing of their own except for the clothes they wore. These might only be a loin cloth and a blanket. When they became **ascetics** they would even reject their names and would perform funeral rites over a clay image of themselves. They were dead to the world. Ascetics believe that by denying themselves material things and disciplining the body in this way they can free the spirit.

This kind of asceticism was not available to most of the men who listened to the Gurus and became their disciples. They did not belong to the higher castes and their families were often so poor, and in need of every available pair of hands, that it would have been irresponsible to leave them. Anyway, the Gurus didn't think that the ascetic path led anywhere except, perhaps, to haumai.

KEY IDEA

There is always the danger of self-denial becoming a form of selfishness.

'Practising self torture to subdue desires only wears out the body. The mind is not subdued through fasting and penances.'

(First Guru, AG 905)

Celibacy has never been regarded as a virtue by Sikhs.

The married life is the right life

Sikhism insists that every adult should marry, if possible. It may be that some disability renders marriage impossible or undesirable, or there is an inequality in the ratio of men to women, as after a war, but the norm for Sikhs is the married state. Only Guru Harkishan was unmarried and that was because he died at the age of eight. The fourth Guru, Ram Das, composed a hymn called **Lavan** which is used at weddings. In this way he showed that marriage is more than a social contract. It is part of God's plan and order. Nowadays Sikh marriages take place in the presence of the Guru Granth Sahib.

The importance of the family is a feature of Indian life. In most Indian languages there are special words to distinguish between maternal and paternal grandparents. (None of the problem of 'Which gran are you talking about, Mum?' that happens in the English language!) **Nani** means your mother's mother, **dadi** is your father's mother. There are special words, too, that can be used when you are speaking about other relatives.

A head of family

It is customary to have a head of an extended family. Among Sikhs this may be a man *or* woman and need not always be the most senior member, but it usually is. Shortly after the head of a family has died senior members will meet to appoint a successor. If this is a man someone will tie his turban in public, to acknowledge that he has been chosen, so that no one may dispute his position. In the case of a woman there is no ceremony. The decisions she makes are likely to be passed on to the family by one of her sons.

The extended Sikh family is a great support group. If any child becomes orphaned it will be adopted by relatives. If the parents or grandparents are unable to care for themselves one of their sons will look after them. This is usually the youngest one. He is likely to have least responsibilities and still need help and guidance from his parents.

How the family works

This is the story of one Sikh family in the Punjab. The father died leaving five sons and two daughters as well as his widow. The oldest son went out to work and put his next brother through college. This son then looked after the family while his older brother went to college. This process continued until all the sons and daughters had received higher education. Next came the marriage of the two daughters, the elder first, of course, in the Indian tradition, and the weddings of the sons, in order of age. The widow went to live with her oldest son. In this example the children set up their own homes rather than living under the same roof. (In India it is not usual for most students to receive grants to help them pay for higher education.)

The family decides

Extended families may choose marriage partners for their children, because it is a matter of concern to all the family when a new member joins it. They may not fit in. Imagine a girl from the city who has been used to servants (a common experience, not a sign of great wealth as in Britain), finding herself on a farm where she is expected to milk the cows. She might never even have seen one!

Families may also choose their children's careers. For example, a farming family had no need for a younger son to work on the farm. Mechanization had meant that the father and older son could manage. They decided that the younger son should train as an accountant so that he could keep the books and deal with the tax inspector!

Some idea of the importance of the family in Sikh life can be seen from the way in which close friends will be called 'brother' or 'sister'. To be made an honorary family member is a mark of great respect.

The family is important to Sikhs

Sikh marriage is a religious act. In some countries a civil wedding may have to be performed in a register office. Sikhs accept this but the couple are only properly married when the ceremony has taken place in the presence of the Guru Granth Sahib. In Britain this will normally be in a **gurdwara**, the Sikh place of worship. In a country with India's climate it may be in the open air, even on the flat roof of a house. The place is unimportant but it is usually in the bride's home district. Engagement parties and other activities which may be arranged are also unimportant. It is the witness of the Guru Granth Sahib that matters. This is a way of showing that God sees the marriage and blesses it.

Arranged marriages (see page 191) are not really in keeping with the ethics of Sikhism. The Gurus had arranged marriages and arranged them for their own children, but that was the custom of the day. No opportunities existed for young men and women to meet outside family gatherings, and Sikhs may not marry close relatives. In practice this means they must not share any of the same great grandparents.

An open-air wedding in India

Today, in Britain and in the Punjab, young Sikhs may have a considerable say in their marriages. However, parents and perhaps other relatives still like to feel included in the choice of partner. Love marriages are not altogether trusted. The married life is seen to be the way in which God intended human beings to live. Its purpose is to fulfil God's wishes, not to curb or legalize sexual urges or just to procreate, though naturally there is a hope that a marriage will result in children.

Sometimes shoes may be given as wedding presents. They belong in pairs. One is no good without the other.

THINGS TO DO

► Try to see a video of a Sikh wedding, or attend one if you can. Sikhs would welcome you, though there will be crowds of people present if it is on a Sunday. How is the importance of the Guru Granth Sahib as witness of the wedding shown?

FOR DISCUSSION

► Guru Nanak said:
'They are not man and wife who have only physical contact. Only those are truly married who have one spirit in two bodies'

(AG 788)

What do you think he meant?

Weddings bring two families together

Remarriage of widows

Widows were often thought to be unlucky in the India of Guru Nanak's day. The Gurus would have none of this. They permitted widows to remarry, just as widowers had always done, but they said that if a woman did not want to, she was under no obligation to remarry and no pressure should be brought upon her to do so. Whatever she decided to do she should be treated as a full and respected member of her family and of the Sikh community.

In the past, a widow might marry the brother of her deceased husband to become his second wife. When it happened the wedding would not take place in the presence of the Guru Granth Sahib, because the arrangement was purely social. It was a way of caring for the widow and her family. The community would be present to show its approval. Under Indian law it is now illegal to have two wives.

FOR DISCUSSION

▶ How can a Sikh family care for a widowed sister-in-law and her family today in India?

Divorce

Divorce is – reluctantly – permitted by Sikhs but marriage is intended to be for life and its failure is an upset to family pride. Consequently the family does all it can to hold a marriage together. Sikh grounds for divorce are desertion, insanity, the impotence of the husband, habitual cruelty, adultery and change of religion. A fairly common reason was the failure of the wife to have children, though this could once lead to the husband taking a second wife, so long as the first one gave her agreement.

As in many other matters Sikhs will be influenced by the laws of the land in which they live. In 1976 the government of India allowed divorce by mutual consent. Sikhs have accepted this. They do not ask for their own courts or Sikh codes of family law to be introduced.

Even though Sikhs believe that marriage should be for life, there is no religious objection to the remarriage of divorced men or women. Of course, this takes place in the presence of the Guru Granth Sahib. As with the remarriage of widows or widowers it is unlikely to be celebrated in the same festive atmosphere as the wedding of two young people.

Polygamy

Three of the Sikh Gurus, Guru Arjan, Guru Hargobind, and Guru Gobind Singh, had more than one wife. Sikh aristocrats sometimes followed this custom but the teaching of Guru Nanak was that:

'A Sikh should follow the instructions of the Guru and not imitate his lifestyle.'

(AG 933)

He recognized that the Gurus' standards could be too high or, on the other hand, Gurus being mortals were as capable of error as other people. Only God is perfect. Anyone who adopts human beings as heroes always take a risk.

Bhai Gurdas, a very famous Sikh who helped the fifth Guru, Arjan, to compile the Sikh scriptures, expressed the view that:

'A Sikh should have one wife and treat other women as sisters and daughters.'

(Var 6; pauri 8)

On the whole this has been the Sikh way. However, two exceptions have been accepted by Sikhs generally, which have already been mentioned. In 1956 India made polygamy illegal. It is also illegal in Britain. If Sikhs still wish to practise polygamy it means that the couple have to live together as common law husband and wife, after a gurdwara marriage. Sikhs would recognize the children of such a union as legitimate and they would enjoy full rights of inheritance.

FOR YOUR FOLDERS

▶ Explain why Sikhs might allow a man to have two wives.
▶ What grounds can a Sikh woman have for divorce?

FOR DISCUSSION

▶ A Sikh woman is not allowed to have more than one husband. What reasons do you think Sikhs might give for this?

Sikhs believe that sexual activity is normal and acceptable. The sexual urge is part of the make up of all creatures and is implanted in human beings by God. However, the sex act is an expression of the union of husband and wife. There is no place for it outside marriage. It may be important in a marriage but it is not to be considered an end in itself. It is a way of expressing a deeper union. Guru Nanak said:

> 'Real union between husband and wife occurs when the heart of one dies in the other's and they become one as a necklace of pearls with the passing of a thread through them.'
>
> (AG 58)

The natural and proper place which sex has in life can be abused. Sikhs argue that pornographic books and films, prostitution and lust leading to adultery, are all indications of how it can get out of control or be exploited. This is another aspect of haumai (see page 188), putting self first, which is the main reason for life getting out of order according to Sikh teaching. The Gurus did not underestimate the power of this tendency. They warned husbands:

> 'Do not cast your eyes on the beauty of another's wife.'
>
> (Guru Nanak AG 274)

Wives were told:

> 'There can be no happiness without virtue.'
>
> (Guru Nanak AG 56)

In Sikh teaching the primary wifely virtue is chastity. Virginity is a bride's badge of respectability.

Sex outside marriage

Sex outside marriage has no place in Sikhism. Young people in their teens or even earlier become aware of their sexuality and are likely to become physically attracted to one another. They may not be able to exercise the restraint which adults should be capable of in such circumstances. This is a major reason why Sikh parents are anxious about their sons and daughters going to disco dances, parties, and dating. There have been cases of Sikh fathers murdering daughters who became pregnant. These are well known in the community. While such conduct cannot be condoned, it should be seen as

the desperate act of someone who saw all the values of his culture being threatened by the different standards of western society, and did not know how else to respond. The solution of some Sikhs to this kind of threat is to arrange the early marriage of their sons and daughters.

Birth control

As Sikhs do not believe that the primary purpose of sexual intercourse is to have children, there is no opposition to birth control. Of course this must be completely voluntary. When the Indian government introduced a policy of compulsory male sterilization during the Emergency of 1975, Sikhs were united in their opposition to it. It violated basic human rights and was seen as tampering with the God-given natural form. For the same reason, Sikhs do not agree with circumcision and do not cut their hair. There may be genuine health reasons which make a vasectomy necessary, or the removal of the ovaries or other parts of the body. Sikhs will accept these but believed there were *not* valid reasons for the government's actions.

Abortion

In recent years most countries in which Sikhs live have legalized abortion. Sikhs believe that human life begins at conception, so abortion is morally wrong. The sanctity of human life is not to be violated. If conception is the result of rape this *might* be a justification for terminating a pregnancy. Sikhs do not accept the possibility of a child being born with severe mental or physical abnormalities as being sufficient reason for an abortion, though in such situations Sikhs recognize the rights of parents to make their own decision. (See page 211, amniocentesis.)

Celibacy

This may be a way of life which someone chooses to adopt. If the motive is spiritual development and implies a belief that the married state is inferior to the celibate, Sikhs would reject this as wasted effort (see page 190).

Homosexuality

This is not new but it does seem to be something the Gurus did not encounter for they did not comment upon it in their teachings. In recent times the claim has been made that homosexuality is as natural as heterosexuality, but less common. Sikhs might eventually come to respect that view but traditionally they see it as perversion, performed for totally immoral reasons. Such acts are considered degrading, damaging to the human personality, and as far removed from the true purpose of sex as prostitution is in Sikh eyes.

FOR YOUR FOLDERS

▶ List the methods of birth control that Sikhs would use.
List the methods of birth control that Sikhs would not use.
Give reasons for the Sikh choices.

FOR DISCUSSION

▶ What reasons would Sikhs give for disapproving of pornographic magazines and films showing explicit sex?
▶ Should childless Sikh couples feel inadequate?
▶ What do Sikhs mean when they say that marriage is not just for sex?

THE LAVAN

The first time round is the time for toil, for work in the world as the Lord may decree;
The Word of the Guru the text which we follow, confirming our faith and destroying our sin.
Be firm in believing and ponder God's Name, as prescribed by the scriptures of old.
Give to the Guru devout adoration, renouncing all evil and wrong.
Blessed is she who adores the Lord's Name, for its praises bring radiant bliss.
Nanak declares that the first of our rounds marks the start of our marriage with God.

The second time round is the time for our meeting, the meeting which comes with our only True Lord.
Fear is dispelled and our spirits are cleansed from the filth of our self-centred pride.
The fear we retain is our fear of the Lord as we sing

to his praise and perceive him in all;
The Master is present in all his creation, his being pervading whatever we see.
Within and without he is ever our comrade; come join with his faithful and sing to his praise.
The mystical music resounds in our hearts as we follow the second round.

The third time round is the time for detachment, for freeing our minds from all wordly desire.
Blessed is she who unites with the faithful, for thus she is brought to her Lord.
She who finds God will sing hymns to his glory, the words which she utters inspired by her Lord.
Blessed is she who is found with the faithful, who utters the words of ineffable truth.
God's Name shall resound in the depths of her spirit, the Name we repeat if our fate so decrees.
The third round progresses, God rises within us, and cleanses our minds from all pride and desire.

Our spirits find peace as the fourth round commences, for God comes to dwell in our hearts and our minds.
By the grace of the Guru we know he is present, his sweetness pervading our bodies and souls.
This sweetness flows forth from the love which God nurtures for all who are rapt in his infinite bliss.
Desires they have treasured find precious reward at the sound of his glorious Name.
The bride who is chosen to marry her Lord knows that wonderful Name as it surges within.
Nanak declares that the fourth of our rounds brings our ultimate union with God.

THINGS TO DO

▶ Each of the four verses of the *Lavan* makes a number of points about the relationship of humans and God. Copy each verse, and list the points it makes beneath it.

FOR DISCUSSION

▶ The *Lavan* mentions God and the bride. Do you think it applies to the bridegroom? Can God be regarded as the bridegroom in the *Lavan*?

At the time when Sikhism developed as a religion, the wife of a brahmin, the highest Hindu caste, was as likely to be despised as a low caste man. Blood was considered ritually polluting, so during menstruation and after giving birth women were to be avoided. At all times they were inferior. They had very few civil rights. The better place they enjoyed in the early days of Hinduism had long been lost.

The Gurus taught the equality of all human beings. Sexual differences were merely functional. In the perfect marriage there should be equality (see page 192). Guru Nanak was particularly severe on the attitudes of his day towards women:

'We are conceived and born from women. Woman is our life-long friend and keeps the race going. Why should we despise her, the one who gives birth to great men?'

(AG 473)

All the Gurus were male, a fact explained by the culture of the day. No one would have followed a woman guru. However, within 20 years of the death of Guru Nanak, Guru Amar Das had appointed women to be preachers and missionaries. At the first Baisakhi initiation ceremony, in 1699, the wife of Guru Gobind Singh, Mata Sahib Kaur, helped prepare the **amrit**, a nectar of water and sugar crystals sanctified by the chanting of hymns composed by the Gurus. A woman taking part in such an activity would have polluted it in the eyes of many Hindu Indians. To this day, women may perform any function and hold any office in the Sikh community.

Practical difficulties

The difficulty which Sikh women face is the practical one of living in a man's world. It has not been considered important that they should be educated. Until recently a woman would not continue in a paid job after marriage. She might help on the farm or in a family business, but not in the work she had been doing while single. Her husband was expected to keep her. Her place was in the home.

In Punjabi culture a girl is **paraya dhan**, the property of others: first of her father, then of her husband. Her birth is unwelcome because she will be a source of expense, without any return. The family doesn't give boxes of sweets to relatives and friends when a daughter is born, as they do when a son is born. When she is married her in-laws will expect a **dowry**, even though it is illegal in India. Long ago the Gurus said this was wrong.

Practical responses

In 1976 the Sikh women of Smethwick decided to give a reminder of the Gurus' teaching to the community. At the annual gurdwara elections they registered their disapproval of the way in which affairs were being managed by voting in a committee of women, with one man! Since then there have been a number of women elected as president or secretary of a gurdwara and there are Sikh women magistrates, councillors, doctors and teachers. The Supreme Religious Council of the Sikhs, the **Shiromani Gurdwara Parbandhak Committee** in Amritsar, elected two women members for the first time in 1981.

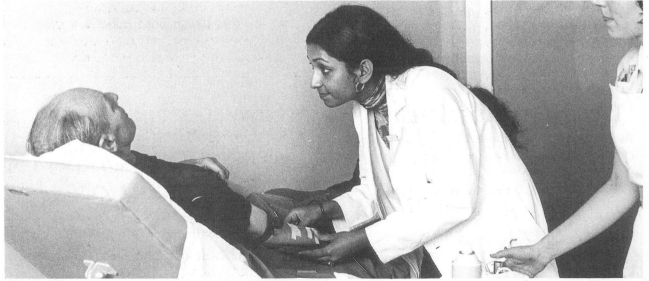

Sikhs should not believe that a woman's place is in the home!

The Gurus appointed women to positions of responsibility

Changes

Young men in Britain may be like their fathers and may prefer marriage to a quiet Punjabi girl rather than a western, educated, career-minded woman, but such marriages increasingly end in divorce and are being discouraged by Sikh leaders. A 60 year old wife may walk the traditional three paces behind her husband in Southall or Leicester, but young Sikh couples are more likely to be seen strolling hand in hand. This is a rare sight still in India and one which often brings disapproval, as would dressing in anything but the most modest of clothes. Even saris are unacceptable to some Sikhs, as they leave the arms bare.

Customs are changing but Sikh women have still to struggle to obtain the rights which the Gurus intended them to have, because of conventional ideas about behaviour.

Sati

One of the evils of Indian society, which reformers denounced for hundreds of years before it was made illegal in 1829, was the practice of **sati** or **suttee**. A wife would commit suicide by burning herself to death on her husband's funeral pyre. Long before 1829 the Sikh Gurus said that sati was evil and condemned it.

Guru Amar Das attacked its purpose, saying that it had no value:

'They should not be called satis who burn themselves with their husband's corpses. They are satis who die with the sheer shock of separation.

They also are satis who live modestly and contentedly, waiting upon the Lord whom they remember each morning when they wake up. Wives burn themselves on the funeral pyre with their husbands. If they have deep love for their spouse they will suffer physical and mental anguish without doing that. If they do not, what good will burning do? Whether the husband be alive or dead, such a wife is distant from him.'

(AG 787)

FOR YOUR FOLDERS

► Sikh women can take the name 'Kaur' instead of their husband's name. How might this help them establish personal independence?

► It was fairly common for girl babies to be killed at birth in the Punjab. The Gurus condemned this practice. Why?

► The word **sati** means *virtuous woman*. What kind of qualities does Guru Amar Das say such a woman should have?

FOR DISCUSSION

► 'The task for Sikh women is to overcome Punjabi culture.'

FOR YOUR FOLDERS

► How do Sikh attitudes to the birth of a daughter differ from those of Punjabi culture? Why?

► What is a role model? Why should Sikh women value Mata Sahib Kaur as a role model?

► What are the main reasons for Sikh women being second class members of their community?

Sati and **Suttee** are both accepted variations of the same word.

Caring for the body

Sikhs regard the body as a temple built by God which should be looked after with care. Its natural form should be respected and kept maintained, and one of the Sikh ideals is uncut hair. To an outsider this may seem trivial. Where is the harm in cutting the hair? Sikhs would reply that the Gurus kept their hair uncut. It is in the natural form, unspoiled, as God intended it to be. For this reason Sikhs do not circumcise their male children nor do they accept cosmetic surgery. Vasectomies, or the removal of the ovaries or womb as ways of achieving birth control do not have Sikh approval, although the removal of the womb because it was cancerous would be accepted without hesitation as being necessary. Sikhs believe that body hair should not be shaved off to improve physical appearance, but it can be removed in preparation for an operation. Incidentally, Sikh teaching about the hair also says that it should be combed regularly and kept clean. Sikhs may not always wash it when they take their daily shower but they probably do so about twice a week.

Smoking tobacco or taking drugs clouds the mind, and damages lungs, the heart and other parts of the body. In Guru Nanak's day it was quite usual for drugs to be taken. When the Guru had an audience with the emperor Babur, at a town called Saidpur which had just been captured, he was offered a drink containing opium. He replied that he was 'hooked' on praising God. The third Guru, Amar Das, said:

'By drinking wine one loses sanity and becomes mad; one loses the power of discrimination and incurs God's displeasure.'

(AG 554)

FOR YOUR FOLDERS

▶ Make up a short story to explain what is meant by 'power of discrimination'.

Drinking beer, wine and spirits – or any other form of alcohol – is considered wrong by Sikhs. They believe that alcohol weakens and damages the body and would point out the effect which it has on the kidneys. They would also say that it takes away, or at least weakens people's ability to think clearly. For example, drunken drivers are likely to think themselves as safe a driver as they normally would be, even though the evidence is clearly that they are a danger to themselves and others.

Sikhs believe that the mind should always be clear so that it can respond to God's will. They would say that concern for others is also important, but the first reason is so that they can be aware of God.

The Sikh Code of Discipline, the **Rahit Maryada**, says:

'Sikhs should not partake of alcohol, tobacco, drugs, or any other intoxicants.'

A Sikh who smokes and who has been initiated into the Khalsa family must undergo the initiation rite again. Nothing could better show how bad smoking is considered to be than that.

FOR YOUR FOLDERS

▶ Why might Sikhs say that God is displeased with wine drinkers?
▶ 'The uncut hair is a mark of identity.' What do Sikhs mean when they say this?
▶ Imagine that you are a Sikh parent with a son or daughter at college, who decides to cut their hair.
  (a) Write the letter from the son or daughter giving reasons for their decision.
  (b) Write your letter expressing your feelings and saying why you think they are wrong.
▶ What do Sikhs mean by 'cleanliness is part of godliness'?

Suicide

As the human body is a gift from God, Sikhs do not accept suicide as this damages it and destroys life. The Gurus spoke out very strongly against the Hindu custom of sati. This was a ritual by which a wife would commit suicide on her husband's funeral pyre (see page 197). Sikhs believe that life is given by God. It may be happy or sad. It may be long or short. Nobody has the right to shorten it by their own act. Guru Nanak said:

'God sends us and we take birth. God calls us back and we die.'

(AG 1239)

He also said:

> 'Who knows how we shall come to die? Who knows what manner of death will be ours?'
>
> (AG 555)

Sikhs believe that all these things are in God's hands and nobody should meddle in them. However, Sikhs realize that despair can drive people to take their own lives. Those who do are not condemned. They are given full Sikh funeral rites. This death is also seen to be God's will, but God would not be said to have caused it.

Euthanasia

Euthanasia is also called *mercy killing*, ending someone's life when any joy or pleasure has been replaced by pain and misery, day in and day out. For someone to do this without the consent of the 'victim' would be murder, but what if someone were asked to do it? What if the 'victim' were too ill to ask for relief? Answers are not as simple as people might like them to be. A person who is unconscious could be put on a life-support machine for years. Should this be permitted?

For most people in India, including Sikhs, these are not problems. People do live to a good old age but life-support machines are only to be found in a few hospitals in the largest cities. Sikhs haven't really needed to make up their minds on such matters. In the West, today, two views could be taken. One might be that nature must be allowed to take its course. Death should not be resisted in such cases, which are clearly different from the kind of situation where a sick or injured person can be restored to normal health. The other view is that it is the quality of life, not its length that matters, so if a person has reached a stage where they are merely a living corpse, euthanasia would be acceptable so long as there were legal and medical safeguards to make sure that it was voluntary. The Sikh is taught to remember:

> 'The dawn of a new day is the herald of a sunset. Earth is not your permanent home.'
>
> (Ravidas, AG 793)

These are words used in the funeral service. Each evening Sikhs are supposed to meditate upon some other words:

> 'Know the real purpose of being here and gather up the treasure under the guidance of the true Guru. Make your mind God's home. If he abides with you undisturbed, you will not be reborn.'
>
> (Guru, AG 13)

GURU AMAR DAS MISSION

Guru Amar Das Mission is a U.K. registered Charity. Its primary role is to initiate as well as to assist Primary Health Care Projects in the rural areas of Punjab. Our Charity in particular, funds Eye Camps. It also assists Charitable Hospitals or Trusts, especially those caring for Leprosy sufferers. There is an enormous amount of work to do to help alleviate blindness and suffering in our motherland for which we need your help. We have the expertise to ensure that donations given are properly utilised and accounted for. Please help generously. You may send us a single donation, or pay by deed of covenant, or pay a small sum monthly, or remember us in your will. Next time you have a function to celebrate any occasion, be it a wedding, festival or just a party, do us a good deed, please make a collection on behalf of those who are blind and cannot see their loved ones, or who cannot earn a living because they have been disabled by an accident or a disease like leprosy. Help us to help those who need your help. You may contact any one of us listed below. If you would like to assist us in any way or become a Sevak in our Charity, or represent us in your area, please do not step back, join us, we need your help. You will be most welcome. If you wish to sponser an Eye Camp in the memory of a loved one, we will be able to advise and assist you or organise it on your behalf. Just think of the happiness and the joy, this could bring to those who are blind but can be cured by a simple operation. You can help someone to see again for a little as £10.00. The blessings of these needy people are upon you. Kar Sawa, Kha Mewa, Waheguru Ji Ka Khalsa, Waheguru Ji Ki Fateh.

Sikhs believe that the body matters, not just the soul

199

Work

Work should not be a chore for Sikhs. It is a religious duty. In the India of Guru Nanak's day there were men who taught that it was right to spend the whole of one's time in meditation or going on pilgrimages to holy places. Such people ate little but depended on those who did work to feed them. Guru Nanak said:

'Is it not shameful that a holy man should beg from door to door?'

(AG 903)

He had no time for men who were religious professionals, priests, astrologers or hermits. He criticized them saying:

'Cursed is the life of those who trade in the name of God.'

(AG 1245)

In the time of the Gurus, poor Hindu villagers had to work every day until they died. There were no sickness benefits and no retirement pensions. Life was hard, death could be a relief! These manual workers were often despised, yet holy men would beg from them. The Gurus said that work was a way of serving God and something to be proud of so long as it was honestly done.

'Every work is noble if performed in the right way.'
(3rd Guru, Amar Das, AG 568)

The only work that the Gurus said that Sikhs should avoid is anything which is dishonest or exploits others. Many Sikhs would include the sale of tobacco or alcohol, or organizing gambling among these unacceptable jobs.

For some Indians, begging is their profession. Sikhs disapprove of this. This means that Sikhs should try to help beggars find other work of a socially useful kind. Sikhs themselves should never beg.

Wealth

Two stories about Guru Nanak are usually told by Sikhs when they are discussing attitudes to wealth. One is about his meeting with Malik Bhago and Bhai Lalo.

The second story is about another rich man.

GURU NANAK, MALIK BHAGO AND BHAI LALO

Malik Bhago was a rich and important man in the town where he lived. When Guru Nanak went there Malik Bhago naturally thought that the Guru would stay with him. Instead he went to the shack which was the home of a very poor man, Bhai Lalo. Malik Bhago was deeply offended and made sure that the Guru knew how he felt! He asked the Guru to come to him to explain his insulting behaviour. When he came to Malik Bhago, Guru Nanak told him that his food was impure. His bread was made with the blood of the people he exploited. Bhai Lalo's was pure, made with the milk of honest work.

DUNI CHAND

Each time Duni Chand got another 100 000 rupees he hoisted a pennant over his house. Several flags flew from the building. Guru Nanak met Duni Chand and asked him to keep a needle for him and let him have it back in the next world. Duni Chand was delighted to have been honoured by the Guru. He ran home to tell his wife of the way in which Guru Nanak had given him the opportunity to serve him. His wife laughed and asked him whether the Guru had told him how to carry the needle to the next world – she had seen cremations and nothing much seemed to survive! A more down-to-earth Duni Chand went back to the Guru, who told him that only faith and a reputation for good deeds live on so he had better put his trust in God and begin to serve his fellow human beings instead of exploiting them. He became a Sikh, built a place of worship, and started to care for his needy neighbours.

FOR DISCUSSION

▶ These are some of the verses found in the Guru Granth Sahib relating to wealth. Read them and then discuss the questions written under them.

● *'The bounty of nature is there to be used. There is enough for all but in this world it is not shared justly.'*

(1st Guru, Nanak, AG 1171)

● *'He who gathers wealth by oppressing others is cursed by them. The relatives for whose comfort and pleasures this was done do not stay in this world forever.'*

(5th Guru, Arjan, AG 42)

● *'Blessed is the godly person and the riches they possess because they can be used for charitable purposes and to give happiness to others.'*

(4th Guru, Amar Das, AG 1246)

● *'Be grateful to God whose bounties you enjoy; be compassionate to the needy and the people you employ.'*

(1st Guru, Nanak)

● *'He who eats what he earns through hard work and gives with his own hand, he alone knows the true way of life.'*

(1st Guru, Nanak, AG 1245)

▶ In the light of these verses what seem to have been the main faults of
(a) Duni Chand
(b) Malik Bhago
from a Sikh point of view?

▶ Do you think the Gurus would approve of someone giving away all their possessions to become an ascetic? (An ascetic is a person who lives a very strict life, praying, fasting, probably leaving the family and having no possessions.) Give reasons for your decision.

▶ Why might Guru Nanak think it better actually to give to the needy with your own hands rather than put a ten pound note into a collecting box?

▶ What would Guru Arjan suggest were better things than wealth to pass on to our relatives? Why?

THINGS TO DO

▶ Act out these two stories, trying to get inside the minds of the main characters. Work out how Bhai Lalo felt when the Guru went to his home, or how Duni Chand came to his senses.

(If you have Sikhs in your class you should discuss whether the part of the Guru can be acted. Some Sikhs would not like this, and care should be taken not to give offence.)

FOR YOUR FOLDERS

▶ Do these stories actually condemn wealth? If so, why? If not, what do they condemn?
Why do you think these kinds of story have been kept alive by Sikhs?

Leisure

Sikhs are as fun loving as anyone else. They go on holidays, to football matches and to concerts. They read novels and paint. The Indian cricket team usually has one or more Sikhs in it and they are to be found in the hockey teams of several countries. Guru Nanak, however, spoke against watching plays and dancing:

'Dancing and plays are lower activities of the mind.'

(AG 465)

Gambling, smoking and drinking alcohol are also forbidden to Sikhs who still say that the best use of leisure is meditation.

'Some pass their time in gambling dens, others intoxicated with drink, and others robbing people of their wealth and possessions. Pious people devote their time to contemplation.'

(1st Guru, Nanak, AG 914)

Pray, work and give

On page 186, three things were mentioned, **nam japo**, **kirt karo** and **vand chako** – 'pray, work, and give.' **Seva** or community service covers them all. It is one of the distinctive aspects of Sikhism. The Gurus stressed the importance of devotion to God. After all, their main purpose was to enable seekers to know God, especially those who belonged to the lowest Hindu castes or were so-called **untouchables**. However, they also believed that God was worshipped not only by meditating and singing hymns but also by working hard instead of shunning the world, and by caring for instead of rejecting *all* human beings. He warned:

> 'Wandering ascetics, warriors, celibates, sannyasins, none of them obtains the fruit, [liberation], without performing seva.'
>
> (AG 992)

> 'A place in God's court can only be attained if we do service to others in this world.'
>
> (AG 26)

Worship and compassion went together:

> 'There can be no worship without performing good deeds.'
>
> (AG 4)

> 'The rain of your gracious glance falls wherever the poor are cared for.'
>
> (AG 15)

Bhai Gurdas, a relative of the fifth Guru wrote:

> 'A sign of divine worship is the service of one's fellows.'
>
> (Var 14:7)

> 'The sign of a good person is that they always seek the welfare of others.'
>
> (Var 20:12)

Some Hindus of Guru Nanak's time would not help people outside their family or caste group. They sometimes believed that suffering was the result of **karma**, that is the effect of actions performed in a previous life. The illness or handicap, therefore, was the will of God, a kind of divine punishment. It would be wrong to interfere with it. Another belief which might have prevented people helping those in need was the fear of being made ritually impure by touching a person of a lower caste.

By no means all Hindus shared these beliefs. Guru Nanak was born a Hindu and he did not. He taught his followers to reject such ideas and provided ways by which he and they could put his teachings into practice. One was **langar** (see page 216), another was sharing sweet **karah parshad**, after a service in the Gurdwara. Both of these stressed equality by making everyone eat together. **Seva** was Guru Nanak's method of teaching humility and responsibility towards all those in need. It was an important lesson that was not easy to learn.

Washing the steps of a gurdwara is an act of seva

GURU NANAK AND HIS SONS

Guru Nanak had two sons. Not long before he died he realized that the men and women who had accepted his teachings would need someone to guide them when he had gone. One of his sons, Shri Chand, might seem to be the obvious choice. (His brother wasn't very interested in religion.) One day the Guru decided to test him and to teach his other companions a lesson. He was washing his hair and a bowl which he was using had fallen into a ditch. The Guru asked his sons to fish it out. They refused. Lakhmi Das said it was not fit work for a Guru's son to do. Shri Chand, a very pious young man, said that the filth in the pool would make him impure. Another Sikh, Lehna, scrambled down the bank without being asked, got the bowl, washed it and returned it to Guru Nanak. It was Lehna who eventually became the second Guru. He was given a new name, **Angad**, which means *my limb*, or *part of me*, by Guru Nanak, who realized that he shared his own outlook.

Another example which Sikhs often call to mind is **Amar Das**, the man who became the third Guru.

AMAR DAS

For many years Amar Das carried water every day for many miles, so that Guru Angad could bath. This was how he learned humility. Shortly before Guru Angad died he asked his son to bring him water but the son refused. He thought that he was too important to do such work and, besides, the weather was hot and the journey was long. Without being told Amar Das picked up the large water pot and fetched the water. At the time he was about 70 years old. (He lived to the age of 95.)

Sikhism teaches that there is no stigma attached to service. On the contrary God commands it.

Today Sikhs learn seva in the gurdwara, doing simple but tiresome jobs like washing up the dishes and scrubbing down the tables, or cleaning the walkway round the pool in large gurdwaras in India. The dirt from thousands of pairs of feet can make them very messy. However, seva should also be given to anyone in need.

Seva even in times of war

Only a few of the most famous examples of seva can be given. Perhaps the best known of all was performed by **Bhai Ghanaya**. When Sikh and Mughal forces were fighting one another in the days of Guru Gobind Singh (1666–1708) he gave water to the wounded of both sides on the battle field. Some Sikhs were angry at him helping their enemies. They took him to the Guru who questioned him. When Bhai Ghanaya said he saw neither Mughal nor Sikh but only the Guru's face in all who were suffering the Guru commended him and gave him ointment to treat the wounds.

A more recent story of a similar kind was told by Lt General Harbaksh Singh, Commander in Chief of the Indian Army in 1965 during a war against Pakistan.

I was stopped at one of the welfare stalls on the Grand Trunk road by a string of young girls stretched across the road. They urged me to eat some puries and parshad. While so engaged I noticed a bus full of uniformed personnel halted under a tree and the occupants being served by the girls with the same food as I was eating. I was told that they were Pakistani prisoners of war from the front. I walked up to the junior commissioned officer in charge of the prisoners to enquire why they had not been blind-folded as per instructions. Before the officer could answer the girls shouted in unison, 'It is not his fault, we ordered the Pakistanis' eyes to be unfolded so that they could eat with comfort'. I did not have the heart to take action against the officer. Such is the magnanimity of the Punjabis. I was reminded of Bhai Ghanaya.
(*Spokesman Weekly*, 28th annual number 1979, page 73)

In 1982 when thousands of people gathered at East Midlands airport to welcome the Pope, Sikhs from Coventry provided them with tea and cold drinks.

During the 1985 coal strike in Britain, gurdwaras gave food parcels to mining families and provided free meals in gurdwaras.

Sikhs also contribute to Christian Aid, Oxfam, Ethiopian Famine Relief and many other caring agencies. Little of what Sikhs do may catch the attention of the media, which are not usually interested in such news items. Sikhs do not wish to attract publicity because the motive of seva should be pure, a desire to serve in the way that God cares for humanity, out of love, not from a wish for reward or to win worshippers by offering them bribes.

'Those who love God love everybody.'
(Guru Nanak, AG 557)

FOR YOUR FOLDERS

▶ There are some Sikhs known as **seva panthis** who give their lives to helping others. What is the difference between these and ascetics?

FOR DISCUSSION

▶ Why did Guru Nanak place so much emphasis on seva?
▶ What is the difference between work and seva?

Morality and suffering

Sikhs accept that suffering is real. The aim of the religious person must be to rise beyond it or **transcend** it. For example, they would point to the way a person can forget toothache when someone invites them to a party! Much suffering can be explained with little difficulty. Sikhs believe that there are moral laws which they ignore at their peril. They have the same effect on rich and poor, wise or foolish. Guru Nanak put it very simply:

'Whoever will taste poison will die.'

(AG 142)

FOR DISCUSSION

▶ Think of some examples of what Sikhs might consider to be moral laws.

The mystery of suffering

The reason why many things in life happen, however, will remain a mystery. Guru Nanak taught that:

'The more we find out, the more there is still to discover.'

(AG 5)

Suffering is one of those mysteries which will never be solved. The Gurus taught that **Akal Purukh**, the **Timeless Being**, God, is the only one who knows. Our difficult task is to accept that:

'From the beginning of time pain and pleasure are written in humanity's fate by the Creator.'
(Guru Nanak, AG 1054/18)

Why some people seem rarely to be suffering while others who are more religious, more moral, have a hard time of it, only God knows. Both, however, are from God.

'Both poison and nectar are made by the Creator;
both fruits grow on the tree of this world.
Everything is in the Creator's hands.
We are given to eat as much of them as it pleases God to give us.'

(AG 1172/9)

The torture and martyrdom of Guru Arjan

It might seem unfair that the mugger prospers while the victim is maimed for life. Sikhs would agree that it would be unfair if God had not provided human beings with a spirit which is greater than all suffering, which can endure and overcome pain.

Faith can overcome pain

Through contemplating the glory of God and discovering the inner presence of God, Sikhs believe a spirit of detachment and indifference to pleasure and pain can be developed. The better anyone knows God the more willing they are to become subject to God's will. The person who is developed spiritually should be able to share the words of Guru Nanak, making them their own:

'Lord, when I am happy I will worship you only; when I suffer, I will not forget you.'

(AG 757)

A story is told of the fifth Guru, Arjan, when he was being tortured by soldiers of the Mughal Emperor. A Muslim, the well known Sufi mystic, Mian Mir, was allowed to see the Guru and offered to try to use his influence to help him. Guru Arjan replied, 'It is God's will and I am at peace with God's name on my lips.'

Guru Tegh Bahadur, the ninth Guru, managed to face a cruel death in the same way.

Haumai

Pain can be overcome by faith but Sikhs would not say that God has put pain and suffering in the world to force people to turn to him. This would be just as immoral as any father or mother using threats or promises to win the obedience or love of their children. Humankind has been given freedom to accept or reject God's love as they wish. God wants a willing, free response from them. Sikhs do not believe that those who reject God's love will be punished eternally as a consequence. This kind of punishment is the result of **haumai**, self-centredness (see also page 188). It is self-inflicted.

Haumai-based conduct also causes suffering to others. For example, the selfish person is likely to drive whilst under the influence of drink, or take drugs. They know that they could cause an accident that could harm someone else, but they believe themselves to be clever enough or lucky enough to keep out of trouble. Much suffering in the world is inflicted by human beings on one another; there is

no need to try to put the blame on God. Sikhs argue that human beings should have sufficient moral sense and concern for other people not to cause suffering and to prevent this kind of misery.

Suffering for others

Finally, there is also a form of suffering which people should be willing to face and endure for others. The ninth Guru, Tegh Bahadur, died because he defended the cause of religious freedom at a time when the Mughal emperor threatened it. In 1975–7, during the Emergency, when the Indian government suspended many civil rights, 40 000 Sikhs protested against the Emergency and volunteered to go to jail to defend civil liberties.

Evil

For Sikhs, God is the source of everything. Even evil is from God. God has put some plants in the world which are poisonous and others which are life-giving. It is the same with opportunities to live good or bad lives. People have to choose. If they make bad choices they should not blame God for giving them free will. Sikhs speak of five evils. They are lust, anger, greed, attachment, and pride.

FOR YOUR FOLDERS

▶ List the five evils. Explain why these are the ones Sikhs single out. (Thinking about haumai may help you.)

FOR DISCUSSION

▶ How would a Sikh answer the question, 'Why is it that suffering rather than pleasure causes us to question the existence of God?'

▶ Think of an example of 'innocent suffering'. Discuss how a Sikh might explain it.

▶ What might a Sikh mean by saying 'God doesn't make us suffer so that we might believe in God; but it is only by believing in God that we can overcome suffering'?

Sikhs believe that the one God is the source of all life. That is a basic Sikh teaching. God has no colour or form. Male and female, black, brown or white, are only functional distinctions. To discriminate on grounds of race, religion or gender is wrong according to Sikh beliefs.

In practice it is not easy to keep to these principles. For example, Sikh women have to struggle to win the respect and status which the Gurus said they should have (see page 196).

It is the same with regard to prejudice of other kinds. Sikhs were converts from Hinduism for the most part. Even today only 5 per cent enter Sikhism from any other religion. Converts from Hinduism have always tended to bring two things with them into the Sikh community, the **Panth**.

Two Hindu influences

One influence is good, the famed **tolerance** which Hindus have of other religions. It is seen in the relation which Sikhs still have with Hindus. There is a saying in Punjabi, '**Roti beti di sanjh**', which means *they eat together and intermarry*. In principle there is no opposition to mixed Sikh–Hindu weddings. However, there is opposition to marriages with members of other faiths because of strong cultural differences, or because that religion requires conversion. (For example, any woman marrying a Muslim man must become a Muslim; a Muslim woman may not marry a non-Muslim.)

This respect for other religions is seen most clearly in the Guru Granth Sahib. It contains the teachings of six of the Sikh Gurus but it also has many writings by Hindus of various castes, and Muslims. The Gurus never claimed that the truth was to be found only in Sikhism.

The other influence of Hinduism on Sikhism has been less good, the **caste system**. This is an important part of Hinduism. Hindu society is based on social divisions based on ritual purity. The purest caste, the **brahmins**, are at the top. The most impure, the **shudras**, are at the bottom. Outside it are people who were called **untouchables** because it was thought that even their touch could pass on this impurity. Their shadow could make food impure if it fell on it. Hindus believe that people are born into a caste and remain in it for the whole of this life.

The Gurus condemned the caste system. People should be respected for other qualities:

'Know people by the light which illumines them, not by their caste. In the hereafter no one is regarded as different from another on grounds of caste.'

(Guru Nanak, AG 349)

'All castes and special clothing are like dust.'
(Guru Nanak, AG 352)

However, after conversion Sikhs still had to marry and they still had their Hindu relatives. They continued to work at their traditional occupations in those days. Naturally, they clung to many of their old ways. Sikhs were also a small minority of the population. Whatever they had tried to do would have had little effect on the rest of the village or family. For example, they might have wanted to show their rejection of caste by intercaste marriages, but if no other family would agree and they could only marry beyond second cousins, they would have difficulty finding a partner.

Sikhs have never managed to shake off the caste system entirely, especially in the area of marriage. Jat marries Jat, Khetri marries Khetri, and so on. The sense of being a member of one of these groups may be stronger in Britain than in India. In one town there may be a Bhatra Sangat Gurdwara, Ramgarhia Sikh Gurdwara, and Singh Sabha Gurdwara, each attended by a different section of the community. Prejudices are sometimes encouraged to preserve separation.

Ritual purity and pollution

'Untouchability', the belief that there are people who are born impure, remain impure and pass on impurity by touch, was ridiculed by Guru Nanak:

'All impurity contracted by touch is mere superstition.'

(AG 472)

Many so-called untouchables entered the panth because they believed in the message of the Gurus as well as hoping to be accepted by a society which said all people were equal. To their dismay some found that although they could worship together in the gurdwara, socially they were still rejected. Sometimes they found the same attitudes among Christians and Muslims. Some of them followed the leadership of a great untouchable, **Dr Ambedkar**, and became Buddhists. Others looked to past teachers. Leather workers or **chamars** called **Ravidas** their Guru. He was a cobbler whose hymns are in the Guru Granth Sahib. They often look like

Sikhs, and worship like them, keeping the turban and beard. They continue to respect the Sikh Gurus and use the Guru Granth Sahib in worship but they call themselves **Ravidasis**. The Sikh Guru Ram Das would not have tolerated any prejudice against chamars or any other similar group. He wrote:

'Ravidas, the cobbler, praised his Lord for a brief time and from a low caste wretch was purified and all four castes fell at his feet. Namdev loved the Lord. Though people called him a shudra calico printer the Lord turned away from the high castes and instead hugged him, his devotee, to his bosom.'

(AG 733)

FOR YOUR FOLDERS

▶ Find out more about the caste system, from pages 96–7 of this book and other books on Hinduism.

FOR DISCUSSION

▶ What reasons can you think of for caste discrimination by Sikhs even though the Gurus denounced it?
▶ What did Guru Nanak mean by saying that 'All impurity contracted by touch is mere superstition.'?

THINGS TO DO

▶ Consider this story.
Shortly before Guru Nanak died his followers began to argue among themselves about his funeral. Those who came from a Hindu background wanted it to be done in their way. The Guru must be cremated. 'No,' said those who had been Muslims. 'Babaji must be buried, that is the proper way.' Guru Nanak overheard the discussion. He called the disciples to him. 'What you must do when I die is cover my body with a cloth overnight. Place flowers on either side of me. In the morning come and see whose flowers are still blooming and whose have faded. Those whose flowers are blooming may deal with my body after their own custom.' This satisfied the Sikhs. When the Guru died they did as he had instructed them. One group put flowers on one side, one on the other side. In the morning they returned together to find both lots of flowers were blooming as though they had been freshly picked – but the body had gone! We don't have to ask whether the story is historical fact or not. That would be to miss the point as much as the Hindu and Muslim devotees did!
▶ What is the message that the Guru wanted to put across?

"Singh Sajo Lahar"

(Become Sikhs movement)

Over the years, Harijans have been discarding Hinduism which, because of its caste-ridden society denies them the right as human beings, and opting for a religion which at least guarantees them equality in the brotherhood of man. Now the trend is in favour of Sikhism because, as they contend, it is so akin to Hindu way of life.

Opined a fiery youth, Daulat Ram: "All our lives we have been treated by all villagers as dirt because we were chamars (shoemakers). Now we have decided to renounce our faith and adopt a new one."

A deputation of these Harijans visited Gurdwara Sisganj in Delhi last year. Since then, more than 1,000 have embraced Sikhism.

The Sikh missionaries have now spread out to all villages in the Terai region and preach the message of fatherhood of God and brotherhood of mankind.

207

102 THE NEEDY

The extended family is the basis of caring among Sikhs, but there are times when the family cannot care for its needy members. Then seva has to take on particular forms and the panth has to take action. On 30 October, 1902, an organization was set up to provide such help. It was called the **Chief Khalsa Diwan**. One of its first acts was to open an orphanage in Amritsar. This was on 11 April, 1904. Since then thousands of children have been brought up in the **Central Khalsa Orphanage**.

After the assassination of the Indian Prime Minister, Mrs Indira Gandhi, on 31 October, 1984, anti-Sikh riots took place in Delhi and elsewhere. Many Sikhs were left homeless; thousands of widows and orphans were left in a country where state welfare facilities are few. The **Sikh Women's Association** was created by Mrs Satwant B. Singh and other young women to give help in the form of food-kitchens, clothes, bedding, and furniture. The **Nishkam Sikh Welfare Council** and **Delhi Sikh Gurdwara Board** helped children with books and stationery for school, repaired damaged houses, gave weekly rations of food, and provided pensions. An international organization, the **Sikh Forum**, raises money in Britain and other countries as well as India for these families but it has extended its contributions to help victims of disasters world wide, Sikh and non-Sikh.

Care for the elderly

Improved hygiene and medical care has resulted in an increase in the number of elderly people in India. Most Sikhs remember the warning which Guru Ram Das gave his eldest son:

'It is the greatest sin to quarrel with parents who have given you birth and brought you up.'

(AG 1200)

They interpret it positively, care for and respect their parents. Bhai Gurdas wrote:

'When a man acts in a morally irresponsible manner towards his parents his religious acts and worship are futile.'

(Var 37:13)

However, patterns of family life are changing. The nuclear family is replacing the extended family, young people are finding work in Bombay or Madras, thousands of miles away from the Punjab and are living in small flats. This all means that there may be no one to care for the elderly. The gurdwaras in India and in Britain often act as day care centres where the elderly can meet, chat and be fed, but in 1959 the main Sikh care organization, the **Chief Khalsa Diwan**, set up an old people's home at Tarn Taran, near Amritsar. It is called the **Bhai Vir Singh Bridh Ghar**, after one of the Punjab's greatest poets. (It means *Home for the old*.) In 1959 it had places for 30 people, now it cares for almost 100.

The handicapped

Guru Nanak cared for a leper called Nuri whom he found living in a small hut on the outskirts of the Punjab village of Dipalpur. Others may have avoided him, but the Guru helped him find a faith which enabled him to accept his condition. The third Guru, Amar Das (1479–1574), cared for and healed patients suffering from tertiary fever at Goindwal, his headquarters. He also nursed back to health a leper, Prema, who had lost his limbs. The fifth Guru, Arjan (1563–1606), built the first leprosarium in the Punjab, at Tarn Taran. It still exists. Guru Har Rai (1644–1661), ran a free dispensary and even treated the Dara Shikoh eldest son of the Emperor Shah Jahan who had demolished a gurdwara in Lahore and built a mosque on the site. The boy Guru, Har Kishan (1656–1664), died of smallpox caught while caring for victims of the disease. In the community prayer of the Sikhs, **Ardas**, he is remembered as the one 'a glimpse of whom erases all suffering'. Guru Gobind Singh (1666–1708), the last Guru, taught some blind Sikhs to play musical instruments so that they could earn a living by performing kirtan in gurdwaras. This kind of work lives on. In 1935 the Chief Khalsa Diwan opened a home for the blind in Amritsar. Two famous musicians, Bhai Gopal Singh and Surjan Singh, were educated there. Two well known British blind ragis are Sital Singh Sitara of London and Gian Singh Surjeet of Gravesend.

Clinics and hospitals

The Sikh panth considers healing and caring as part of its religious heritage. Indian gurdwaras often have clinics attached to them, for example, there is an eye clinic at Gurdwara Bangla Sahib in Delhi, and a homeopathic dispensary at Gurdwara Singh Sabha, Simla. A gurdwara at Bangkok in Thailand organizes a bloodbank as well as a dispensary. A large hospital is attached to the Golden Temple at Amritsar.

The celebrations took place in 1969 of the 500th anniversary of Guru Nanak's birth. It inspired Sikhs to do such things as establish a hospital and medical school in Bombay. In Delhi doctors volunteered their services to a free hospital which they opened for poor people.

The pingalwara, Amritsar

The most famous Sikh **pingalwara**, or home for disabled, is in Amritsar. Bhagat Puran Singh lived in Lahore. As a young man he decided to devote his life to seva. He cared for destitute people, accompanied the sick to hospital and undertook the cremation of those who died and had no relatives to perform the funeral rites. In 1947 he joined the refugees fleeing to Amritsar, carrying a disabled and mentally handicapped young man, Piara. He had cared for him since Piara was abandoned on the steps of a gurdwara as a baby. He continued to look after sick and disabled refugees in Amritsar. At the time this book was written he was still looking after Piara and over 300 men and women. Some are mental patients, others are lepers, limbless or terminally ill, or the homeless families of men who are in prison.

Sardar Ishar Singh Chopra ran a similar pingalwara at Ranchi in the state of Bihar. It was opened in 1969 and has cared for over 20 000 patients, of whom 5000 have had surgical appliances fitted. His son, Dr Amarjit Singh Chopra and father-in-law, Sardar Amar Singh Chhatwal (editor of *The Sikh Courier*, London), bought land at Ranchi and are building a 350 bed hospital for the disabled, helped by donations from supporters world wide.

TO FIND OUT

▶ If there is a Sikh community near where you live try to discover what charities they support.
See if they can tell you more about the charities mentioned in this section or about other charities organized by Sikhs.

FOR YOUR FOLDERS

▶ Explain why Sikhs think it is important to help the needy. You may need to refer back to earlier sections of the book.

FOR DISCUSSION

▶ Is Sikh voluntary work of the kind done by Bhagat Puran Singh needed more in India than in Britain?
▶ **Bhagat** means *one who is devoted to God.* How did Bhagat Puran Singh show this?

Sikhs believe that God cares for everyone and that they must too. Their hospitals and schools are open to all

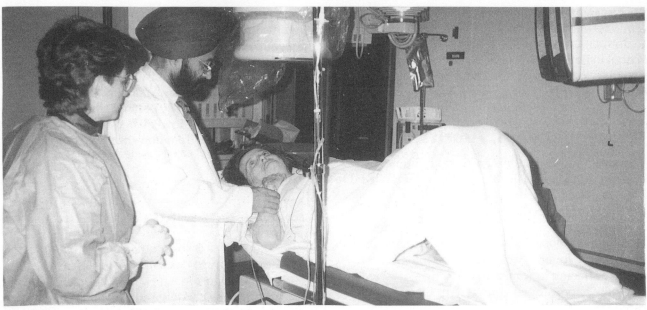

In caring for patients, the Sikh doctor is following the example of the Gurus

Medical care

From earliest times Sikhs have cared for the sick by building dispensaries and hospitals. Guru Nanak is described as healing lepers in some of the stories about his life. Leprosy was a dreaded disease at that time, and still is. In those days, however, it was considered incurable and likely to be passed on to anyone who touched a leper. Guru Arjan set up a hospital for the care of lepers at the Punjab town of Tarn Taran at a time when little care was available for the sick outside the family, and they were left to form support groups of their own, if they were lucky, and live together until they died.

Medical work is still at the heart of Sikhism. Many Sikh men and women are doctors or surgeons, yet more are nurses. India is a country which cannot afford to employ all the doctors it trains, which explains why some of them have migrated to Europe or America. India depends on volunteers and voluntary contributions to make up for services which the government cannot afford to provide. Sikhs do this by setting up clinics or dispensaries and day wards at gurdwaras. Here medical care is given free of charge and minor operations can be performed.

Problem areas in medical ethics

Advances in medical research are making Sikhs think about some other issues related to the body.

Transplant surgery

One of the great scourges of India is **blindness** caused by diseases of the cornea. This can be cured by **corneal grafting**. Sikhs are encouraged at death to donate their eyes to eye banks so that this can be done. 'Eye camps' are set up in rural districts, where patients who are blind or have poor sight can be brought and the simple operation which gives them back their sight can be carried out. In 1987 a Sikh set up a **Life After Death Society** in Calcutta, with the object of educating the public about the necessity of donating the entire body for transplant, medical research and educational purposes, instead of cremation or burial. About 40 000 Indians die of kidney failure alone each year. Mr H. Singh, its convenor, wrote:

> 'Our modest effort in the past year has led to the formation of branches in six cities including Calcutta, Bombay, and Delhi.'
> (*Spokesman Weekly*, New Delhi, June 20, 1988)

Transplant surgery poses no ethical problems for Sikhs. The third Guru wrote:

> 'The dead may be cremated or buried, or thrown to the dogs, or cast into the waters or down an empty well. No one knows where the soul goes and disappears to.'
> (3rd Guru, Amar Das, AG 648)

Once someone has died their body is merely like

the discarded skin of a lizard, or some other animal that leaves its skin behind when it is outgrown. The soul or spirit, the **atman**, has no more use for the body so it can be used for transplants or research. In practice, many Sikhs do not like to think of the bodies of their loved ones being treated in this way, so they are only slowly accepting the idea of donating parts of the body.

> *'Let as many Sikhs as possible donate their eyes and other usable parts of their bodies after death, by legally signing such donation papers in collaboration with local or neighbouring hospitals. In the name of the Guru, let the Sikhs sacrifice portions of their bodies after death, as he did while living.'*
> (*Sikh Phulwari*, Vol 6, no 1, July–Sept, 1988)

The **Guru Ram Das Mission** is a UK organization which enables hospitals and eye clinics to be set up in rural Punjab.

Amniocentesis

This is a modern method which was developed to detect abnormalities in the foetus, but it can be used for finding out the sex of a child while it is in the womb. It is creating a problem in India where parents sometimes ask for an abortion if the child is a girl, because Indian cultures tend to prefer boys to girls. Sikhs reject this trend.

Genetic engineering

This is a process which involves altering the structure of human cells. It can be a means of preventing parents passing on hereditary illnesses to their children. Many Sikhs still feel that this is a way of tampering with the natural body which God has given. However, some doctors argue that this is God-given knowledge which should be used to help those who suffer from these disorders. Certainly they approve of parents using contraceptives if they do not want to run the risk of bringing such children into the world. Once born, however, such a baby should be cared for with as much love as any other. Any child is a gift from God.

Sikhs do not agree to experiments being carried out on aborted foetuses, as human life is believed to begin at conception.

Artificial insemination

There are two forms of artificial insemination. The first one involves fertilizing the egg or ovum of a woman with the sperm of her husband. This is often done outside the woman's body, to produce a 'test-tube' baby. The fertilized egg is implanted to the woman's womb. If the woman's husband is sterile, the second form may be used, which involves fertilizing the egg with the sperm of another man.

The insemination of a wife with the sperm of someone other than her husband is morally wrong according to Sikh teachings. There is a stigma attached to it which is similar to adultery. Even if the husband were to give consent, and the donor were to remain anonymous, the possibility of the husband feeling inadequate and jealous could put the marriage at risk. Adoption is the acceptable solution, or being willing to live with the childless state acknowledging it to be God's will. For the same kinds of reasons surrogacy is not acceptable.

In vitro fertilization, or 'test tube babies', would not be objected to by Sikhs. They would, however, look for adequate safeguards to make sure that only the sperms and ovum of a married couple were used.

FOR YOUR FOLDERS

▶ Many of the terms used in this section may be new to you. Write them down, then look in a dictionary for a definition. (You may need a very up-to-date one.) Then write one or two sentences giving the Sikh view of each one.

FOR DISCUSSION

▶ Why should Sikhs allow their organs to be used for transplants? Do you think that they would permit their bodies to be used for medical research?

The Khalsa

In 1699 Guru Gobind Singh called upon Sikhs to become members of a distinctive family known as the **Khalsa**, the pure ones. Sikhs have to consider political involvement from the point of view of the Khalsa. Its members must wear the special uniform which marks out a Sikh to this day, the **five Ks**. (These and community rules are discussed on pages 214–15.)

New members of British society sometimes have to struggle for their way of life to be recognized

War and peace

DHARAM YUDH

The Khalsa was also called upon to obey a code of conduct which included a readiness to fight in a just war, a **dharam yudh**. 'Dharam yudh' means *war in defence of righteousness*. This is only allowed if:

- It is a last resort.
  Guru Gobind Singh said, 'When all other means have failed it is permissible to draw the sword.'
- There should be no wish for revenge.
- Any land or property captured during the war should be returned as soon as possible; there must be no looting or harming civilians.

- The army should be made up of soldiers committed to the cause; mercenaries should not be used.
- The minimum force necessary must be used.

Guru Gobind Singh fought 14 defensive battles. He won many of them but after a victory he never took land or booty, held captives for ransom, or damaged the place of worship of other religions.

SANT SIPAHI

The Sikh should be a **sant sipahi**, a saint-soldier, who is devout and who does not drink, does not smoke and will not molest the womenfolk of his opponents. He must also refrain from looting.

This saint-soldier ideal does not leave room for pacifism but in today's world Sikhs recognize that it is almost impossible to obey the code of the dharam yudh. Civilians cannot be protected from mass bombing during air raids, for example. Sikhs would hope that organizations like the **United Nations** might be able to solve international problems and avert the need for countries to go to war.

There may be individual Sikhs who are pacifists. India, where most Sikhs live, has always had armed forces made up of volunteers, so it is impossible to be certain. It is **conscription**, a law compelling men and perhaps women to join the forces, that really forces people to make up their minds whether it is right or not for them to fight.

REBELLION IN A JUST CASE

The Gurus often criticized unjust rulers. Guru Nanak spoke against the Mughal Emperor Babur who conquered northern India between 1520 and 1526. He was no more brutal than other invaders, perhaps. However, when Guru Nanak saw with his own eyes the suffering of women and children, at a town called Saidpur, he complained to the emperor about their treatment and asked that they should be released. Babur had intended to enslave them, but he set them free.

Guru Gobind Singh wrote a letter in Persian to the Emperor Auranzeb. It is called the **Zafarnama**. It told him that subjects had a right to rebel against **tyrants**, that is, unjust rulers who oppress their subjects. It included the words: 'When all other means have failed it is permissible to draw the sword.'

Sikhs, therefore, believe that subjects may rebel if they have no other way of obtaining justice.

All the Gurus were subjects of Mughal emperors and obeyed them up to a point where they had to choose between conscience and the emperor. This should always be the Sikh position. If possible, Sikhs serve and support the state but if there is a clash God must come first. States are seen as necessary for the protection and wellbeing of the people. They have a right to loyalty as long as they do this. Guru Gobind Singh wrote:

'Without power righteousness [dharam] does not flourish,
Without dharam everything is crushed and ruined.'
(Dasam Granth)

THE IDEAL STATE

At the end of Sikh worship a special prayer, Ardas, is offered. It ends with the sentence:

'The Khalsa shall rule, no hostile powers shall exist.
They will all submit, frustrated. Those who enter
the Khalsa for shelter will be protected.'

Some Sikhs see this as a slogan and battle cry, dating from the 18th century, expressing the hope that one day there will be a Sikh state. Others say it conveys the ideal for any state in which Sikhs can exist happily, living out their religion in peace.

GYANI ZAIL SINGH

Gyani Zail Singh is an example of a Sikh who has played a major part in politics. He rose to the position of President of the Republic of India, the world's largest democracy. Unfortunately, during his term of office, the Indian government sent the army into the Golden Temple to root out dissidents. They had made it the focus of their protest against what they alleged were injustices to Sikhs. Many Sikhs argued that Gyani Zail Singh should have resigned in protest against the government's actions. This dispute has often made Sikhs forget that, whatever the truth of the matter, a Sikh has been head of state of a country of over 800 million citizens.

FOR YOUR FOLDERS

▶ Write a letter to the emperor Akbar from Guru Amar Das, giving your reasons why pilgrims to Hardwar should not be taxed.

THINGS TO DO

▶ A number of boroughs in Britain have had Sikh mayors or councillors. Try to find out what part Sikhs take in the civic life of a town near you which has a Sikh population.

FOR DISCUSSION

▶ Guru Nanak said:

'He alone should sit on the throne who is worthy of it.'
(AG 351)

What qualities of kingship do you think he had in mind?

India has had a Sikh head of state, President Gyani Zail Singh

The Sikh Gurus lived at a time when it was easier for them to criticize unjust rulers than teach about crime and punishment. They had no power to punish people who stole, murdered or committed any other crimes. That was the duty of the village council or a local judge. If members of the Sikh community became criminals they would be required to leave. If they showed sincere regret they would be readmitted. Sikhs should avoid contact with wrongdoers:

> 'He who associates with evildoers is destroyed. Being fed on poison his life goes to waste.'
>
> (AG 1343)

Community rules

There were community rules which Sikhs had to obey. These now form the **Code of Discipline** or **Rahit** of the Khalsa. When men and women are initiated into this family they must make certain promises. These are:

- To pray daily using the special hymns which the gurus said they should recite and meditate upon.
- To pay tithes, one tenth of their income, for the use of the community.
- To keep the five Ks–the uncut hair (**kesh**), comb (**kangha**), circle of steel on the right wrist (**kara**), the sword (**kirpan**) and the short trousers (**kaccha**), usually worn as an undergarment.
- Never to remove the hair, by shaving, or using creams or a razor on the legs.
- Not to eat **halal** meat, that is meat slaughtered according to Islamic law. (This was to show their difference from Muslims and because Muslim prayers would have been said over the animal before it was slaughtered.)
- Not to commit adultery.
- Not to use tobacco in any form.

Should any of these vows, known as **kurahts**, be broken the offender will be excluded from the congregation until they keep the rules. (A person who said they were sorry for cutting their hair but still kept it short would not be considered a serious

Preparing the sugar and water solution used in initiation. Once initiated, a Sikh must keep the Rahit faithfully

penitent.) The sangat might decide that such a person would have to be re-initiated.

There are other rules which are considered to be less serious. These are called **tankhas**, things which Sikhs should not do. (The word actually means *salary*. Sikh humour sometimes uses a word which means the opposite to that which is intended.) They are:

● Not to dine from the same dish as an uninitiated person.
● Not to dye or pluck out white hairs.
● Not to receive money in return for a daughter's or son's hand in marriage.
● Not to use narcotics or intoxicants.
● Not to perform a ceremony which violates the principles of Sikhism, (examples might be taking part in a marriage to which one of the partners had not consented, or conducting a non-Sikh ceremony).

Sometimes these breaches of discipline are overlooked. It would be difficult, for example, to be a member of a family where some are initiated and others not, and avoid eating together. However, where a breach is really offensive, for example a Sikh attending the gurdwara while he was drunk, five chosen Sikhs from the sangat would decide on a punishment. It might be cleaning the shoes of worshippers, sweeping out the gurdwara or washing the steps. The task should not be too harsh or humiliating, but should provide the rule-breaker with the opportunity to show real penitence.

> **Note** Not everyone who undertakes these jobs has broken the Sikh code. Many may be doing it as an act of seva. See pages 202 and 203.

The purpose of the punishment of criminals

If Sikhs had the power to punish criminals they would ask that punishments should be sensible. They should protect society, so sometimes offenders should be sent to prison. However, they should also provide opportunities for criminals to return to society and become useful citizens.

Capital punishment

Sikhs accept the view that society may take the life of those whose crime is so terrible that their fellow citizens consider that they have forfeited the right to live. However, they would use capital punishment sparingly and never in a spirit of revenge. The execution should be carried out as painlessly as possible. If the death penalty were to be used, Sikhs might say that there are crimes worse than murder that might deserve it. It is claimed by Sikhs that when Maharaja Ranjit Singh, a Sikh, ruled the Punjab at the beginning of the 19th century none of his subjects was executed.

Torture

This was a common punishment in the time of the Gurus. Sikhs have always opposed the use of any form of cruelty against human beings. Confessions gained by threats or promises are not reliable. Sikhs consider mental torture, perhaps threatening violence against the family of someone who is being questioned, as bad as, or worse than physical torture. The Human Rights movement is something which Sikhs support through membership of organizations like Amnesty International.

FOR YOUR FOLDERS
▶ Write down the words 'rahit', 'kuraht' and 'tankha' and explain what each of them means.
▶ Why is it wrong for Sikhs to pluck out or dye white hairs?
▶ Why is the giving of a dowry by Sikhs wrong?

FOR DISCUSSION
▶ Why would Sikhs discourage their children from mixing with bad company?
▶ What crimes might a Sikh consider worse than murder? Why?

This is a new issue for anyone to consider. Its importance only became recognized in the 1980s. For some Indian Sikhs, thinking about pollution and the environment is something of a luxury when they are struggling to survive. They might say that it is a rich person's problem as they gather wood to provide fuel to cook a daily meal.

This can still be a very real issue. Bhagat Puran Singh (see page 209), has written pamphlets and campaigned against the policy of the Indian government in cutting down forests to provide more land for agriculture. This deprived the poorer villagers of wood for fuel.

To some extent this problem has been overcome. Punjabis are now among the richest of India's inhabitants, though poverty still exists. Most people have electricity in their homes, or kerosene stoves. However, one of the main reasons for the wealth of the Punjab is the 'green revolution'. The Punjab is naturally a rich region. It has good weather. There is a constant supply of water provided by rivers which flow from the Himalayan mountains and are fed by melting snow. Irrigation canals carry the water to the fields. High-yielding types of corn, sugar cane and rice have helped farmers to benefit from the climate but this success has created two new problems. One is that the level of water in the rivers has become lower. The water table is now so low that villages need to bore deeper tube wells to provide a water supply for people in their homes. A second is that the use of nitrates as fertilizers threatens to damage the soil and pollute the rivers as surplus water drains back into them. Farmers, naturally, want to continue getting the best yield that they can.

When Sikhs look at this kind of issue – the over exploitation of natural resources – they must look at the teaching of the Gurus about Creation to find out what kind of solutions they should adopt.

The felling of trees leads to deforestation and deprives people of wood for fuel

The Gurus taught that the world belongs to God. In fact, one of the names given to God is **Karta Purukh**, the Creator. Sikhs don't bother themselves with explanations of how the universe came to exist but they do believe that God is:

'. . . the One who builds and demolishes, there is no other.'

(AG 934)

Guru Nanak said:

'The universe comes into being by God's will.'

(AG 1)

The word used is 'comes' not 'came' because Sikhs believe that creation is a continual process. It is still happening.

Sikhs also believe that God is within creation. Guru Nanak said:

'I see the Creator pervading everywhere.'

(AG 21)

A Sikh environmental lobby might put together the idea of God as Creator and of God in Creation to argue that the irresponsible use of the Earth's resources could almost be regarded as injuring God.

Vegetarianism

Some Sikhs are vegetarian for moral reasons, others simply because they have kept to the practices of the Hindu community in which they live. There tend to be three moral reasons for vegetarianism.
- Meat can cause spiritual pollution to the eater.
- The one spirit lives in all creatures. It is this one spirit which gives them life. The spirit is God. To take life is to injure God as well as one's fellow beings.
- The cost of producing meat is so great that it is wrong to use it for these purposes while so many people go hungry.

Sikhs should reject the first reason as they ought not to believe in this kind of pollution. The only kind that Guru Nanak accepted was moral pollution, caught from bad company, evil thoughts, and behaving badly. Food itself does neither good nor harm. The second and third might be reasons which Sikhs would give.

The Gurus, however, did not provide any direct teaching on vegetarianism, leaving it to the conscience of individuals. Their concern was with

helping their followers achieve spiritual liberation. So Guru Nanak said:

'All food is pure, for God has provided it for our sustenance.'

(AG 472)

In gurdwaras only vegetarian food is provided so that no one sharing in the meal, known as **langar**, will be offended. This tradition goes back to the beginnings of Sikhism.

Hunting

By the time of the sixth Guru, Hargobind (1606–1644), the Gurus had become powerful political leaders as well as spiritual guides. Guru Hargobind kept an army and lived like a prince. He hunted in the manner of rulers of his day, sometimes with the Mughal emperor himself. The tenth Guru, Gobind Singh, also had a taste for this pastime. He once wrote:

'I enjoyed myself on the banks of the River Jumna and saw amusements of many kinds. I hunted many tigers, nilgai [antelope], deer and bears.'

(Bachitar Natak)

Today, Sikhs would leave decisions on hunting to the individual conscience but would clearly distinguish between it and things like bear-baiting which have always been condemned for their cruelty. The wilful causing of suffering to others is wrong.

FOR YOUR FOLDERS

▶ What do Sikhs believe about God and Creation? How might it influence their thinking about the environment?

FOR DISCUSSION

▶ In matters like hunting, where Sikhs are left to make decisions according to their consciences, what considerations are likely to affect their choice?

Maharaja Ranjit Singh

Service

The Gurus were not merely concerned with personal or social matters. They gave attention to the needs of humankind as a whole. They built their teachings on firm social foundations. This is why they rejected the monastic ideal, which involves a life of withdrawal and segregation, in favour of the love and service of their fellow human beings. They also emphasized the **panth**, the total Sikh community, and the **sangat**, local fellowships. Their purpose should be to serve one another.

Respect for all faiths

The panth and the sangat should help Sikhs to achieve spiritual liberation and live in peace. Their duty to non-Sikhs is that of helping them to enjoy conditions in which they can follow their own **dharma,** or way of life, peacefully. The Sikh scriptures contain many writings by Hindus and Muslims. This indicates that Sikhs believe that God speaks through other religions, not only through the Sikh Gurus. This must mean that if a Sikh state were ever established it would be one in which all religions were given equal respect. In fact, there *was* a kingdom ruled by a Sikh for a short period of time. The ruler was Maharaja Ranjit Singh. His reign in the Punjab lasted from 1801 until 1839. Although books sometimes describe the Maharaja's rule as the Sikh Empire it was not one in which Sikhs enjoyed special privileges. They were able to practise their religion in peace but so were the other religions of the Punjab, Hinduism and Islam. During that time Hindus and Muslims, as well as some Europeans, were employed by him. The offices of state were not monopolized by Sikhs.

Maharaja Ranjit Singh was a **pragmatic** ruler. This means that he thought about the immediate needs of his people and his position and adopted policies to meet them. He didn't work from some kind of master plan. Sikhs today would need to turn to the Gurus' teachings to provide principles upon which to build the ideal society. They would certainly have approved of the Maharaja's policy of respectful tolerance. Guru Gobind Singh put this principle forward in these words:

> *'To recognize the oneness of all humanity is an essential pillar of Sikhism. Some call themselves Hindus, others call themselves Muslims but humanity worldwide is made up of one race.'*
>
> (*Akal Ustal* 85:15)

Honesty in public life

Sikhs demand honesty in public as well as in private life. Guru Nanak spoke out strongly against corruption. He said:

> *'There is none who does not give or receive a bribe. Even the king administers justice only when his palm is greased.'*
>
> (AG 350)

Rulers should not expect privileges. They are only fulfilling their calling and deserve respect only if they do their job well, that is for the good of the nation as a whole.

> *'Only one who is worthy of it should sit on the throne.'*
>
> (Guru Nanak, AG 1039)

Elsewhere he said:

> *'A king remains installed on the throne by virtue of good qualities.'*
>
> (AG 992)

In Guru Nanak's India, kings were the people with power. Today he would demand good qualities and worthiness of presidents, prime ministers, and democratically elected governments.

The defeat of poverty

While there are poor in the world, Sikhs cannot feel that their view of a perfect society is being achieved. The Gurus condemned wealth which ignored poverty. Guru Nanak expressed this important principle in these words:

> *'Only he who earns a living by the sweat of his brow and shares his earnings with others has discovered the path of righteousness.'*
>
> (AG 1245)

As long as there is one needy person Sikhs should not relax their efforts for human welfare.

Equality

An ideal society would be one which respected equality in matters of race and sex as well as religion and job and wealth opportunities. Guru Gobind Singh's vision was for one race, the human race. Earlier in the book it was seen that women may perform every function in the Sikh religion (see page 186). Sikhs would support organizations like the United Nations which try to create a just and free world order.

Summary

The Sikh ideal is of a society which combines divine truth with human good. At the end of their congregational prayer, Ardas, Sikhs say, '**Raj karega khalsa**' which means *the Khalsa will rule*. What they ask is that God will use them to establish the kind of world in which the principles mentioned in these pages will flourish and be the birthright of everyone.

FOR YOUR FOLDERS

▶ List the Sikh principles mentioned in these pages. How should they affect Sikhs in their everyday lives?

FOR DISCUSSION

▶ Does Sikhism seem an easy religion to follow? Give reasons for your answer.
▶ Sikhs would tell you that they often fall short of their ideals. What reasons might they give for this?

An artist's impression of the meeting of Emperor Babur and Guru Nanak

Justice

Sikhism approves of every clause in the **Declaration of Human Rights**. In fact, Sikhs would say that they embody the teachings of the Gurus. They would look at the clauses about justice and remember Guru Nanak's meeting with Babur, the great Mughal emperor whose army was invading the Punjab. They met at Saidpur, now called Eminabad. The Guru had been taken prisoner when the town was captured. Guru Nanak complained about the cruel treatment of prisoners and the way in which innocent victims of war, civilians, were threatened with slavery. The result was that Babur released them.

Once Guru Nanak compared God to a potter. He said:

'Call no one high or low. God, the one potter has made all alike. God's light alone pervades all creation.'

(AG 62)

FOR YOUR FOLDERS

► Look at the Declaration of Human Rights.
► Which passages in the Declaration might Sikhs say the verse quoted above covered?
► Which clauses in the Declaration do you think Guru Nanak would have quoted to Babur if it had existed when Babur destroyed Saidpur?

The ninth Guru, Tegh Bahadur, lived during the reign of the Emperor Aurangzeb. This zealous Indian ruler wished to convert all his subjects to Islam. His policy included the destruction of Hindu temples which were replaced by mosques. Sometimes force was used to make converts, even though Islam teaches that there should be no compulsion in religions. People should be free to choose for themselves. The Guru took the side of those Hindus who were being persecuted. He was arrested and given the choice of death or conversion. He chose death and was executed in Delhi in 1675.

The right to work

The Gurus commended their followers to work hard at any job which was honest and to keep other people in mind when it came to using one's earnings (see page 202). A very famous Sikh, Bhai Gurdas, a distant relative of the third, fourth, and fifth Gurus, described the true Sikhs in these words:

'They labour to earn an honest living and distribute part of their income for the benefit of others. They have touched the perfect Guru and their hands have become holy, so they will not touch the body of another woman or the property of others.'

(Var 6:12)

FOR YOUR FOLDERS

► Try to link this verse with any parts of the Declaration.
► If there are any sections of the Declaration which have not been covered so far, list them and then look through the Sikhism sections (pages 186–221) to see whether you can find anything which might help you to decide what views Sikhs might have. (The Index should help you in your search.)

FOR DISCUSSION

► Why does Sikhism support so many principles of the Declaration of Human Rights?

Universal Declaration of Human Rights

Article 1 All human beings are born free and equal in dignity and rights. They are endowed with reason and conscience and should act towards one another in a spirit of brotherhood.

Article 2 Everyone is entitled to all the rights and freedoms set forth in this Declaration, without distinction of any kind, such as race, colour, sex, language, religion, political or other opinion, national or social origin, property, birth or other status.

Furthermore, no distinction shall be made on the basis of the political, jurisdictional or international status of the country or territory to which a person belongs, whether it be independent, trust, non-self-governing or under any other limitation of sovereignty.

Article 3 Everyone has the right to life, liberty and security of person.

Article 4 No one shall be held in slavery or servitude; slavery and the slave trade shall be prohibited in all their forms.

Article 5 No one shall be subjected to torture or to cruel, inhuman or degrading treatment or punishment.

Article 6 Everyone has the right to recognition everywhere as a person before the law.

Article 7 All are equal before the law and are entitled without any discrimination to equal protection of the law. All are entitled to equal protection against any discrimination in violation of this Declaration and against any incitement to such discrimination.

Article 8 Everyone has the right to an effective remedy by the competent national tribunals for acts violating the fundamental rights granted him by the constitution or by law.

Article 9 No one shall be subject to arbitrary arrest, detention or exile.

Article 10 Everyone is entitled in full equality to a fair and public hearing by an independent and impartial tribunal, in the determination of his rights and obligations and of any criminal charge against him.

Article 11 (1) Everyone charged with a penal offence has the right to be presumed innocent until proved guilty according to law in a public trial at which he has had all the guarantees necessary for his defence.
(2) No one shall be held guilty of any penal offence on account of any act or omission which did not constitute a penal offence, under national or international law, at the time when it was committed. Nor shall a heavier penalty be imposed than the one that was applicable at the time the penal offence was committed.

Article 12 No one shall be subjected to arbitrary interference with his privacy, family, home or correspondence, nor to attacks upon his honour and reputation. Everyone has the right to the protection of the law against such interference or attacks.

Article 13 (1) Everyone has the right to freedom of movement and residence within the borders of each state.
(2) Everyone has the right to leave any country, including his own, and to return to his country.

Article 14 (1) Everyone has the right to seek and to enjoy in other countries asylum from persecution.
(2) This right may not be invoked in the case of prosecutions genuinely arising from non-political crimes or from acts contrary to the purposes and principles of the United Nations.

Article 15 (1) Everyone has the right to a nationality.
(2) No one shall be arbitrarily deprived of his nationality nor denied the right to change his nationality.

Article 16 (1) Men and women of full age, without any limitation due to race, nationality or religion, have the right to marry and to found a family. They are entitled to equal rights as to marriage, during marriage and at its dissolution.
(2) Marriage shall be entered into only with the free and full consent of the intending spouses.
(3) The family is the natural and fundamental group unit of society and is entitled to protection by society and the State.

Article 17 (1) Everyone has the right to own property alone as well as in association with others.
(2) No one shall be arbitrarily deprived of his property.

Article 18 Everyone has the right to freedom of thought, conscience and religion; this right includes freedom to change his religion or belief, and freedom, either alone or in community with others and in public or private, to manifest his religion or belief in teaching, practice, worship and observance.

Article 19 Everyone has the right to freedom of opinion and expression; this right includes freedom to hold opinions without interference and to seek, receive and impart information and ideas through any media and regardless of frontiers.

Article 20 (1) Everyone has the right to freedom of peaceful assembly and association.
(2) No one may be compelled to belong to an association.

Article 21 (1) Everyone has the right to take part in the government of his country, directly or through freely chosen representatives.
(2) Everyone has the right of equal access to public service in his country.
(3) The will of the people shall be the basis of the authority of government; this will shall be expressed in periodic and genuine elections which shall be by universal and equal suffrage and shall be held by secret vote or by equivalent free voting procedures.

Article 22 Everyone, as a member of society, has the right to social security and is entitled to realization, through national effort and international co-operation and in accordance with the organization and resources of each State, of the economic, social and cultural rights indispensable for his dignity and the free development of his personality.

Article 23 (1) Everyone has the right to work, to free choice of employment, to just and favourable conditions of work and to protection against unemployment.
(2) Everyone, without any discrimination, has the right to

equal pay for equal work.

(3) Everyone who works has the right to just and favourable remuneration ensuring for himself and his family an existence worthy of human dignity, and supplemented, if necessary, by other means of social protection.

(4) Everyone has the right to form and to join trade unions for the protection of his interests.

Article 24 Everyone has the right to rest and leisure, including reasonable limitation of working hours and periodic holidays with pay.

Article 25 (1) Everyone has the right to a standard of living adequate for the health and well-being of himself and of his family, including food, clothing, housing and medical care and necessary social services, and the right to security in the event of unemployment, sickness, disability, widowhood, old age or other lack of livelihood in circumstances beyond his control.

(2) Motherhood and childhood are entitled to special care and assistance. All children, whether born in or out of wedlock, shall enjoy the same social protection.

Article 26 (1) Everyone has the right to education. Education shall be free, at least in the elementary and fundamental stages. Elementary education shall be compulsory. Technical and professional education shall be made generally available and higher education shall be equally accessible to all on the basis of merit.

(2) Education shall be directed to the full development of the human personality and to the strengthening of respect for human rights and fundamental freedoms. It shall promote understanding, tolerance and friendship among all nations, racial or religious groups, and shall further the activities of the UN for the maintenance of peace.

(3) Parents have a prior right to choose the kind of education that shall be given to their children.

Article 27 (1) Everyone has the right freely to participate in the cultural life of the community, to enjoy the arts and to share in scientific advancement and its benefits.

(2) Everyone has the right to the protection of the moral and material interests resulting from any scientific, literary or artistic production of which he is the author.

Article 28 Everyone is entitled to a social and international order in which the rights and freedoms set forth in this Declaration can be fully realized.

Article 29 (1) Everyone has duties to the community in which alone the free and full development of his personality is possible.

(2) In the exercise of his rights and freedoms, everyone shall be subject only to such limitations as are determined by law solely for the purpose of securing due recognition and respect for the rights and freedoms of others and of meeting the just requirements of morality, public order and the general welfare in a democratic society.

(3) These rights and freedoms may in no case be exercised contrary to the purposes and principles of the UN.

Article 30 Nothing in this Declaration may be interpreted as implying for any State, group or person any right to engage in any activity or to perform any act aimed at the destruction of any of the rights and freedoms set forth.

Booklist

Readers who would like to have more knowledge of the religions which they are studying in this book are encouraged to turn to some of the following publications.

GENERAL BOOKS

Five World Faiths, Ed. W. Owen Cole (Cassell)

Six Religions in the Twentieth Century, W. Owen Cole and Peggy Morgan (Stanley Thornes and Hulton)

A Dictionary of Non-Christian Religions, Geoffrey Parrinder (Hulton)

BOOKS ON SPECIFIC RELIGIONS

Buddhism, Holly and Peter Connolly (Stanley Thornes and Hulton)

Buddhism, Sue Penney (Heinemann Educational)

Christianity (a dictionary), Alan Brown and Judy Perkins (Batsford)

Christianity, W. Owen Cole (Stanley Thornes and Hulton)

Christianity, Joe Jenkins (Heinemann Educational)

Christianity, Sue Penney (Heinemann Educational)

Hinduism, V.P. (Hemant) Kanitkar (Stanley Thornes and Hulton)

Hinduism, Sue Penney (Heinemann Educational)

Islam, Ali Ashraf (Stanley Thornes and Hulton)

Islam, Rosalyn Kendrick (Heinemann Educational)

Islam, Sue Penney (Heinemann Educational)

Judaism, Arye Forte (Heinemann Educational)

Judaism, Sue Penney (Heinemann Educational)

Sikhism, Sue Penney (Heinemann Educational)

Sikhism, Piara Singh Sambhi (Stanley Thornes and Hulton)

INDEX

Publisher's acknowledgements

The Publishers would like to thank the following for permission to reproduce copyright material:

Tsultrim Allione, p. 26; James Belither, pp. 29, 36–37; D.G. Butler, *Many Lights*, Fowler Wright Books Ltd, p. 108; Catholic Truth Society, pp. 46, 48, 50, 51, 58, 61, 65, 70, 72, 74; Christian Aid, p. 68; Zarina Choudry, p.130; Church of England Board for Social Responsibility, pp. 47, 50, 52, 59, 64, 74; W. Owen Cole, *Mandala*, Foundation for the Preservation of the Mahayana Tradition, P.O. Box 1778, Soquel, California 95073, USA, p. 33; Thubten Dadak, *Mandala*, p. 17; His Holiness the Dalai Lama, pp. 24, 28, 31, 32, 36, 37, 38–39; Nichidatsu Fujii, p. 38; Gaia Books Ltd, p. 73; E.P. Gee, *The Wildlife of India*, Harper Collins, p. 108; The Venerable Maha Ghosananda, p. 34; Guru Ram Das Mission, UK, p. 198; *The Guardian*, p. 85; Geshe Kelsang Gyatso, *Universal Compassion* (1988) Manchester Institute Tharpa Publications Ltd, and *Meaningful to Behold* (1980) Wisdom Publications, pp. 24–25, 27; Thich Nhat Hanh, pp. 34, 35; John A. Hardon, S.J., *Modern Catholic Dictionary*, Robert Hale Ltd, p. 50; Liz Harris, *Holy Days*, Summit Books, Simon & Schuster Consumer Group, p. 155; Sahaib Hassan, An Introduction to the Sunnah, p. 122; *Illustrated Weekly of India*, p. 106; Islamic Relief Somalia, p. 135; Carl G. Jung, *Memories, Dreams and Reflections*, Random House Inc., p. 77; D.D. Karve, New Brahmans: Five Maharashtrian Families © 1963 The Regents of the University of California, p. 98; Noor Inayat Khan, *Jataka Tales* (1985) East-West Publications (UK) Ltd, p. 30; Billy Lucas, p. 69; Martin Luther King Jnr, (1967), p. 44, 45; Upendra Maharathi, tr. The Dhammapada, pp. 7, 12–13, 18, 20; Manchester University Press, *Textual Studies for the Study of Sikhism*, ed. McLeod, p. 194; Juan Mascaro, tr. The Dhammapada (1973), p. 56, Penguin Classics, London. Reproduced by permission of Penguin Books Ltd, p. 6; Thomas Merton, p. 76; Methodist Board for Social Responsibility, pp. 50, 52, 54, 59; Daishin Morgan, pp. 12, 14, 15, 32; *Muslim Voice*, p. 140; New English Bible © 1970 by permission of Oxford and Cambridge University Presses, pp. 42–76; Chushin Passmore, pp. 20, 33; Reverend Nan Peete, p. 63; Simon Phipps, p. 71; Thubten Pemo, *Mandala*, p. 27; T.W. Rhys Davids, tr. *The Questions of King Milinda*, p. 41; Chogyam Trungpa Rinpoche, *Shambhala: The Sacred Path of the Warrior* (1984). Reprinted by arrangement with Shambala Publications, Inc., 300 Massachusetts Ave., Boston, MA 02115, p.40; Lama Zopa Rinpoche, pp. 10, 16, 21, 31, 33; H.

Saddhatissa, p. 40; *Sikh Phulwari*, p. 210; Singapore Buddhist Federation, p. 19; The Society of Friends, pp. 49, 66; The Springs of Chinese Wisdom published by Search Press, p.22; *The Spokesman Weekly*, pp. 202, 207, 210; John St. John, Religion and Social Justice (1985), Wheaton, pp. 54, 62, 76; *Sunday Observer* (*Bombay*) *Ltd*, p. 85; Ajahn Sumedho, pp. 23, 29; Sigalavada Sutta, pp. 8–9; Robert Thurman, p. 41; Camilo Torres, *Revolutionary Priest: The Complete Writings and Messages of Camilo Torres*, ed. John Gerassi, Jonathan Cape Ltd, pp. 57, 66; Turtle cartoon, *Mandala*, p.16; Archbishop Desmond Tutu, *Hope and Suffering*, Harper Collins Ltd, pp. 54, 65; United Nations Office of Public Information, Declaration of Human Rights, pp. 221–2; Jean Vanier, p. 68; Andy Weber and Tharpa Publications (1985, 1989), illustrations on pp. 6, 8, 10, 12, 13, 18, 21, 24, 25, 37, 39; Martin Willson, p.27; World Council of Churches, pp. 60, 70, 71; Lama Thubten Yeshe, pp. 15, 21

Thanks are also due to the following for permission to reproduce photographs: Andes Press Agency/Carlos Reyes pp. 44, 50, 54, 56, 59 (top, left), 68, 95; Heather Angel pp. 140, 182; Barnaby's Picture Library p. 145; Robin Bath p. 28; Camera Press pp. 36, 45, 55, 64, 65, 117, 174; J. Allan Cash Ltd pp. 38, 76, 104; A.S. Chopra p. 209; Colorific/David Turnley/Black Star p. 67; Mark Edwards/Still Pictures pp. 97, 107, 119; Format Partners/Stephanie Henry/Maggie Murray pp. 46, 59, 63 (bottom), 66, 70, 73; Sally and Richard Greenhill pp. 47, 53 (left), 128, 136, 210; Group Against Smoking in Public p. 160; Robert Harding Picture Library pp. 154, 179, 181; Hutchison Library pp. 26, 48, 78, 111, 125, 138, 146, 187, 189, 191, 192 (right), 214; Impact Photos/Colin Jones p. 216; Jewish Care/Sidney Harris p. 173; Magnum Photos/Eugene Richards/Salgendo pp. 57, 60; Network/Barry Lewis/Mike Goldwater pp. 53 (right) 177; Ann and Bury Peerless pp. 30, 95, 102, 218, 220; Popperfoto pp. 112, 170 (both); H. Sagoo pp. 196 (both), 212, 213; Peter Sanders pp. 114, 123; Claude Sauvageot p. 77; Liz Somerville pp 157, 163

All other photographs were supplied by the authors.

The Publishers have made every effort to trace copyright holders. However, if any material has been incorrectly acknowledged, we would be pleased to make the necessary arrangements at the earliest opportunity.